W9-CRM-009

YOU WILL ALSO BE INTERESTED IN

CHINA'S CRISIS

BY LAWRENCE K. ROSINGER

A penetrating and outspoken discussion of the realities of the Chinese situation, by the Research Associate on the Far East of the Foreign Policy Association.

THIS IS A BORZOI BOOK

PUBLISHED IN NEW YORK BY *ALFRED A. KNOPF*

John McGilvrey Maki was born in Tacoma, Washington, of Japanese parents, in 1909. From the time he was three weeks old he was cared for by Mr. and Mrs. Alexander McGilvrey and grew up as a member of their family. They legally adopted him in 1918. He was educated in the public schools and at the University of Washington, Seattle, where he received his master's degree in English literature. Turning to Japanese studies, he served for a year as a teaching fellow in the Far Eastern Department of the University of Washington, then spent more than two years studying in Japan. He returned to the University of Washington, where he taught subjects related to Japan until 1942. Since that time he has been doing war work for the government in Washington, D.C.

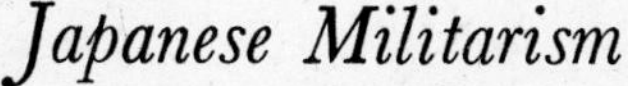

Japanese Militarism

Japanese Militarism

ITS CAUSE AND CURE

By JOHN M. MAKI

1945

ALFRED A KNOPF · *NEW YORK*

FIRST EDITION

To the Memory of my foster-father

ALEXANDER McGILVREY

CONTENTS

PREFACE

OUR WAR *against Japan has been long and costly in both men and treasure. Yet we still have not revealed clearly that we know what we are fighting for. We have fought to avenge Pearl Harbor and the victims of the infamous "March of Death" in the Philippines, to kill "the little yellow monkey-men" and, occasionally and in a vague sort of way, "to rid the world of Japanese militarism."*

The lack of a clearly defined set of war aims against Japan has certainly not impaired the fighting efficiency of the armies and the naval and air forces that have been piling defeat after defeat on the Japanese enemy. But as the final defeat of Japan comes nearer and the problems of the peace loom larger, we must have a clearer conception of the nature of the ideas that we are fighting in our war against Japan. This book has been written in the hope of bringing into clearer focus the aims of the ideological war. We shall not have won the war until the peace has been firmly established, and it can be so established only after the crushing of the ideas on which Japanese militarism and aggression are based.

It would be impossible to list here the names of all who have helped me, directly or indirectly, to formulate my thinking about Japan. I am greatly in debt to my classes at the University of Washington, whose interest — and, at times, lack of interest — forced me to do much of the research and the thinking on which the book is based. George E. Taylor, the head of my department at the University, and Harold M. Vinacke of the University of Cincinnati have been particularly unstinting in the aid and counsel they have given me.

I must, of course, assume sole responsibility for the ideas set down in these pages. They are the fruit of my research and my thinking at the University and are not related to the work I have been engaged in since my departure, on leave, from the University in the spring of 1942.

I should like to add that the names in this book are set down according to the Japanese usage: the surname is written first and the given name second. Japanese historical figures are referred to by their given names rather than by their family names.

JOHN M. MAKI

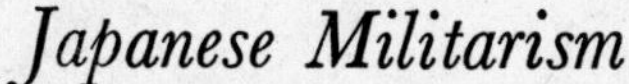
Japanese Militarism

Chapter I

THE WAR AGAINST JAPAN

The war against Japan is a war against people and a war against ideas. The United Nations are winning the war against people, but they have yet to give convincing evidence that they are attacking the ideas that have made Japan dangerous. Defeat of the people will mean victory in the war; but only the defeat of the ideas will make possible a peaceful Japan.

The United Nations have demonstrated that they have learned how to defeat the Japanese people in war. After the first six months following Pearl Harbor, the Japanese Army and Navy seemed to be all-victorious and all-conquering. The sneak attack on Pearl Harbor gave the Japanese Navy temporary control over much of the vast Pacific. The invasions of the Philippines, the Netherlands East Indies, Malaya, Burma, French Indo-China, and Thailand demonstrated that the Japanese armies were not only fitted to fight a modern amphibious war, but were also trained in the techniques of jungle-fighting, a type of warfare almost completely unknown to the armies of the United Nations.

Since the middle of 1942 the United Nations have learned rapidly and well to fight the type of war that had overwhelmed them. The infantrymen of the United States, China, and the British Empire have learned the art of jungle-fighting so well that they now surpass the Japanese at their own game. The United States Navy has outfought the Japanese Navy whenever they have met; it has conquered the vast distances that characterize the sea war in the Pacific, and has mastered the complex problems of logistics. The airmen of the United Nations have also succeeded in re-writing the tactics of air warfare in new and strange theatres of war where few Americans, for example, had ever been. All this has called for the exercise, in unbounded quantities, of courage, skill, intelligence, hard work, and the application to the art of war of the creative imagination.

The result has been that we have been able to bring to bear on the Japanese armed forces in the Pacific theatre an overwhelming array of men, ships, planes, and weapons. Consequently, we are killing Japanese at a rate that indicates that we shall certainly win the war, no matter what Japan's leaders may do.

If we could carry the war against people to its logical conclusion and kill seventy-two million Japanese, we should not have to worry about the winning of the war of ideas. Modern weapons have not yet reached the point where they can annihilate a nation; we must accept the fact that there will be a good many million Japanese still living when this war comes to an end. The war of ideas involves these people. If we can shatter their indoctrination by means of a crushing military defeat and provide a new ideological basis for their political and economic structures, we shall prepare them to return again to the society of nations as well as protect ourselves against the outbreak of another war in the Pacific.

The Japanese militarists, if they have a master plan for the eventual conquest of the world, want us to fight a war of killing and to forget the importance of the extermination of the ideas out of which has grown their power. A militaristic Japan can survive terrific casualties inflicted on both military personnel and civilians, as did imperial Germany during the war of 1914–18; but a militaristic Japan will disappear if the ideas on which it has been erected are rooted out. Nothing would please the militarists more than to see us concentrate solely on the killing of Japanese. Simply by killing we shall never attack and destroy militaristic ideas; we shall only be reducing the number of believers and practitioners of militarism. A reduction in the number of the militarists and their followers will not destroy Japanese chauvinism or Japanese aggression. We must see to it, if we are truly to win the war, that the ideas and attitudes of the Japanese which have made Japanese militarism possible are destroyed as completely and as certainly as the industrial structure that is arming the fighting forces of Japan.

We shall fall into a number of misconceptions if we do not see the war clearly as a war against ideas. It would delight the militarists of Japan to see it turned into a racial war between Asiatics and Caucasians. Japanese propaganda has worked busily to arouse within the peoples of Asia the consciousness that Japanese armies are fighting for an "Asia for the Asiatics." They have sought to create the illusion that all Asiatics are fighting against the Americans and the British. By playing on the racial theme for the rest of Asia, Japan is attempting to disguise her real aims toward Asia. She is no more fighting for "Asia for the Asiatics" than the Germans fought for a "Europe for the Europeans." The slogan, "Asia for the Asiatics," attempts to conceal the Japanese aim to dominate all of Asia for her own glory and for her own profit. The leaders of Japan know that with Japan's superior military power vis-à-vis the rest of Asia, her superior industrial machine and her superior mastery of technology, an "Asia for the Asiatics" would in reality be an "Asia for the Japanese."

If Japan can also dupe her enemies into believing that this war is a racial war, she will have succeeded in diverting our attention from her dangerous ideology. If we fall into the trap of regarding the war as racial, we shall put it on an emotional basis that has no connection with the war against the ideas on which Japanese aggression is built.

We must remember that there are still millions of Asiatics fighting against the Japanese. They are fighting because they have learned from bitter experience that the words of the Japanese aggressor do not match his actions. They know that Japanese aggression, Japanese brutality, Japanese exploitation, and Japanese master-race consciousness do not recognize the kinship alleged in the phrase "Asia for the Asiatics."

To place the war in the Pacific on a racial basis would be as politically ridiculous and immature as it would have been to call the war against Germany a war against "Aryans." In Europe we fought against the political ideology of the Nationalist Socialist Party; in the Pacific we are fighting against the ideology of the Japanese militarists.

The war in the Pacific is not a war to redress the wrongs that have been done to China and to the other areas that have been occupied by Japan. The Cairo Declaration announced the intention of the United States, Great Britain, and China to see to it that Japan was stripped of all the fruits of her aggression since the first Sino-Japanese War of 1894–5. This intention, admirable as it is, has little true political reality as far as the war is concerned. It is like forcing a bandit to return stolen property to his victims without taking any positive action to reform him. The redress of wrongs in the Pacific is merely one of the incidental products of the war against Japan. It has no true relation to the war against the ideas which led Japan to commit those wrongs. It is simply a demonstration to the Japanese that unsuccessful crime does not pay.

We have declared repeatedly that we are fighting to crush Japanese militarism and aggression, but we have tended to confuse these concepts with individuals whom we call "militarists." Our thinking is that as soon as we get rid of these "militarists" we shall have created conditions under which the Japanese people will willingly renounce militarism and aggression. Sometimes we think that the "militarists" are a few top generals and admirals supported by fanatical officers; sometimes we include a larger percentage of the population, adding, for example, the secret societies. But again we fall into the dangerous error of associating the evil in Japan with certain persons whose elimination will almost automatically bring about the political rehabilitation of the Japanese people.

In a sense, militarism and aggression are only the tactical objectives of our war against Japan. The strategic and true objectives are the ideas, the attitudes, the historical currents, the social institutions, and the economic structure that have given rise to militarism and aggression. We can bring a temporary end to Japanese aggression by driving her out of her conquests. We can bring a temporary end to Japanese militarism by eliminating her present Army and Navy. We must strike much deeper to exterminate them once and for all.

It is not strange that our thinking about the war with Japan is dominated by the fact that we are simply warring against people and various groups of people. It is a direct inheritance from our pre-war thinking about Japan. We thought that Japan was dominated by a power-mad group of militarists who had subjugated the people and who were embarked on a career of aggression. We also thought that Japan would be kept out of war with the rest of the world by a group of "liberals" who were supposed to think as we did and would not let Japan declare war against her great and good friend, the United States.

We were thinking in about the only terms that we could. We had no real understanding of the fundamental currents of Japanese society and of Japanese history. Indeed, almost all our thinking about Japan and the Japanese was hemmed within the framework of our own experience. We made the "militarists" the villains of Japan because we hated war, not because we understood what they really were. We failed to see their organic connection with the life of Japan and the Japanese.

On the other hand, we completely overestimated the influence of the "liberals," not only because we regarded them as a bulwark between us and war, but also because we thought they were representative of Japan simply for the reason that they seemed to think as we did. We failed to understand that because they were like us they were non-Japanese, and therefore almost powerless within Japan.

One barrier between us and a true understanding of the Japanese was the fact that almost all our knowledge about both the land and the people came through the eyes of foreigners who lived in Japan. The vast majority who wrote and talked about the Japanese were honest; they reported accurately, in most cases, those particular segments of Japanese life, those Japanese or those material achievements in Japan that most impressed them. They saw only those aspects of Japan with which they were in closest contact. Most of them knew only the cities and the famous tourist spots of the country. Even those who knew the Japanese more intimately in rural areas or in places remote from metropolitan centres were barred from a complete understanding because they were teachers and missionaries, and the very nature of their work tended to give them a somewhat distorted view of the Japanese. Most important, however, is the fact that all foreigners in Japan were really a group apart. Their very complexions revealed to the Japanese that they were strangers and therefore guests within Japan. The behaviour of the Japanese in their presence tended to be more circumspect than would normally be the case.

By far the greatest gulf between us and an understanding of the Japanese was the lack of a common frame of historical reference. In spite of a great diversity of national traditions and national interests in the Occident, all nations share or have known a common historical tradition. It is composed largely of the classical tradition, Christianity, the Reformation, the Renaissance, the Industrial Revolution, the revolutionary wave of the eighteenth century, communism, capitalism, the democratic tradition, and more recently, nazism and fascism. These provide us with a frame of reference for understanding with a fair degree of accuracy many developments in the Western world.

How much more difficult it is for us to understand Japan, which has never known any of the above in the form that they have been produced in the Western world. She has never been immersed in the current of the classical tradition. She has had Christianity within her borders for almost four centuries, but Christians were few and both they and their religion were persecuted. In addition, it has most definitely been an importation with no relation to Japan's past traditions. There has been nothing in Japanese spiritual or political development which equals the impact of the Reformation as a protest against established authority. There has been no great and sudden burgeoning of human intellect, human talent, and human experience comparable to the Renaissance. Japan cannot point to a great intellectual tradition such as has been built up in the Occident. The introduction of Western machine techniques into Japan in the nineteenth century was a rough equivalent of the Industrial Revolution, but they were introduced, not developed as the result of pioneering in the field of science. In a sense, Japan by-passed the Industrial Revolution by picking it up at a time when it had reached its full flowering in the Occident. Neither did there appear in Japan the social and political consequences of the Industrial Revolution as they were known in the United States and Europe. Japan has never experienced a revolutionary wave, if by that is meant a sudden and violent protest against established political authority. Communism has been introduced into Japan, but although a few scholars and students have been allowed to study it as one of many political and economic theories, it has been ruthlessly suppressed as a political movement. Capitalism, in the form of monopoly capitalism, has probably reached its great peak of development in Japan, but it developed not out of a laissez-faire economy, but out of the standard Japanese pattern of economic oligarchy. The democratic tradition has not existed in Japan, for there has been nothing which has promoted the participation of the people in government. It is only with nazism and fascism that there is any comparison with Japanese ideologies and institutions. Yet even here are some significant differences.

Japan is what she is to-day because she is a product of her history. She is also what she is because of certain things that have not occurred in her history. The absence, at least in terms of their historical influence, of many of the elements listed above, has had almost as important an effect on Japanese history as their presence might have had.

What are some of the main currents in Japanese history? What have been the ideas that have determined the development of Japanese institutions? It is possible to list several basic concepts which will provide some clues to an understanding of the enemy that we are fighting to-day in the Pacific.

First, Japan has been dominated from earliest times by a political oligarchy. The groups which have dominated the oligarchy have varied from time to time, but the general pattern of government by oligarchy has never been departed from. The Japanese people have always been the obedient servants of the small group of men who have ruled Japan. The rôle of the people in government has been simply to carry out the decisions of the few who have controlled Japanese society. Before the modern period in Japanese history that meant primarily to fight the battles of one section of the oligarchy against another; in modern Japan it has meant carrying out the plans of aggression of the militarists.

Second, for centuries the machinery of government has been in the hands of men from a military class. This has accustomed the people to obeying and to respecting men who won, retained, and exercised power by means of the sword.

Third, Japanese economy has been controlled by an economic oligarchy as small as the political oligarchy. Through most of Japanese history the political oligarchy has coincided with the economic oligarchy. The monopolization of wealth by the few has strengthened the oligarchic form of government.

Fourth, the institution of the emperor has played a dominant rôle in Japanese politics. The position of the emperor, both at present and historically, is a complex problem, partly religious, but mainly political. The emperor has been an integral part of the structure of Japanese politics, although his rôle for centuries has been passive, rather than active. It is only in terms of his historical position that the real significance of his present rôle in Japanese politics can be understood.

Fifth, the rôle of foreign influences has been of key importance in Japan. The nation on the positive side has been greatly in debt to foreign countries for both institutions and material objects; but as important in terms of Japanese historical development as these have been, the strong current of anti-foreignism has been equally significant. The Japanese have been highly selective in their approach to the things which have come to them from over the sea. While accepting material objects and institutions which could be fitted into the established framework, ideas that might have undermined the basic concepts of Japanese politics and economics have been rigidly excluded.

The oligarchic structures of Japanese politics and economics, the domination of the powers of government by the military group in Japanese society, the rigid control of Japanese ideas, and the concept of emperor worship have been the foundation for the establishment of an authoritarian government within Japan and the exercise of a policy of war and aggression in foreign affairs. These must be the major and the ultimate objectives of our war against Japan; these are the roots from which the evil weeds of aggression have grown. We are in the process of destroying the weeds, but if we do not destroy the roots as well we shall again be involved in war with Japan.

The destruction of Japan's armed forces will be the first step in the direction of the reorientation of Japan. The stresses and strains that follow in the wake of defeat in a long war may serve to tear down the political and economic oligarchies and perhaps even to bring to an end the antiquated worship of the emperor. If these things come to pass, then it will be the duty of the victorious United Nations to encourage the introduction into Japan of new ideas that will enable the Japanese people to attain something resembling political maturity and political responsibility.

The soldiers and sailors of the United States and her allies are bringing about the total defeat of the Army and Navy of Japan. They are making certain that in this war Japan will not win control of the world, and that she will be forced to give up the ill-gotten gains of her aggression. Their task has been and will be difficult; their sufferings have been great. Their courage, their stamina, their resourcefulness, and their intelligence have not only stopped Japanese expansion, but have laid the necessary foundation for a complete victory over Japan, both militarily and politically.

As the military phases of our war against Japan approach a climax, the responsibilities of our statesmen grow greater. It is they who must clinch the victory over Japan by making it political as well as military. Their responsibility will not end with the enunciation of the formal peace terms for Japan. The surrender of the Japanese Army and the Japanese Navy, the demilitarization of Japan, the destruction of her structure of heavy industry, the punishment of Japanese war criminals, and the wresting from Japan of her territorial conquests are not the true concern of the statesmen. The terms of the peace that will cover those problems will be simply the verbal stamp of approval in diplomatic language of the accomplishments of our fighting men. True statesmanship, if it is to be applied to the problems of Japan, must build on the accomplishments of the fighting man. It must go beyond the battlefield and attack Japanese ideas and institutions. Statesmanship must destroy the roots of Japanese militarism; our fighting forces are lopping off its branches.

The responsibility of the statesmen in the problem of Japan is almost overwhelming. If their work fails, thousands of Americans and millions of their allies will have died in vain. If their work fails, new millions will die in a greater war in the future.

The war against Japan is a total war. While suffering on the American home front (apart from the bereavement of families through the death of relatives on the battlefields) has been virtually non-existent, American resources, human and material, have been mobilized to an extent never before witnessed in order to make victory over Japan certain. The result of total war should be permanent peace. If our statesmen exercise for the building of the peace only a fraction of the intelligence and the imagination that have been expended in winning the war, they will be well on the way toward ending forever the threat of Japanese militarism.

The major attacks on Japanese ideas will probably not come

until after the war itself has ceased. It will be in the vital post-war period that the greatest blows against the dangerous ideas and institutions of Japan must be struck. It will be the task of our statesmen to see that the Japanese people are encouraged to rid themselves of the men, the ideas, and the institutions which have made them the slaves of the military oligarchy. The Japanese people are not fitted to do this task alone; they have not revealed the political leadership or the political consciousness necessary for an effective attack on the present order.

Our statesmen must attack the political, economic, and social structure in Japan that has encouraged the development of militarism. They must do this first by not encouraging the retention of individuals or institutions which are organically connected with Japan's past and second, by doing everything possible to encourage the Japanese people at large to adopt ideas and institutions which will supplant the old.

We are pledged to force Japan to accept unconditional surrender, to invade her home islands, and to occupy the country for an indefinite period. We know that we have the military strength to attain these ends. This means that our statesmen will be actually in Japan where they will be in a position to exert direct pressure on the situation within Japan.

We can look back through Japanese history and perceive how Japanese militarism has welled out of Japanese life. We can understand how the war in the Pacific was inevitable as far as Japan was concerned, because of the forces that drove her leaders and her people to militarism and aggression. The past explains the present, and if we study both carefully we can work to build a future Japan which will not threaten the world again.

The task of re-orientation will be a difficult one. The major responsibility will be on the shoulders of the Japanese people. We shall not know until, and if it is accomplished, whether or not they have the capacity to recast their lives. We can aid them by not underwriting anything in Japanese life which will be the possible foundation for a return to the militarism and aggression that will be crushed, at least temporarily, in the present war; and by releasing for them the ideas that have so long been denied them by their government.

The war against Japan and the Japanese will continue to be

bitter. Many thousands of Japanese will have to die; our losses will not be light. Yet we shall defeat the Japanese people, and our victory will place us in a position where we shall be able to win the war against the evil ideology which has weighed heavily on them, and which has resulted in the temporary subjugation of many of their neighbours.

Chapter II

THE POLITICAL OLIGARCHY

Oligarchy has been the characteristic form of government in Japan. Government has been from the earliest times by the few and for the few. It has never been responsive to the will of the people nor has it ever acted for their good except as it might further the interests of the oligarchy. The composition of the oligarchy has varied in the course of Japanese history, but its aims have always been the same: to monopolize economic wealth and to maintain political control of the country.

Rule by oligarchy has determined the form of political change in Japan. During every period of great political change, the Taikwa Reform in the seventh century, the collapse of the court aristocracy and the emergence of the warrior class in the twelfth century, the unification of the country under the rule of the Tokugawa family in the early seventeenth century and the collapse of feudalism in the nineteenth century, the struggle for political control has taken place at the apex of Japanese society. It has never taken the form of a struggle of the ruled against the ruling, but of one faction within the ruling oligarchy against another. Revolution has never challenged oligarchic rule in Japan.

The oligarchy has always resisted changes, political, social, or economic, so sweeping that the basic attitudes on which the acceptance of oligarchy rested would be shaken. It has always controlled political movements so that while changes have been possible inside the framework of oligarchic rule, wider participation in government has not been. The great changes that came over Japan in the last half of the nineteenth century illustrate this well. On the surface Japan went through one of the greatest revolutions that any nation has ever experienced. The old social distinctions were swept away, new political institutions were introduced, a spectacular change took place in the economy of the country. Yet in spite of all this the oligarchic form of government was not abandoned, but was even more firmly established by the use of new techniques of education and propaganda, and new instruments of government.

Rule by oligarchy furnishes a key to the understanding of much that has taken place in modern Japanese history. It accounts in a large part for the fact that Japan has been the ideal soil for the propagation of authoritarianism. There has been no democratic tradition, no theory of responsibility of the governing to the governed. On the contrary, the acceptance of oligarchy is so thoroughly ingrained in the Japanese people that authoritarian control is regarded as the norm in government. It is for this reason that the arbitrary acts of the Japanese government in both domestic and international affairs have gone virtually unchallenged by the mass of the Japanese people.

The earliest Japanese historical records date from the eighth century A.D. The society described in these records was essentially oligarchic in nature, and set the pattern for the evolution of the Japanese state. It was made up of a number of clans which were small, politically and economically independent units. They were built around a core of men and women of the same blood, who were supported by groups of serfs and slaves who lived under their domination.

The affairs of each clan were believed to be under the guidance of a clan god from whom the members of the clan were supposed to have been descended. The god guided the clan's destinies and was responsible for its prosperity and safety. The clan chief was the religious and secular head of the clan, and enjoyed a rôle in many ways similar to that of the emperor today. The clan chief was the supreme figure within the clan, although all the clansmen were supposed to be related to him by blood.

Common descent from the clan god, and therefore common blood, was the determining factor in so far as membership in the clan *élite* was concerned. Sometimes the relationship was close and at other times distant, but it had to be, otherwise the clansman could not claim the privileges of his position.

The clansmen were the politically and economically dominant

group within the clan. Politically their power arose from their close association with the clan chief. Economically, although they were not concerned directly with the business of production, either of agricultural products or other types of goods, they enjoyed control of the wealth produced by the clan. Thus, the clans dominated by a small group at the top anticipated the organic growth, along oligarchic lines, of the Japanese state in later centuries.

The clan system was essentially lacking in centralization. The imperial clan (later to develop into the imperial family), the most powerful one, was the only unifying factor, and its control was informal rather than formal. It enjoyed a position of supremacy only because it had more men under arms. It controlled directly a greater area of land than any other clan and at the same time its prestige guaranteed the allegiance of some of the minor clans whose holdings adjoined those of the imperial clan, but there was no machinery for centralized administration. This was not sufficient if Japan was going to develop into a state resembling nationhood.

The steady growth in the power and prestige of the imperial clan, the development of Japan's relations with the continent, the impetus imparted to Japanese life by these new foreign influences, and the growing complexity of life inside Japan as a result of her own natural development made it inevitable that some great change would come over the face of the country. The issue was brought to a head in the seventh century by the struggle for power between the imperial clan and its nearest rival, the Soga clan. The victory of the former insured its position as the core of the new government, and paved the way for the establishment of a central administration under the guidance of a group of able statesmen.

The dominant position of the chiefs and their clansmen made it necessary for steps to be taken to guarantee their position in the new Japan, unless they were to be completely eliminated. They could not be forced from their holdings without precipitating a major struggle for power, a struggle which the victorious Imperial forces might not have been able to push to a successful conclusion. The statesmen who engineered the Taikwa Reform in the middle of the seventh century A.D. therefore took steps to see to it that the privileged groups in the clans were confirmed in power under the new government structure, rather than deprived of it. As a result, they became the new court aristocracy in Japan, the ruling oligarchy which was to control Japan for some five centuries.

The Taikwa Reform is one of the most important events in all Japanese history, for what it did in effect was to make Japan a nation, by introducing the concept of government by a supra-local authority, and by setting up the machinery for a centralized administration. In addition it firmly established the oligarchic structure in both the political and economic life of Japan. The Reform ranks with the Meiji Restoration as an epoch-making event in Japanese history and like the Restoration it was a process rather than an event, extending over roughly half a century, beginning in A.D. 645.

The far-reaching effects of the Reform may best be appreciated by listing what it accomplished. First of all, it abolished the clan system. This was indeed a revolutionary step in terms of Japanese society as it was then organized. However, as has been the case during every turning point in Japanese history, the revolutionary nature of the change was apparent rather than real. The system was abolished, but the economically and politically powerful groups within the framework of the clans, far from being dispossessed, became dominant in the new political and economic order in Japan. In a sense, the Reform was nothing more than a reorganization of the ruling class of Japan.

Secondly, a centralized bureaucratic system which revolved around the newly created court aristocracy was set up. It was through this bureaucracy that the clansmen retained their political and economic ascendancy in Japan. The aristocratic and oligarchic structure of Japanese society under the clan system was maintained in the new Japan, although the new forms of political and economic organization were radically different from the old.

Next, the emperor emerged as the absolute head of the Japanese state as a result of the Reform. All the land was his and all the people were his subjects, according to the new theory of sovereignty. This theory has persisted until today.

In addition to the political changes that were wrought in Japan by the Taikwa Reform, there were economic changes no less spectacular. But the privileged economic group in the clan system remained the privileged class in the new society. The old vested interests simply became the new vested interests. The ease and rapidity with which the political changes were pushed through were due in a large part to the fact that the economic balance of power was not disturbed.

Compared with the relatively simple organization of even the most powerful clans in pre-Taikwa Japan the new bureaucracy, based on the Chinese model, was complicated in the extreme. In the undeveloped Japan of the seventh century it is difficult to see how many of the offices in the new government structure could have been anything more than mere forms. Nothing more than the skeleton of the more important sections of the bureaucracy will be described here. The great number of offices and bureaus with all their subdivisions and sections would require some pages in even summary form.

At the apex of the new system was the emperor, as was to be expected in terms of the motivation of the Taikwa Reform. Although the emperor was to be the ruler of the new country, the very complexity of the system that was nominally under his control guaranteed that he would be not much more than a figurehead, relying on his advisers. Directly under the emperor was the Department of Shinto. The importance of this religious body in the political hierarchy is understandable in terms of the dual political and religious rôle of the emperor. Also under direct control of the emperor was the Great Council of State. This included the four principal ministers of state and also numbered among its members a number of counselors and secretaries.

The four principal ministers were the prime minister, whose office was created in 671, the great minister of the left, the great minister of the right, and the great minister of the centre. It was they who held the real power to rule the country. Ranged under them was a complicated hierarchy of counselors, controllers, secretaries, recorders, scribes, and ministers of the principal government departments.

An examination of the eight ministries of the government reveals that they were designed not so much for efficient administration of a nation as for the creation of a number of sinecures for courtiers for whom a living had to be provided, and the establishment of an elaborate system for the control of the affairs of the Imperial Court. The names of the eight ministries are impressive enough. They were: the Ministry of Central Affairs (primarily concerned with affairs in the Imperial Palace), the Ministry of Ceremonial, the Ministry of Civil Administration, the Ministry of Popular (or People's) Affairs, the Ministry of War, the Ministry of Justice, the Ministry of the Treasury, and the Ministry of the Imperial Household.

The bureaus and offices making up the ministries belie the high sound of their titles. Under the Ministry of Central Affairs, for example, were the following offices and bureaus: the office of the Empress' Household, the offices of painting and palace etiquette and the bureaus of Imperial Attendants, of palace storehouses, books and drawings, court ladies and divination. The Ministry of Civil Administration contained the bureaus of music and of Buddhism and aliens, the office of mausolea, and the office for burial and mourning. Far from dealing with matters of finance, the Ministry of the Treasury contained offices for metal work, housekeeping, lacquer, wardrobe, weaving, and reception of tribute. The other ministries were organized along similar lines.

There is little in the organization of the bureaucracy to indicate that it was designed to be the machinery for the efficient administration of a nation. From the standpoint of practical politics the system worked well enough. It kept the oligarchy in power and the relation between political office and economic power was maintained to the advantage of the oligarchy.

In spite of its obvious defects as a system for effective administration, the new bureaucracy did give Japan the form of a state. The political organization did not go much beyond mere form, but at least the new Japan represented a distinct advance over the loose system of the clans. Some Japanese scholars have declared that the concept of nationhood was imported into Japan along with the Chinese model for the bureaucracy. Under the new system all factions in Japan were to be subordinated to the imperial will. There was no longer to be any opportunity for a threat to the imperial family of the nature of that of the Soga clan. The emperor was the central figure of the bureaucracy, with the bureaucracy itself acting as adviser to the emperor, and as the instrument through which the will of the emperor was expressed. The form was that which was to be strictly adhered to in subsequent Japanese political history.

The bureaucracy was the ideal instrument through which the system of government by oligarchy could be continued. As a matter of fact the new oligarchy of court aristocrats was infinitely more powerful than the old under the clans. The court aristocrats were a ruling class made up of individuals with common interests in the control of government and with a common aim in perpetuating their economic domination of Japan. In pre-Taikwa Japan there had been no true identity of aim among the men who dominated the clans. Their interests were limited by the extent of the land they controlled. There was no cutting across the boundaries of clan control and joining in a common promotion of common interests.

The bureaucracy was composed of those who had held positions of power in clan society. Naturally, the most influential members of the most powerful clans were given the most important positions in the new bureaucracy. Japan was now controlled by a closed aristocracy. There was no opportunity, even theoretically, for a low-born person to rise to a position of influence in the state. Although the Chinese examination system was set up, only members of the aristocracy were eligible to take the examinations for official appointments, thereby eliminating even the theoretically democratic aspect of the Chinese system. No poor but intelligent lad in Japan was given even the chance of breaking into the bureaucracy.

This bureaucracy, closed as it was to outside influences, could be controlled by one powerful group within it. That is exactly what came about. The Fujiwara family, whose progenitor, Kamatari, had played an important rôle in bringing about the Reform, rose to a position of complete dominance within this bureaucracy of aristocrats. The family's rise to power will be described later.

Below the central bureaucracy and responsible to it was a system of local administration. The local officials were to carry out the edicts of the central bureaucracy, and to collect the taxes and transport them to the capital. The local offices and the emoluments connected with them were given to the members of the minor clans, and thus their loyalty to the new government was insured by exactly the same means as had been used in connection with the central bureaucrats.

Through the political aspects of the Taikwa Reform Japan was given at least the form of a centralized administration, but a truly centralized governmental structure was not to come for many centuries. The topographical barriers to effective communications, the *sine qua non* of an effective central administration, could not be overcome even though the Taikwa Reform set up a system of post-horses, postal communications, and road maintenance. In addition, the concept of a centralized state as an entity over and above local control was foreign to Japanese psychology at that time. Strong local control as expressed in the more or less patriarchal relationships of the clan system was natural. Nothing in the Taikwa system effectively supplanted the relationships of the old order.

The Heian period (794–1152) was the time when the power of the civil oligarchy reached its highest peak, and then disintegrated. The court aristocracy maintained its monopoly of government office, controlled the wealth of Japan, and created the most aesthetic culture that Japan was ever to know. But, like all aristocratic societies, it contained within itself the seeds of its own destruction, and, as great as its cultural contributions were, it lacked a vital spirit which would have raised its cultural contributions to the peak of true greatness. It was the greatest period in the history of Japanese civilization, but it contributed little that has enriched the civilization of the world.

The very factors that made for the greatness of the Heian aristocrats contributed to their downfall. The qualities that were to create brilliant literature and one of the most aesthetic societies in world history were not those that would contribute to the maintenance of a firm grip on the reins of government and the control of the economy of the country. The aristocrats were responsible for their own downfall as surely as they attained to greatness because of their superior qualities.

What was the state of Japanese society at the beginning of the ninth century when the Heian age began? By this time the Taikwa reforms were as firmly established as they could be, the new government had gone through its "shake-down" phase, and the court aristocracy had developed a sense of oneness.

Japan had also developed a sense of nationality. The new government gave the nation a sense of cohesiveness that could not have developed under the system of clan society. Japan's contacts with China, then one of the world's great powers, no doubt filled the leaders of the new Japan with a desire to emulate their great neighbour. But the new Japan was still very small indeed.

As far as the structure of Japanese society was concerned, the court aristocrats were definitely established as a class, and with both economic and political power concentrated in their hands they were in a position to compound that power. This is exactly what they did. Within this new aristocracy there was already developing a monopoly within a monopoly. The influential Fujiwara family was beginning to develop a control over key positions within the imperial court that rivaled the ascendancy that the aristocracy held over the nation as a whole.

The other important group in Japanese society at this time was the Buddhist priesthood. Because Buddhism was also a virtual monopoly of the aristocrats, the priests were beginning to loom as both economic and political factors in Japan. Their close association with the aristocrats placed them in a position where they could gain special economic rights for their temples, and wield political influence.

The common people, as has been true in all periods of Japanese history, were the basis without which the rulers of Japan could not have existed. But they had no rights and no voice in the government under which they were able to eke out a meagre existence. In the literature of the Heian period there are but a few references to them. The haughty aristocrats of the time wrote of them as if they were strange beasts who spoke and acted not like men, but like a sub-species of the human race.

As the Heian age continued, more and more political power became concentrated in the hands of the Fujiwara family. It was the great Kamatari who, during the political turmoil when the Soga family was making its bid for supreme power, laid the foundations for the influence of the Fujiwara family. The result of his work was that the Fujiwara family was given a position only slightly lower than that of the imperial family itself.

The accession of the Fujiwara to its position of unchallenged supremacy in the court bureaucracy was slow. During the eighth century there were signs that the family was beginning to capitalize on its favoured position, but in the early part of the Heian period the emperors were still not completely under Fujiwara control, and other families still enjoyed high office within the bureaucracy.

The position of the Fujiwara family, as the rulers within the ruling class, was firmly established by the middle of the tenth century, which was the beginning of the most brilliant period in the history of the Heian court. By that time the Fujiwara had gained complete control of all the important offices within the bureaucracy. Since the positions in the bureaucracy were appointive, the Fujiwara were able gradually to extend their control by placing only members of their family in important positions. Thus, the more power they gained the better were they able to extend it.

The Fujiwara family instituted the system of exercising control over the emperor by furnishing Fujiwara daughters as imperial wives and concubines. This close association with the imperial family gave the Fujiwaras tremendous prestige and guaranteed their accession to a dominant position in the imperial court. Fujiwara men were leading government officials, scholars, poets, writers, artists, and everything else within the court.

Control over two offices – those of *sessho* (regent) and *kwampaku* (civil dictator) – guaranteed the family absolute political supremacy within the bureaucracy. The title of *sessho* was granted to the leading member of the Fujiwara family while the emperor was still a small boy, and after the emperor attained his majority the office of *kwampaku* was assumed by the leader of the Fujiwaras. Control of these two offices meant that the Fujiwara family controlled the emperor.

The great period of Fujiwara control covered the hundred years between the middle of the tenth century and the middle of the eleventh century. This century of Fujiwara greatness coincided with the most brilliant period of Heian civilization. Fortunately, we have in Lady Murasaki's great novel, *The Tale of Genji,* an excellent picture of the life of the times, and we can see in it both the greatness and the weakness of the lives of the court aristocrats.

The greatness of the civilization of the Heian period, as it is reflected in the literary works of the times, was in the aestheticism that permeated the lives of the courtiers. Poetry, appreciation of nature, music, dancing, elegant conversation, and many other polite arts were all inextricably woven into the daily life of the court nobles and their feminine companions. These pursuits were as effeminate as they were aesthetic and, of course, served to smother any qualities of leadership in the nobles.

But from the same sources we can also learn of the amount of gossip and intrigue that went on inside the restricted society of the imperial court. Good marriages, promotions in court rank, appointments to good positions in the bureaucracy, schemes to discredit rivals, impressive but apparently empty court ceremonies, all these and similar minor affairs seem to have constituted the principal political tasks of the court nobles. Malicious gossip about manners, morals, clothes, poise, and social graces was used of course to help attain certain of the political ends mentioned above.

Concentration on such cultural, social, and petty political affairs could not but distract the nobles from the more serious business of both state and personal affairs. Not only did their grasp on government begin to slip, but they also began to neglect their personal business affairs. Their private estates were regarded simply as a source of income which would allow them to continue their lives of peace and ease in the capital. They cared little about who administered the estates or how they were administered as long as they received enough to maintain them in the state to which they had accustomed themselves. They were absentee landlords at their worst.

The Fujiwara family, being the principal figures in the imperial court, could not escape the baneful influence of the society that they had done so much to create. The family was to suffer from a lack of able leaders as time went on. When the crucial period came the Fujiwara family was able to protect neither its own interests nor those of its class, the nobility, against the warriors who slowly and gradually slipped into the position of power once held by the civil oligarchy. By the end of the twelfth century the court aristocrats had lost all political and economic power and were never again to play a major rôle, as a class, in Japan.

The military oligarchy which fell heir to the power that slipped from the hands of the aristocrats dominated Japan for seven centuries — from the middle of the twelfth century until the middle of the nineteenth century. The warrior class did not maintain iron control over the entire nation at all times during this long period.

At times its rule was lax and restricted to local areas. At other times the centralization of military control was complete. But during these seven hundred years the military, as a class, enjoyed complete control of Japanese society,

The advent of the warrior class was one of the decisive facts of Japanese history. This added the military element to the already established oligarchic pattern. Not only did the warriors dominate the Japanese economic and political systems, but they created the conditions for the acceptance of modern militarism in Japan. When the warriors came to power in the twelfth century they ended forever the rôle of the court nobility in Japanese affairs and instituted a system that effectively kept political power out of the hands of the emperor. Thereafter Japan was to be governed by a feudal militaristic régime which established enduring political and economic relationships which have survived until today.

Seven centuries of military oligarchy molded Japanese society into such a form that it was inevitable that Japan, once emerged into the modern world, would adopt an authoritarian form of government and embark on a policy of military aggression. Such a government and such a policy were accepted as natural, for they were firmly imbedded in the Japanese attitudes toward government which had been developed over long centuries. The military oligarchy, ruling by virtue of its armed strength and held accountable by no higher authority, developed to a high degree government by men rather than government by law. To them law was not a series of rules which would act as a check on the arbitrary exercise of power, but a means of imposing controls on those who might challenge their authoritarian rule. By the end of the feudal period in the mid-nineteenth century the rule of authority was so firmly entrenched that the foreign theories of government and of law that were imported into Japan had no more than a superficial effect on Japanese political attitudes.

The emergence of the warrior lords as a body of men who could and did successfully challenge the supremacy of the court nobles was a slow process. Their appearance was the result of the operation of unplanned economic and political forces, unlike the almost architectural construction of the civil bureaucracy by the men who guided the Taikwa Reform.

The Taikwa Reform had made no provision for the establishment of a true military arm as a part of the new government. The bureaus of the new central government handling affairs which were normally military were either minor or delegated with duties which were military only in the formal sense. Furthermore, the men who were charged with the duty of supervising the military functions of the bureaucracy were without real interest in the martial arts. They were given military offices which were for the most part sinecures, carrying with them imposing titles and comfortable grants of land. Besides, interested as they were only in the affairs of court, they were temperamentally unsuited for the business of war.

The military class, as a consequence, developed slowly and in areas outside the capital. Its growth was quiet and natural in the provinces, where neither the interest nor the authority of the civil bureaucracy effectively extended. There is little evidence that the warriors themselves were conscious of the extent of their slowly developing power and influence.

The spearhead of the new class consisted of the warrior lords. Their environment was the provinces where their economic power developed on the estates held by the court nobles. Certain of the warrior families were off-shoots of the court nobility and even of the imperial family itself. Imperial princes and other high nobles were, on occasion, willing to sacrifice their chances at the imperial court for a more exciting and perhaps more rewarding life in the provinces. The Fujiwara monopoly on positions in the bureaucracy made it difficult at times for men of ability to exercise their talents. In an environment where the ability to plot and to win favouritism was an all-important consideration, men who wanted to exercise their talents as administrators and who were frozen out by less able associates had no recourse but to seek new fields of endeavour outside the capital. Imperial princes and other influential members of the court gave up any claims that they might have to the throne or to important positions within the bureaucracy, and became commoners. A part of the settlement usually included the grant of land or of estates in the provinces. These formed one group out of which the new warrior class was to develop.

Another group that contributed its share was made up of the

provincial nobles who remained almost completely unaffected by the Taikwa Reform. These families were not absorbed into the new aristocracy, principally because they were too far removed from the capital. They retained their autonomy and their control over their estates, to emerge prominently in the new society that was slowly developing in Japan.

Still a third group was composed of men who became the chief administrative officials on estates owned by the nobles. These officials, through the apathy of their overlords and through their own shrewdness, to say nothing of their undisputed occupancy of the estates, became the virtual owners, with sufficient men under their command to protect their interests against both competing neighbours and possible interference from the real owner of the estate who resided in the capital.

A final group of warriors was made up of men who had been sent out in command of the imperial troops in order to quell uprisings of the Ainu, a proto-Caucasoid people who inhabited most of Japan before the present racial group became dominant. These men, instead of returning to the capital, remained in the provinces, where they became provincial lords and developed their own estates.

The common foot-soldier was the backbone of the power of the lords, but did not share in the powers that the warrior lords were gaining for themselves. Some of the foot-soldiers had been sent on the campaigns against the Ainu and remained attached to their lords when they settled in the newly conquered areas. Others developed on the estates of nobles because of the central government's increasing dependence on the lords for the maintenance of order within the country. They organized their serfs in order to maintain peace and order and to protect the estate against possible attack from neighbours. The more war-like of the peasants became specialists in the bearing of arms.

By the middle of the twelfth century two families emerged as the leaders of the new warrior group, but as yet they were without apparent consciousness of the strength of their position. These families were the Taira and the Minamoto. Both traced their descent back to the imperial family, having been founded by imperial princes who had decided to give up their rights to the throne. Neither family, as has been true of all such groups in

Japanese history, was particularly unified. Since the families had many branches, it was not unusual for Taira to fight against Taira and Minamoto to fight against Minamoto.

The Taira family, the first to accede to a position of power, had its strength in the western part of Japan. It was more closely connected with the Fujiwara family, still a dominant group in Japanese politics at this time, than was the Minamoto family, and consequently was in a better position to gain an influential place in the government. Its close connection with the imperial court was to be both an advantage and a disadvantage. Because of its relations with the court it was in a position of trust which made it relatively easier for it to seize power, but it was also infected by the aestheticism and effeminacy of the court.

The Minamoto family, on the other hand, had the centre of its power in the eastern part of Japan around the Kwanto plain. It had played a leading rôle in the subjugation of the Ainu and had remained in the eastern part of the country. The Minamoto, not the Taira, definitely established the warriors as the dominant group in Japan, although the latter first gained control of the country.

The Gempei period ("Gem" refers to the Minamoto clan and the "Pei" to the Taira clan) is one of the most dramatic periods in Japanese history. This fifty-year period from 1150 to 1200 has become one of the richest sources of literary inspiration in all Japanese history. Dramatic events followed each other with such bewildering rapidity that the story of the times is almost impossible to follow.

In the brief period of less than half a century the Fujiwara family's hold on political and economic supremacy in the land loosened and fell away. Coupled with this was the equally dramatic advent of the warrior clans, the Taira and the Minamoto. The meteoric rise of the Taira was matched only by the suddenness of their collapse. But the Minamoto, apparently crushed by the rapid rush of the Taira, recouped their fortunes in a short period and dealt a fatal blow to the aspirations of their former conquerors. As if the turbulent rise and fall of the fortunes of these three families were not enough, the Gempei period also saw Fujiwara fight against Fujiwara, Taira against Taira, and Minamoto against Minamoto. Struggles over the succession both to the throne and to the leadership of the clans added still more confusion to the political situation. Intrigue was interlocked with intrigue and betrayal was piled on betrayal. A simple recounting of these events is almost as powerful as the most inspired work of the literary imagination.

To match the political struggles was the economic upheaval that accompanied them. First of all, when they came to power the Taira gained control of extensive tracts of land in the western part of Japan. Large parts of these lands were turned over by the Taira to the men who had helped them in their wars. But with the crushing of the Taira, the Minamoto clan came into control of the lands once held by the former, with the result that still another apportioning of land was carried out.

The people of the times, impressed by all these events, regarded the age as heralding the end of the world. In addition to the great changes that were coming over the affairs of men, the nation was visited also by a succession of storms and plagues that seemed to indicate that nature was in as great a turmoil as society. The crumbling of the brilliant culture of the aristocracy, which had shone like a light over the rest of the nation, must have been another ominous portent. Buddhism, with its emphasis on the evanescence of the affairs of men, was also being dramatically supported by the events that were taking place. The rise and the fall of the Taira and the Minamoto, to say nothing of the Fujiwara, came at the time when they seemed to be at the peak of their power and prosperity. Their collapse occurred when their future seemed to be most secure. Buddhists could scarcely ask for better proof of the validity of their views than the events which were taking place with such rapidity all around them.

The warriors did not seem to realize at first that they had arrived at a supreme position in Japan. At the beginning of this brief period their rôle was scarcely more than that of mercenaries who fought the battles for the Fujiwara and the court nobles. It was not until the Taira had emerged in a rôle of paramount importance that the warriors seemed to realize that they had in their hands the military strength, if they cared to exercise it for their own ends, that would guarantee to them the supreme power. But the Taira were unable to free themselves from the effeminacy and aestheticism of the court nobles, and they in turn were deposed by the Minamoto, who had a keener appreciation of the importance of their rôle on the stage of Japanese history.

Taira Kiyomori, one of the great men of Japanese history, was responsible for the success of his family. He was the first member of the warrior class to be appointed to the position of prime minister, an honour given him in 1167. He was definitely a man of action, without the polish that was demanded of men who were thought worthy of holding such high positions in the bureaucracy. The courtiers regarded him as an uncouth interloper, and hated him for it. He attempted to control the emperor by the same methods that the Fujiwara had used. His daughter became the wife of an emperor, and their son later came to the throne. This, of course, made Kiyomori the grandfather of the emperor, and presumably placed him in the same position of control that his more illustrious Fujiwara predecessors had enjoyed.

The major flaw in his thinking was that he believed that the members of his family would have to become courtiers in every sense of the term, if they wished to rule the country as they should. He failed to perceive that the qualities that had made the court aristocracy admired were not those of successful administrators. He died in 1181 and with him died the brief power of the Taira family. He apparently saw the danger that the Minamoto clan still held for his family, but he was powerless to eliminate it. Like the great Toyotomi Hideyoshi who was to follow him some four centuries later, Kiyomori left behind him no member of his family who was worthy of succeeding him.

Three years after his death the Minamoto clan administered a crushing, but not decisive, defeat to the forces of the Taira at the famous battle of Ichi-no-tani, not far from the present city of Kobe. The final blow to the hopes of the Taira family was delivered in 1185 at the battle of Dan-no-ura. The Taira, rallying their forces for a final attempt to stave off defeat, massed a fleet at the western end of the Inland Sea. In a sea battle off Dan-no-ura, not far from Shimonoseki, the Minamoto forces crushed those of the Taira, firmly establishing their own rule, and ending forever the Taira aspirations to power.

Minamoto Yoritomo not only established his own family in power, but instituted the system that was to keep the warrior class in control of Japan until the end of the feudalism. Born in 1146, he died fifty-three years later, after having crushed all rivals and established a system which he believed would insure his family's retention of power.

Yoritomo saw clearly that the centre of administration would have to be moved from the imperial capital if a successful government were to be set up. Intrigues in the imperial court into which the Taira family had permitted itself to be drawn with fatal results to its ambitions, had undermined the government's power. Consequently, Yoritomo set up his capital in Kamakura in the Kwanto region, not far from present-day Tokyo, to serve as the actual administrative centre while the imperial court was kept in isolation in Kyoto. This geographical separation of the aristocrats from the centre of political administration ended their hopes to revive their power. No longer were they to be in a position to take direct part in the government of the country.

Though he had planned wisely and well for the future of his family, Yoritomo failed to erect a secure structure. He, like his predecessor, Taira Kiyomori, was destined to be the first and only member of his family to enjoy great political power.

Yoritomo was responsible for the creation of the office through which the warrior class was to dominate Japan for seven centuries. That was the office of *sei-i-tai-shogun* ("subduing-barbarian-generalissimo") to which Yoritomo himself was appointed in 1192. The title is usually shortened to *shogun* which means simply "general," but in terms of the functions of the office "military dictator" is perhaps a better rendering. The title had existed for some centuries and was originally given to the commanders who directed the campaigns against the Ainu, hence the "barbarian" in the title. Yoritomo gave the office the special administrative sense that it retained until it was finally abolished in 1867.

The *shogun* was the warrior administrative and political chief of Japan for almost seven centuries, from the time that Yoritomo established his government until the military oligarchy was brought to an end in the nineteenth century. The office remained, of course, the monopoly of the most powerful military families except on a few occasions not long after Yoritomo died, when his successors to power appointed youthful imperial princes and members of the Fujiwara family as puppet occupants of the office. At times the *shogun* was almost as much of a figurehead as the emperor, but the office was vested with the right to administer the country, and the fiction of the *shogun's* powers was maintained as religiously as that of the emperor's.

The military administration of the country was organized parallel with the old bureaucracy of the imperial court. The latter was permitted to continue to exist, although it was completely without power. The offices were mere titles and the work was nothing more than empty play. The military administration held all actual power to rule the country, and the *shogun* as its head was the real ruler of the country.

The emperor continued to be theoretically the supreme source of political power. These two fountainheads of power were neatly harmonized by the device of maintaining the emperor as the titular head of the government and as the actual source of all political power. The *shogun* was merely the deputy of the emperor, carrying out the actual business of administration by virtue of the fact that the emperor had bestowed on him the right to do so. Broadly speaking, the emperor was the spiritual head of the state and the *shogun* the temporal head. In all the centuries that the institution of the *shogun* continued in existence there was not a single attempt by any *shogun* to usurp the throne.

Seven centuries of rule by the *shogun* firmly rooted the tradition of rule by warriors in the political soil of Japan. By no means all of the *shogun* were military dictators. Some were children; others dilettantes; and still others nonentities. But almost without exception they came from families who were recognized as having warrior blood.

The Kamakura period (1183 to 1333) should have been the age of the power of the Minamoto family, but almost immediately after Yoritomo's death in 1199 the government that he had built up fell under the control of the Hojo family, which was that of Yoritomo's wife.

With the accession to power of the Hojo family, a curious system of regents gradually developed, until in time the real rulers of the country were exercising political control four times removed from the actual source. Child-emperors and child-*shogun* were controlled by regents, and then by tutors from the powerful Hojo family. This peculiar system is one of the most remarkable political developments in Japanese history.

The emperor remained at the head of the Japanese state, at the peak of the political hierarchy. His political power, although theoretically still great, was weaker than it had ever been before. During the period of the civil oligarchy the emperor was at least physically close to the source of political power. His court in the capital city was the centre around which revolved all the activities of the civil bureaucracy, even if the Fujiwara control of his person was such that he could not exercise any direct influence on government. But with the removal of the capital to Kamakura, a geographical gulf was added to the political one that separated him from the power that was theoretically his.

During much of this period the *shogun* shared the powerless position of the emperor. The Hojo family, when it wrested power from the hands of the Minamoto, did not abolish the office of *shogun,* as it might well have done. Instead, it decided to control the *shogun* and to act through him, just as Yoritomo had planned to control the person of the emperor. Following the death of Yoritomo's son, the Hojo appointed members of first the Fujiwara family and then the imperial family, as *shogun*. These *shogun* were mere children at the time they were appointed, their average age when nominated being less than ten years.

Behind the child-emperors and the child-*shogun* there stood the regents, members of the Hojo family, to whom was entrusted the actual business of ruling the nation. Hojo Tokimasa was the first regent, as he had himself appointed to the position in 1203. But even these officials were destined to become puppets. Of the last four of the eight who were appointed to this office, two were under ten, one under fifteen, and only one was an adult when he was given the office. During the latter part of the rule of the Hojo family the final source of power, four degrees removed from the theoretical head of the state, was in the hands of the mature members of the family, whose rank was relatively low.

The Hojo family was crushed in 1333, and the power to rule the country passed into the hands of the Ashikaga family, which monopolized the shogunate for about two and a half centuries.

The period of Ashikaga rule was the most turbulent in Japanese history, and there is some justification for calling it the "Dark Ages" of Japan. But these two hundred years, from the mid-fourteenth to the mid-sixteenth century, might more accurately be regarded as a period of transition, a time when certain newly developing streams in Japanese politics, economics, and society were struggling to reach the surface. It was a period of transition characterized by disorder and chaos, but at the same time by the germination of new ideas and of new concepts that were to result in the appearance in Japan for the first time of a true unity and a true nationhood. The very turbulence of the times served to keep the warriors in a position of prominence in Japan. Though no family controlled Japan, the dominant position of the warriors was unshaken.

It was an age of violence and rebellion, with the sense of personal loyalty almost completely lacking in men's relations with each other. Betrayal, always a key factor at times of political stress in Japan, became almost the standard mode of behaviour. The emperors were to plumb the depths of political impotence and of economic poverty. The Ashikaga *shogun,* although theoretically in possession of the power to rule the country, were so weak that no one paid much attention to them, especially after 1400. They were not only too weak to command order and respect, but even to be considered worthy rivals for political supremacy in the country.

The period was one of almost continuous warfare between the feudal lords. None was strong enough to depose the Ashikaga *shogun,* and none was strong enough to control enough of the country to become politically dominant. The very disunity of the times paved the way for the advent of a strongly centralized government. Political disunity had reached such a stage that things could not possibly get worse; they had to get better.

In less than fifty years at the end of the sixteenth century, the chaos and turmoil of the Ashikaga period were swept away. Three of Japan's greatest men, Oda Nobunaga, Toyotomi Hideyoshi, and Tokugawa Iyeyasu, appeared simultaneously on the scene, and were destined to play important and complementary rôles in the destruction of the old feudalism and the establishment of a strong new centralized authority in Japan. These three men all knew each other personally, and the work of none could have been possible without the work of the others. Nobunaga blasted away the elements in the nation standing in the way of unification; Hideyoshi built the foundation for the new system; and finally

Iyeyasu completed the edifice of authoritarian government which was the forerunner of the modern Japanese state.

Oda Nobunaga (1534–82) traced his descent back to the great Taira Kiyomori. Nobunaga apparently did not possess the qualities of leadership and statesmanship that made his two more famous confreres the outstanding men they were. He is described as being unconventional, rough, and warlike. As befits a man who was destined to take long strides toward unifying the country by means of military conquest, he was bold and headstrong. He was never considerate of the feelings of others and his pledged word seems to have meant little. Yet he was possessed of the qualities of generalship and ruthlessness that enabled him to break some of the forces that were most resolutely standing in the way of unification of the country.

Like other great leaders in Japanese history, Nobunaga was not able to establish the fortunes of his family on a secure foundation. Personally he became all-powerful before his untimely death, but his successor, Hideyoshi, soon removed his descendants from the political scene.

Nobunaga was closely connected with both the imperial family and the Ashikaga family. They were the nominal repositories of political power, and Nobunaga, because of his steadily increasing influence, was bound to come into contact with them. In both 1561 and 1567 he was given imperial orders to restore peace in the capital, which had been periodically swept by revolt and left in ruins. In 1568, he succeeded in restoring order in Kyoto with the help of his able lieutenant, Hideyoshi. He would not have been given these imperial orders had he not succeeded in building up his power by conducting successful military operations against his rivals.

His connections with the Ashikaga were equally close. He virtually made Yoshiaki, the last of the Ashikaga line, *shogun*. Naturally, this placed him in a position where he thought that he was justified in interfering in the internal affairs of the Ashikaga family. Although he had worked for Yoshiaki, he finally broke with him after sending him a memorial criticizing his extravagance, his maladministration, his favouritism, and other shortcomings which made Yoshiaki scarcely an ideal administrator. Following this incident Yoshiaki plotted against him, but Nobunaga had no difficulty in crushing this abortive plot and in exiling him. The exile took place in 1573, and although Nobunaga did not deprive him of office, this brought an end to the Ashikaga line of *shogun*. This move eliminated a weak political element and paved the way for a stronger administration.

Another blow that Nobunaga struck in the cause of unification was the smashing of the power of the Buddhist temples. For many years some of the larger temples in the vicinity of the capital had existed as virtually independent states within the country. They had accumulated large holdings of land which constituted the foundation on which they were able to build up armies. Thus, they were able to protect their holdings against attack from others, and in addition could defy the central authorities, such as they were, to levy taxes or even to bring them under control. Nobunaga struck his greatest blow against the temples in 1571, when he succeeded in storming the great Buddhist stronghold on Mount Hiei near Kyoto. He ruthlessly burned the temples to the ground and put many of the priests to the sword. The blow against one of the holiest Buddhist posts in Japan stupefied the Japanese, but it eliminated a source of grave disorder.

Nobunaga definitely believed that the power, both economic and political, of the temples had to be crushed. He knew that the temples had openly intimidated the government when it had attempted to regulate them, and that a central administration could not function while such entities were allowed to exist independently. The temples had been protected by tradition and had been the beneficiaries of the patronage of the imperial family and the nobles. Numerous grants had given them wealth and immunity from taxation. But their primary function as time went on became not the exercise of their religious duties, but the protection of their secular holdings and the increase of their wealth. With Nobunaga's decisive action their power was crushed and brought completely to an end.

Nobunaga's career came to an inglorious conclusion. He was betrayed by one of his men who, he thought, was a faithful lieutenant. A certain Akechi Mitsuhide turned on him in 1582 and attacked him while he had only a few men with him. Nobunaga fought well, but seeing that he was faced with defeat, he killed himself. Hideyoshi, abandoning a campaign in Western Japan, hastened back in time to avenge the death of his master by killing Mitsuhide.

After Nobunaga's death power soon slipped from the hands of the Oda family. Rivalry developed between his two sons as to which should succeed to the father's rôle, but neither of the young men could match the political astuteness of Hideyoshi. The latter, ostensibly attempting to solve the dispute between the two heirs of the Oda family, selected Nobunaga's infant grandson as his logical successor. Thus gaining control of the Oda family's affairs, Hideyoshi lost no time in assuming for himself the powers that had been so arduously won by Nobunaga. He was to carry forward well toward completion the work of unification that had been started by his predecessor and to lay the foundation for a warrior-dominated military state.

Toyotomi Hideyoshi (1536–98) is virtually the only man in pre-modern Japan who arose to a position of power and influence from among the people. He came from neither the court nobility nor the feudal nobility. His father was a farmer. But lowly as he was in birth he did not have a feeling for the humble. He was from the people rather than of them. By the time he came to power he was completely of the warrior class, and as a matter of fact he was responsible for some legislation that was to weigh most heavily on the farmers.

Through ability and sheer force of will he became one of the greatest men in all Japanese history. His brilliance as a general enabled him to conquer the country. His statesmanship enabled him to bring peace to the nation which had been shaken by internal strife for generations.

Hideyoshi successfully finished the work that Nobunaga had auspiciously begun, namely, the military pacification of the country. Those feudal lords whose power he was unable to break directly, he awed into alliance. Perhaps it would be more correct to say that Hideyoshi and those lords whose power almost equalled his own were wise enough to see that they could accomplish their ends by negotiation rather than by continued fighting, which would serve only to sap seriously their resources. At any rate, Hideyoshi within a few years after Nobunaga's death was able to look around him at a Japan which he dominated either by the force of arms or by diplomatic negotiation.

With the work of military pacification brought to a successful conclusion, Hideyoshi lost no time in demonstrating the powers of statesmanship and of political acumen that were to win him even more fame than did his military ability. In many ways he laid out the pattern of authoritarian rule on which his successors, the Tokugawa, were to build so successfully the political organization that maintained them in power for more than two and a half centuries. His work is best revealed in a series of edicts that he issued during the last fourteen years of his rule.

In 1585 he issued an edict to the effect that a person could not change his employment without the permission of his lord. This was an important step in the direction of freezing the social order. If this edict were rigidly enforced a feudal lord would at all times know not only the number of men on whom he could rely for military service, but also the number of productive workers that he had under his control. Neither would he have to fear that his more influential neighbours might be able to lure away his fighting men and his serfs.

A year later Hideyoshi made the first move in the direction of the stratification of society which proved to be an important factor in the maintenance of social stability during the Tokugawa period. According to the laws that he issued in 1586, no *samurai* (warrior) could become a townsman, i.e., merchant; no farmer could leave the land and work for hire; and no landlord could protect vagrants and men who did not cultivate the soil. The law concerning the *samurai* was an important step in making them a solid core around which the rest of Japanese society could be developed. The law freezing the farmer to his land placed the national economy on a firmer foundation by insuring that the productive capacity of the land would not suffer because of a drift of labour away from the land. Finally, the law concerning landlords was a check on the possible development of private armies that would prove to be a threat to political stability. These laws were to undergo later modification, but they definitely set up patterns of control that were to be typical of Japanese society for many years to come.

One of Hideyoshi's most famous acts was the "Sword Hunt" in 1587. He declared that all farmers had to hand in to the authorities any weapons that they might have in their possession. The obvious reason for this order was to draw a sharp dividing line between the warrior class and the rest of the population. The peasant was no longer to be a part-time warrior, tilling his fields in time of peace and bearing arms for his feudal lord in time of war. The privilege and profession of bearing arms were to be reserved henceforth for the members of the warrior class, thus not only strengthening the authority of the warriors vis-à-vis the great mass of the people, but also establishing their prestige even more firmly.

Other classes of society were also to come under control of his government. Numerous laws regulating *samurai* behaviour were issued by Hideyoshi and his men. For example, he forbade marriages and all other types of arrangements among his vassals without his specific approval. Similar laws became one of the foundations of the power of the Tokugawa family.

Hideyoshi followed a policy of ostensibly rehabilitating the position of the imperial family and the imperial court, but actually he showed them no more real respect than had his predecessors. He revived certain court ceremonies, contributed funds to the emperor and built a palace for the retired sovereign. At the same time he utilized the emperor for political ends, as has been done for centuries in Japan.

His greatest economic work was a land survey covering the entire nation, which was carried out in the six years between 1590 and 1596. The economic dislocation brought about by the civil wars and the breakdown of the system of land tenure made such a step necessary. Probably his primary reason for ordering the survey was to increase his own revenues, by making certain that every parcel of land under his control was contributing the tax that was demanded. However, he took the additional step of arbitrarily ordering that the unit of measure be made smaller. This resulted in an increase of some twenty per cent in the area of taxable land which, of course, automatically increased the revenue of both Hideyoshi and the feudal lords. Another reason for the survey was to equalize the incomes from lands which could be distributed to the feudal lords loyal to Hideyoshi. The bringing of uncultivated land into production was another motive for the survey. With all plots of land accounted for it would be possible to plan a program of reclamation of waste land.

The survey was also a step in the perfection of the fief system which strengthened the financial position of the lords. Financial stability would contribute to political stability by making it possible for the lords successfully to police their lands and to support the number of people under their control. In addition, the financial basis of Hideyoshi's new central administration was strengthened by the survey.

Japanese historians estimate that the income of Hideyoshi and the other feudal lords was increased from thirty to fifty per cent as a result of the survey. The major part of the increase is to be accounted for by the arbitrary decrease in the size of the unit of area, but in addition the discovery of fields which had not been previously reported added considerably. The tax principle established at this time was, in the phrase of the times, "four to the lord and six to the farmer." This proportion, though it varied from time to time and according to the whim of the lord, remained the standard tax rate for many years.

Another important step that Hideyoshi took was to convert the standard for the valuation of land from an arbitrary cash basis to its productivity. Subsequently, value of land was calculated in terms of the amount of rice it would produce. The unit of measure was the *koku,* which is slightly less than five bushels. The extent of a lord's holdings was measured in terms of the number of *koku* of rice that they would produce during the year. Lords granted their retainers lands the yield of which was of course also measured in *koku*. The rice tax was henceforth to be the standard. This move eliminated many other taxes, which, however, were restored later when the nation was beset with economic difficulties.

Hideyoshi had perfected a system which guaranteed his unchallenged political supremacy in Japan, but it was not strong enough to continue his family in power. Tokugawa Iyeyasu broke the grasp of the Toyotomi family on Japan and perfected the structure of control, the foundation for which had been so ably laid by Hideyoshi.

Tokugawa Iyeyasu, the third of the three great figures who brought unity to Japan, was the beneficiary, if not the designated heir, of both Nobunaga and Hideyoshi. It was he who perfected the system after his two illustrious predecessors had broken the forces standing in the way of unification and had built the foundation for an efficient and effective administrative system. Iyeyasu had been a faithful ally to Nobunaga, almost on a footing of equality, as he was the lord of three great provinces and with influence extending across the borders of others. After Nobunaga's death he supported one of his sons against Hideyoshi, but the latter made his peace with Iyeyasu without coming to blows over the question of succession to Nobunaga's power.

His relations with Hideyoshi himself were much more complicated. The alliance that was eventually formed between the two seems to have been founded on the respect with which these shrewd men regarded each other. As a mark of his respect for Iyeyasu, Hideyoshi appointed him a member of the council of five which was to function as a kind of cabinet. These five, drawn from the most influential families of the land, were to discuss and to decide all great political affairs in a spirit of conciliation and freedom from suspicion. Apparently Hideyoshi thought that the appointment of the five men to such a key group would cause them to act as checks on each other's ambitions, and that they would therefore serve the cause of his family more loyally. In addition, he set up other administrative groups and appointed faithful attendants and tutors for his son, Hideyori, whom he had chosen to be his successor and who was only five years old at the time of his father's death.

Iyeyasu broke all active opposition to his rule at the decisive battle of Sekigahara in 1600, the date usually given for the start of the power of the Tokugawa family; but it was not until 1615 that the Toyotomi family was finally wiped out. After his advent to power Iyeyasu permitted Hideyori to retain the great Toyotomi castle in Osaka and the three neighbouring provinces. Hideyori was only seven years old at the time that Iyeyasu came to power, but his mother, Yodokimi, headed his cause. In 1602 Iyeyasu betrothed his six-year-old grand-daughter to the young Hideyori; but that did not prevent him from crushing Hideyori and his followers in the so-called winter campaign in 1614, and the summer campaign of the following year. The two campagns were fought in Osaka around the strong Toyotomi castle that Hideyoshi had carefully built. The winter campaign was indecisive, the castle's fortifications proving too strong even for Iyeyasu's great armies. A truce was arranged, and Iyeyasu, resorting to guile where force had failed, asserted that the truce allowed him to fill in some of the outer moats surrounding the castle and to destroy certain fortifications. The indignant Hideyori party protested against this, but their protests were too late. The summer campaign was easy. The Toyotomi clan was wiped out, and with them went the last armed threat to the Tokugawas.

Tokugawa Iyeyasu (1542–1616), like Oda Nobunaga, was a skilful warrior and like Toyotomi Hideyoshi, a shrewd statesman, but he proved to have both qualities in greater measure than did either of his two illustrious predecessors. If his policy can be summed up in a few words, it was to build up a political organization that would keep his family in control of Japan. The means to attain that policy were equally simple: to establish strict control over all classes of society and to eliminate everything that might possibly weaken the rule of the Tokugawa régime. The isolation of Japan from the outside world was a part of the system. The control of the feudal lords and the imperial court, the stratification of society, and numerous restrictions placed on the life of every inhabitant of Japan were part of the pattern of control that Iyeyasu instituted. The system, based as it was on control, was fundamentally static, yet it concentrated so much authority in the hands of the Tokugawa family that it was able to maintain itself in power for more than two and a half centuries. It also did much to create the political and social attitudes that are the basis for the modern authoritarian state.

The unification and centralization accomplished by Iyeyasu and his immediate successors did not give the Tokugawa family absolute control of every feudal estate in all Japan. The Tokugawa family was simply the most powerful of a great number of feudal families. It had great estates and a large number of warriors to police and to protect them, and in its possessions its rule was supreme. In regard to the other feudal lords the Tokugawa government was primarily concerned with preventing the growth of conditions in their fiefs that would result in political or economic disorder, and with preventing anti-Tokugawa plots. As long as other lords managed their affairs well and displayed no dangerous ambitions, the Tokugawa administration was content to allow absolute rule over their territories. At the same time, however, certain measures were evolved that would prevent the interests of the lords from growing beyond the limits of their fiefs.

The key Kwanto region was the base of Tokugawa power. The Tokugawa family had had its seat in the central part of Japan, to the east of Kyoto, but in 1590 Hideyoshi granted Iyeyasu the eight provinces of the Kwanto in exchange for his ancestral lands. But Iyeyasu did not develop his new holdings until 1604, a year after he had been appointed to the position of *shogun,* when he decided to set up his capital at Edo. He was undoubtedly influenced in his decision by the strategic location of the city. It was on the Kwanto plain, which has been one of the key economic areas in Japan. In addition, its strategic location at the bend of Japan where the coast shifts from an east-west to a north-south direction was at the ideal spot for the maintenance of efficient communications with both the northern and western halves of Honshu.

Edo had been the site of the castle of a small feudal lord for many years, but it had not enjoyed any real importance until Iyeyasu decided to construct his capital there. Economic and political reasons, as well as strategic motives, lay behind his decision to build an elaborate capital city. He saw that the forcing of the feudal lords to contribute men and materials toward the construction of the city would weaken them financially, and would therefore reduce their power of waging war against him. This strategy is observable in the manner in which he exacted men and materials from the lords. Iyeyasu saw to it that the lords had to contribute in direct proportion to their strength and importance. He established an elaborate system of checkers to see that each and every lord contributed exactly what was demanded of him. In the first phase of the construction, 1604 to 1606, the lords in the western part of Japan had to bear the brunt of the cost, and in the second stage, 1607 to 1614, the lords to the east and north had to contribute most heavily.

In addition to sharing the cost of constructing the new capital, the feudal lords had to build and to maintain mansions in Edo, another constant drain on their resources which helped to sap their potential for attacking the Tokugawa. Apparently the construction of feudal mansions in the capital originated merely as a gesture of confidence in the Tokugawa régime, but it soon became a law that every lord had to maintain an establishment in the capital. Besides constituting a financial drain on the lords, this custom also served the practical purpose of keeping the lords where the Tokugawa government could observe their every move.

Edo, built around the Tokugawa castle which later became the imperial palace, was the capital from which the affairs of Japan were administered and in addition it was the secondary seat of all the feudal lords. Hence, the spirit of the city was definitely martial, as the Tokugawa régime was a military one. But with the martial air there was also a strong commercial flavour to the city's activities. The newly rising merchant class naturally flocked to the capital in order to supply the needs of the warriors. They also served as the business agents of the lords. Administration and business were the principal concerns of the leading inhabitants of Edo.

The *daimyo* or feudal lords were divided into two groups, the *tozama* ("outside lords") and the *fudai daimyo* ("traditional lords") . The *tozama* were the lords who had acknowledged Tokugawa supremacy after the battle of Sekigahara. Some of them had actively fought against the Tokugawa while others had been only neutral. In other words, they were the lords who were suspect in varying degree by the Tokugawa government. The *fudai daimyo,* on the other hand, were the lords who had been traditionally associated with the Tokugawa family before the battle. These enjoyed positions of trust within the administration and certain important offices were reserved only for them.

The *fudai daimyo* were placed throughout the nation, so that they could act as a check on possible unfriendly acts against the central government. For example, *fudai* estates were strategically located across the main highways, so that they could block marches on either Kyoto or Edo. *Fudai* estates were also strategically placed so that their men could march on the rear of the *tozama* lords in the event that the latter set out to attack the capital or any other important area.

But the *tozama* lords were not weaklings. Some of the most powerful lords in the country, such as the Shimazu in Kyushu and the Maeda in north-central Japan, were among them. They were so powerful, in fact, that even Iyeyasu prudently decided against attempting to crush them, and allowed them to keep their fiefs intact. Many *tozama* were wealthier and possessed larger estates than the *fudai daimyo*. It was among the *tozama* lords, as a matter of fact, that the greatest opposition to the rule of the Tokugawas developed and it was they who were finally responsible for the fall of the Tokugawa régime.

Many rules were laid down to regulate the conduct of the lords. Although the intent of some of these seems to be moral, at the bottom all were political in the sense that they were designed to preserve the stability of society and of the political order. In 1615 Iyeyasu issued a number of rules regulating the conduct of feudal lords. Both military arts and learning were to be fostered among the members of the warrior class. Militarism, according to these rules, was an unavoidable necessity although not desirable in itself. Drinking parties and other amusements were to be kept within bounds, for drink and women were principally responsible for the loss of estates. Lawbreakers were not to be sheltered by anyone, and any retainer guilty of rebellion or homicide was to be expelled from a lord's holdings, for "savage and unruly retainers are edged tools for overthrowing the empire and deadly weapons for destroying the people."

Neither lords nor retainers nor serfs were allowed to visit other fiefs. This was to prevent the building up of secret armies and to eliminate spying. Also in the category of military controls were the regulations concerning castle construction. All repairs to castles, to say nothing of the construction of new ones, were to be reported to the authorities. "High walls and deep moats," said the order, "are the cause of great upheavals when they belong to others."

The *samurai* were instructed to practice economy. The materials for garments were minutely regulated. This was to enforce economy and to keep the classes separate. Also controlled was the use of palanquins by the lords. On the more positive side, lords of provinces were enjoined to select men of ability to act under them. They were told that the art of government lay in obtaining the right men for the jobs. The lords were expected to observe faithfully all rules and regulations established by the central government. The five most severe punishments were execution, confiscation of estate, domiciliary confinement, reduction in the size of the estate, and shift to another less favourably situated fief.

There were between two hundred and fifty and three hundred

daimyo during the Tokugawa period. The number varied for the reasons outlined above. As can be seen, the *bakufu* ("tent government"), as the Tokugawa administration was called, possessed the power to create or to destroy the lords under them. Although the estates were under the strict control of the *bakufu,* they were at the same time virtually independent kingdoms. The frontiers between the estates were jealously guarded, and the roads entering and leaving them were marked off by gates and barriers through which all travelers had to pass and at which they had to show their credentials.

One of the most unusual forms of control instituted by the Tokugawa government was the system of *sankin kotai.* This system involved alternate residence of the feudal lord in his fief and in the capital. Although the regulations concerning *sankin kotai* varied with the feudal lord and the distance of his fief from the capital, basically they set forth that the lord had to spend a certain period of each year in residence in the capital. The system involved, of course, the maintenance of a mansion in Edo. When the lord left Edo to return to his fief he had to leave his wife and children in the capital as hostages to guarantee his good behaviour. The aims of this system were to impoverish the lords by forcing them to bear the expense of the journey to the capital, to keep them in attendance at the capital so that they would have neither the time nor the opportunity to plot with their neighbours against the government, and finally to force good behaviour by means of the hostage system.

Under the *sankin kotai* system travel was minutely regulated. A feudal lord could not simply leap on his horse and, accompanied by a few retainers, set off for the capital. The time of departure, route, and size of retinue were all regulated by the government. The lords were absolutely prohibited from passing through Kyoto on their way to Edo, a move obviously designed to prevent the seizure of the person of the emperor or the co-operation between lords and the imperial court.

The emperor and imperial court were kept under as strict a control as were the feudal lords. In a sense the control was even tighter, for the imperial family and the court nobles were not permitted to own their own estates, but were forced to depend for their economic existence on the grants that were given them by the *bakufu.* As has already been pointed out, the emperor and his retinue were to spend their time in empty study of ancient customs and of ancient literature. They were kept isolated from all contact with the *daimyo* because of the fear of intrigue.

The pretense of political power in the hands of the emperor was maintained through the preservation of the fiction that the emperor was the ultimate source of political power. The emperor retained the empty power of issuing the formal appointment of the *shogun* to office. One of the most important officials of the *bakufu* was stationed in Kyoto in order to see to it that no plots or intrigues were hatched there either by the nobles alone or in collaboration with the feudal lords.

Because of their exalted position the court nobles were not considered as forming one of the social classes of Japan during the Tokugawa period, and thus to some extent they escaped some of the social controls that were a part of the Tokugawa system of government. But the economic and political controls that were set up around the court were sufficient to insure their docility.

Thus the Tokugawa government kept under control the two groups within Japan, namely, the feudal lords and the court nobility, from which they might expect opposition to their government to rise. The Tokugawa family and its advisers undoubtedly knew the history of their country well, and if they did then they were aware of the dangers of plots that might arise within the ruling oligarchy. However, their control of society extended down through the lower levels.

The central administration that was set up and dominated by the Tokugawa family was known as the *bakufu,* literally, "tent government," a term originated by Minamoto Yoritomo. This was the machinery through which the Tokugawa family ruled Japan. It was the primary centralizing agent that maintained a cohesion in administration in spite of the fact that the feudal lords were really the heads of independent political and economic units. The Tokugawa family was not the *bakufu.* As a matter of fact the *bakufu* was a government for the Tokugawa family, rather than a government by them.

The capstone of the Tokugawa system was, of course, the *shogun.* The office was the monopoly of the Tokugawa family, and in it was seated the power to administer the country as the agent of the emperor, as had been the case in previous periods. The Tokugawa *shogun* had at their disposal a large enough force of armed men to make their position secure, an economic foundation broad enough to support the expense of maintaining such an army, a central administration efficient enough to control subordinate feudal lords, and a carefully thought out system of checks which kept potentially divisive elements under control. Thus, the *shogun* was an effective ruler rather than the holder of an empty title, as he had been so often previously.

The rigid stratification of Japanese society into four classes of warrior, farmer, artisan, and merchant was another means that was used by the Tokugawa in order to insure social and political stability within Japan. Although these social categories were broken down by law when the Tokugawa régime crumbled and the change was later written into the Constitution itself, the effects are still observable in Japan. The glorification of the warrior and the warrior ideal is one example. Perhaps of even greater moment is the Japanese acceptance of the idea that society is made up of a series of hierarchies, extending on the lower level from the relationships existing within the family to the ultimate one, the relation between the subject and the ruler.

At the apex of the social hierarchy were, of course, the warriors. They were the privileged class of Tokugawa society. They monopolized political power; they were economically dominant; they enjoyed the social prestige that naturally accrued to their position of power. They dominated Japanese society even more completely than did the court aristocracy of the Heian period. Not only their political and economic dominance, but also an elaborate code of conduct, contributed to the idea that was constantly drilled into all Japanese that they were a class apart. They were given certain prerogatives, such as the right to bear swords, that not only made them conscious of their position as the socially chosen group of Japanese society, but made every one on lower levels recognize their superiority.

Although they were encouraged to develop a high degree of social cohesiveness within the class, the individuals making up this group varied greatly in both function and character. At the lowest end of the scale were men who took advantage of their position to be little more than bullies and petty gangsters. At the other end were men who were either scholars or statesmen. Others were professional soldiers, medical men, local officials, teachers, and literary men. But no matter what their talents were, the warriors, as a group, were a parasitic class. They produced nothing in the way of economic wealth. Their economic function was simply to encourage production so that their incomes would be maintained at the proper level, and to see to it that the peasants paid all the taxes that were demanded of them.

Second in the social rank were the farmers, although this exalted position was nothing more than a mockery. It was the only honour that they enjoyed and an empty one it was. The peasants bore the complete economic burden of the Tokugawa system and actually supported all classes of society, for they produced rice, the wealth of the times. In return for their economic contribution to Japanese society they were given no political voice. Their only political connection with the *bakufu* was the responsibility of producing the rice that was exacted from them in the form of taxes. They had no control over the amount of tax that was demanded of them, and they could expect neither the *bakufu* nor their feudal lord to use any of the wealth they produced to improve their lot.

Their only means of political expression was rioting. The declining years of the Tokugawa régime witnessed many peasant riots, which, although they sapped the strength of the *bakufu,* did not directly bring about its downfall. The revolts of the peasants were all directed at a purely local cause, an unpopular official, a too-oppressive feudal lord, too heavy taxes. At times they involved as many as several hundred thousand persons, but they all remained basically local in character. Difficulties of travel, effective means of control, and the lack of able leaders prevented the peasants from organizing a mass revolt that might have brought down the entire feudal structure, as in France.

The artisans, the class ranked third, was small and unimportant both politically and economically. It was simply because they worked with their hands that they were placed above the merchants, the lowest on the social scale. They became important only when the extent of their business made them merchants.

Ranked last in the social scale and heartily despised because they did not work with their hands, and because they were interested in money matters, were the merchants, who had begun to appear as a separate class during the Ashikaga period. The warriors incidentally were taught that money was literally filthy and that it was a disgrace for them to concern themselves with financial matters. Although the merchants were on the bottom of the social scale, during the Tokugawa period they became the most powerful economic group. They were also important culturally, because it was they who developed the first truly bourgeois culture in Japan. It was out of the society that they were forced to create for themselves that the popular theatre developed and that an extensive popular literature, with all the faults and all the lively virtues of people's literature, developed. But they were never to become politically powerful. Tokugawa control of the merchants was too strict to permit them to get their hands directly on political power or to govern the nation indirectly by the use of economic pressure. The merchants were never able to free themselves of the social restrictions that were forced on them by the Tokugawa government.

The relatively weak political position of the merchants did not, however, vitiate the strength of the ties that bound them to the warriors. The restrictions that were placed on them by the Tokugawa government actually brought the two groups into close contact with each other and paved the way for a continuation of close co-operation in the modern period after the barriers between the classes had been successfully broken down. The same relationship, in general outline, has existed between big business and government in Japan as had existed between the merchants and the Tokugawa *bakufu* in feudal Japan, namely, control on the part of the central administration, but freedom on the part of the merchants to enjoy the fruits of their investment and their initiative.

The barriers between the classes crumbled to a certain degree, mainly through the operation of economic factors. But the hard fact of the stratification of society was not seriously undermined. If one crossed class lines, he became a member of the class that he entered; he did not act as a rebel to whom all social distinctions were anathema. This attitude toward social relationships persisted, as has been pointed out, even after the system itself was broken down by the new régime that replaced the Tokugawa.

The Political Oligarchy

The entire Tokugawa system was based on control, control exercised through the authority that was the Tokugawa *bakufu's* by virtue of the military power that it possessed. There was no room in the system for protest or for individual initiative in either politics or economics. The one cardinal political rule for the masses was the acceptance of authority. All political and economic decisions were made by the narrow oligarchy that was the *bakufu,* and the feudal lords who, though all-powerful within their domains, were still amenable to the orders of the *bakufu.* The governing class had no responsibilities to those whom it ruled and the sole responsibility of the mass of the people was to obey.

Here during the Tokugawa period were solidified the political attitudes that were to lead logically to the modern authoritarian state in Japan. The transition from the Tokugawa form of authoritarianism to the contemporary form was smooth and rapid, although there was created an illusion that Japan had abandoned her old absolutism. The illusion grew out of the fact that the introduction of new forms of government was mistaken for a fundamental change in the philosophy of government that lay behind them. But the Tokugawa system had to disappear before the new authoritarianism could appear.

Japanese society in the latter part of the Tokugawa period was shot through and through with discontent. It grew out of both the economic dislocations that were being felt increasingly in all levels of society and also out of the oppressive measures of the *bakufu.* There was no great gathering wave of unrest against the ideology on which the political and economic orders were built, but a mounting discontent with the galling restraints of the *bakufu's* rule. Had there been basic ideological disagreement between the malcontents and the Tokugawa régime the whole structure of militaristic, authoritarian government of Japan might have been undermined.

The imperial court, although without political power and kept under economic restrictions, was the seat of a few discontented courtiers who were to play a key rôle in the events that brought about the downfall of Tokugawa rule. It was the courtiers who became the spearhead of the "Revere the Emperor!" movement which was going to be the ideological basis for the attack on the Tokugawa régime. The near-poverty forced on them by the *bakufu* was particularly irritating to the able courtiers, whose studies in earlier Japanese history had convinced them that they were the heirs of a great cultural heritage from which they were being kept by the Tokugawa interlopers. The courtiers did not succeed in bringing about a renaissance of the power and glory of the nobility as a class, but they were an extremely effective component of the political groups that were being mobilized for the final assault on the Tokugawa order.

The effective core of the opposition to the *bakufu* was the *tozama* lords, the group which had always been held most suspect by the *bakufu*. As has already been pointed out, the most influential of these lords had under their control large areas of productive land and formidable bodies of armed men. They had never been completely won over to the Tokugawa colours, and were keenly conscious of the means by which the *bakufu* sought to control them. They were aware of their strength and of the distrust with which the *bakufu* regarded them. Since their fiefs were in the outlying sections of the country it was difficult for the Tokugawa authorities to keep an accurate and continuing check on them or even, for that matter, to send out bodies of men to keep them under control. The *tozama* lords and their retainers did not escape the economic difficulties that were weighing heavily on Japan. They too sought some change in the system that would ease their situation.

Although the *tozama* lords formed the nucleus of leaders that was to attack successfully the Tokugawa structure, it was from among their retainers that the real brains behind the attack on the Tokugawas came. These men were even more suited than their lords to act as leaders, for it was they who were in active charge of the fiefs. They knew the pressing nature of the economic problems that were facing them. They were familiar with the techniques of administration that would have to be utilized by any group that might succeed in overthrowing the Tokugawa. They had the contacts with the merchants who might be expected to finance an anti-Tokugawa movement. These administrators were young, intelligent, and eager to serve their lords and the interests of their country by acting as leaders of the movement against the *bakufu*.

It was from the warriors, too, that the ideological basis along traditional Japanese lines, for the attack on the Tokugawa, came. The warriors, as has been pointed out, were encouraged to become scholars and to develop themselves intellectually as well as physically. A group of outstanding scholars in the eighteenth century founded a school of research in classical literature and historical research. Such men as the great Motoori Norinaga delved into ancient Japanese history and found that according to the ancient records, the sole repository of the right to rule was the emperor, and that the *shogun* had really been usurping the right under the guise of assisting the emperor. Ironically it was a branch of the Tokugawa family itself that contributed most toward the establishment of this group of classical scholars. Using the findings of these scholars as a basis, the anti-Tokugawa forces easily created the ideological basis for their attack. It was the technique of calling for a return to the hands of the emperor of the right to rule, of charging the ruling group with usurping the rights of the throne.

The Tokugawa régime itself was gradually disintegrating. Like all such ruling groups, the line was running poor. After a succession of able men in the first part of the Tokugawa period, the men of the Tokugawa family were losing their capacity to administer and to lead. They were less the leaders that their ancestors had been and more the figureheads for whom the real administrators of the country were acting. This lack of leadership was crucial at a time when the pressure of both events and men on the Tokugawa régime was growing ever stronger.

In addition, the Tokugawa administration was falling into financial difficulties. Although it controlled vast tracts of land, the income was no longer sufficient to maintain the administration in smooth operation. The need for money income became greater and greater, and the resources of the Tokugawa were static. They had cut themselves off from the possibility of significant income from foreign trade. There was no expanding income from the new commercial structure that was being developed under the control of the merchant class. The Tokugawa régime, in other words, had no resources at its command that it could use effectively in order to allay either the political or the economic discontent rapidly mounting around them.

The merchants, undoubtedly the most secure economic group

in the society of Japan, were not unwilling to welcome a change in the régime under which they were forced to live. Tokugawa legislation had kept them under a control that was as strict as it was galling. A change in the rulers of Japan might bring about a relaxation of the controls, they must have reasoned, if the proper financial support were given those who were planning to overthrow Tokugawa rule.

Considerable unrest among the peasants also was evident. The number of peasant revolts during the latter part of the Tokugawa régime was large, for the peasants were the group of all the others that suffered the most economic hardship. But their rôle in the destruction of the Tokugawa régime was indirect rather than direct. Their riots were a part of the widespread discontent that was eating away at the foundations of the Tokugawa power, but the peasants did not march against the Tokugawa as a group. No peasant leaders appeared either to lead their fellows against the central authorities or to demand of the new rulers of Japan a completely new economic deal for the peasants.

Another force, coming from outside Japan, was to play a major rôle in the collapse of the Tokugawa régime. The Westerners were appearing off Japanese shores in increasing numbers and demanding that Japan again open her doors to their trade. Pressure was being increasingly exerted on the Tokugawa to reverse a policy more than two hundred years old. The issue of the opening of the country quickly became a major one in the domestic politics of Japan.

Thus, a complex of economic, political, social, and diplomatic factors was pressing ever more heavily on the Tokugawa régime, and the *bakufu* was becoming increasingly helpless to solve the major problems that were facing it. Events were moving rapidly in the direction of another change in the oligarchy that had ruled Japan for centuries. The "outs" were becoming more and more restless and the "ins" progressively weaker in defense of their position. Japan was on the verge of the most dramatic and most significant change in its history.

The events that brought the Tokugawa régime to an end were at all times kept under control by the small group of anti-Tokugawa leaders who had formulated the plans for the coup and who had at their command the forces necessary to carry them out.

Popular participation in the great political change that swept over the land was confined to the task of fighting the minor battles that Tokugawa resistance awakened. The widespread discontent described above made possible the dethronement of the Tokugawa government, but it did not break into open revolt against the system that created the causes for discontent. Participation in the planning and the execution of the coup was as restricted as participation in the construction of the new government was going to be.

The old order as represented by the Tokugawa régime was gone, and the new rulers of Japan were embarked on a career of reform and modernization that was to confirm in power both them and those who thought as they did. There was still much deadwood to be cleared away, but the direction in which the new Japan was facing was clear.

On April 6, 1868, only a few weeks after the Tokugawa régime had been dispossessed, the famous Charter Oath of the Emperor Meiji was issued in his name. This oath has been regarded by Japanese as one of the most important documents in all Japanese history, primarily because it is supposed to represent the thoughts of Emperor Meiji at the beginning of his reign. It is important because it lists in broad, general outline the entire course of the development of Japan during the Meiji period; but whether it was actually used as a blueprint is another question. However, the things that it foreshadows were all carried out. The Charter Oath reads as follows:

"*1. An assembly widely convoked shall be established, and all affairs shall be decided by impartial discussion.*

"*2. All classes shall be of one mind and administration shall be vigorously carried out.*

"*3. All classes of people shall be allowed to fulfill their just aspirations, so that there may be no discontent.*

"*4. All absurd old usages shall be abandoned, and justice and righteousness shall regulate all action. Uncivilized customs of former times shall be abolished, and everything shall be based upon just and equitable principles of nature.*

"*5. Knowledge shall be sought for throughout the world, so that the foundations of the Empire may be strengthened.*

"Desiring to carry out a reform without parallel in the annals of our country, We ourselves here take the initiative and swear to the Deities of Heaven and Earth to adopt these fundamental principles of national government, so as to establish thereby the security and prosperity of the people. We call upon you to make combined and strenuous efforts to carry them out."

Emperor Meiji was only sixteen years old at the time that the Charter Oath was issued, consequently it is highly probable that this is another instance when the emperor's advisers decided on a step that should be carried out and simply obtained the imperial sanction. One Western writer observes that this Oath is not a declaration of rights, as it is sometimes described as being, but a declaration of intentions.

The first article was undoubtedly written in order to provide a foundation for breaking down the monopoly of government office that had been typical of the Tokugawa system, and that seemed to be emerging in the new state that was being set up. Later it was interpreted to mean that the Emperor had promised the people representative government, and the clause was used by the proponents of a representative government to force more concessions out of the ruling oligarchy.

Articles Two and Three are predominantly moral in tone, and apparently were designed to foster unity of effort. Article Four attacked the feudal practices that the leaders of the new Japan felt were holding back Japan from the progress that was necessary if the country was to build up its strength. A strong Japan could defend itself effectively from possible attack from without, and in addition could bring about the emancipation of the country from the unequal treaties forced upon her when Japan had again been opened to contact with the outside world.

The fifth article was perhaps the most positive of all. It was an open injunction for the nation to look to other parts of the world for inspiration. Western knowledge and Western techniques were eagerly to be sought after and set up in Japan. The leaders who had written the Charter Oath for the young Emperor knew that this imperial sanction would be a long step in the direction of freeing the country from its prejudices against the "Western barbarian."

The Charter Oath is not one of the great political documents in world history, but it was of great significance in the development of modern Japan, for it charted out in rough form the course that the new state was to follow.

The deposition of the *shogun* and the issuance of the Charter Oath did not mean the immediate end of feudalism. But feudalism had to be ended if the new government was to become as strong as its architects desired it to be. There was a fundamental contradiction between feudalism and the centralization that was necessary to make Japan strong. Under the old system each feudatory assessed and collected its own taxes, enacted its own laws for the control of its land and its people, and commanded all troops within its territory. No matter how much control a central authority like the Tokugawa administration might have over these lords, the nation would still not be one. It would still be lacking in a centralized system of laws, a national economy, and a national army. The movement toward the abolition of feudalism was deliberate and carefully planned.

With the abolition of the Tokugawa régime, the imperial court was given jurisdiction over the lands once held by the Tokugawa family. An imperial official was appointed to represent the imperial interests in each fief newly come under the control of the imperial court. The status of the feudal lords themselves remained unchanged.

A major step in the direction of the dissolution of the feudal régime was made in March of 1869, when the lords of the Satsuma, Choshu, Hizen, and Tosa clans presented a memorial to the throne surrendering their lands to the Emperor. These four clans had been the leaders of the anti-Tokugawa movement, and it was really they who became the leaders of the new government in Japan. The lead of these four major families was soon followed by the rest of the feudal lords. By the end of the year virtually all of the feudal lords had presented similar memorials to the throne.

The following quotations from the memorial will give an insight into the motives of the four lords as well as a key to the unfolding of the new order in Japan.

"It is now sought to establish an entirely new form of government. Care must, therefore, be taken to preserve intact both one central body of government, and one universal authority. The land in which your servants live is the land of the Emperor, and the people whom they govern are his subjects. Neither the one, therefore, nor the other can belong to your servants.

"Your servants accordingly beg respectfully to surrender to Your Majesty the registers of the population, and beg Your Majesty to deal with everything as you may think fit, giving what should be given and taking away what should be taken away. They entreat Your Majesty to issue such Imperial decrees as may be deemed necessary with respect to the lands and the people of the four clans represented in this Memorial, and to make such changes as Your Majesty may think proper. They also beg that all laws, decrees, and military regulations, extending even to military dress and accoutrements, may be issued by the Central Government, so that all matters of state, both great and small, may be decided by one and the same authority. In this way both name and reality will be secured, and this country will be placed on a footing of equality with foreign powers."

The old theory that the emperor is both the owner of all Japan and the ruler of all the people is enunciated here once again. Again we can see the spectacle of the real leaders of the country making what is on the surface a tremendous economic sacrifice, but resting secure in the fact that their political control of the country will carry with it sufficient economic returns to recompense them more than enough for the sacrifices they were making in the name of the emperor. They knew that it would be they who would be making the laws that they were so humbly requesting of the throne.

Under the terms of this partial settlement of the problem of feudalism all fiefs were returned to the control of the emperor, and the *daimyo* remained on them as governors. But this measure, too, fell short of the necessary steps that had to be taken if the government was to be truly centralized. The end of feudalism came in 1871. A rather brief imperial rescript announced that the clans were abolished and prefectures established in their place.

In 1877 the last bit of armed resistance to the new order flared up in the form of the Satsuma rebellion. The Satsuma clan had been the leaders in the movement against the Tokugawa régime, but its leader, the great Saigo Takamori, had become disgruntled because his plans had been circumvented on several occasions, most notably in 1874, when he was eager to start an invasion of Korea. The Satsuma clan, traditionally one of the most warlike of all the feudatories, was also dissatisfied with the treatment that the warriors as a whole were receiving. They saw the warriors as a class losing their favoured position in Japanese society. The army was being thrown open to the masses by the institution of the system of mass conscription.

The fighting took place in Kyushu, and the Satsuma clan was defeated after slightly more than six months of campaigning. The most galling thing about their defeat was the fact that it was inflicted by a conscript army, drawn from all classes of society, many from the despised peasant class. These men, without the traditions of the *samurai,* but armed with modern weapons and trained according to modern methods, more than proved a match for the Satsuma *samurai,* who were fighting according to tradition.

This brief flare-up was almost the only bit of serious resistance that the new régime had to face. The transition from the feudal state was carried out with a speed that was as remarkable as it was fortunate for the Japanese nation.

Feudalism as the economic and political structure of the country disappeared with the collapse of the Tokugawa régime, but the feudal psychology remained in Japan as the dominating factor in the establishment of a new form of oligarchic government. This feudal attitude of unquestioning acceptance of the control of authority was the foundation on which the modern authoritarian state was based in Japan. The old class barriers that were erected during the Tokugawa period were swept away and the warriors as a separate and distinct class in Japanese society disappeared, but the whole Japanese nation became imbued with the psychology that was once held by only a percentage of the population. Universal male conscription, for example, instead of sweeping away the concepts of the once proud military class, really extended to all Japanese the ideals of militarism. The traditions of the military class became the traditions of all Japan.

The creation of the modern Japanese state was presided over by men whose roots were deep in the feudal military past of Japan, men who were filled with the ideals of the military class over whose liquidation they had presided. They were willing to sacrifice the special rights and privileges of their class if they could succeed, as they did, in building up a new political structure by means of which they could control the nation. To attain this end, they imported new governmental forms, but they did nothing that would undermine the attitudes toward government and toward militarism on which the old feudal order had been established.

The mass acceptance of the ideas of the feudal world laid the foundation for the regimentation and totalitarian militarism on which the modern Japanese state has been erected. The new authoritarianism of Japan will be described at length in a later chapter. The old political oligarchy disappeared, but was replaced by a new one which proved to be dangerous not only to Asia, but to the world.

Chapter III

THE ECONOMIC OLIGARCHY

The political oligarchy was erected on an economic structure that was dominated by an equally narrow group which, in most periods of Japanese history, was identical with it. The oligarchic structure of Japan's economy has given rise to certain attitudes among the people which have contributed to their acceptance of the political oligarchy.

It has been the task of the Japanese people to create the wealth on which their political masters have built their power. They have not been allowed to enjoy the full fruits of their labour, just as as they have been given no voice in the way in which they have been governed.

The economic oligarchy, like the political oligarchy, had its roots in the organization of the clan society of early Japan. The economic organization of the clans probably varied greatly from clan to clan according to their size, but in all it seems to have been based on the possession of rice-fields. We have some idea of the holdings of the imperial clan and it is probably fairly safe to assume that the same pattern was followed, if not by all clans, then by the more powerful ones that ranked close to the imperial clan in wealth.

The primary wealth of the imperial clan consisted of the imperial rice-fields, the people to till them, and the imperial granaries which were erected near the imperial estates for the storage of the grain from the fields. The fields were not contiguous, but scattered. This was due apparently partly to conquest and partly to the custom of establishing "memorial" rice-fields to honour deceased members of the imperial clan or to perpetuate the names of those who died without issue. The people who tilled the fields were also under the control of the clan.

There seems to have been a rudimentary system of taxation, but perhaps it might be more accurate to call it tribute rather than taxation. Rice was sent to the seat of the imperial clan from the imperial granaries and apparently also from at least some of the other clans. *Corvée* was also exacted from the tillers of the imperial fields. Finally, food, clothing and other products seem to have been contributed in the form of tribute.

The economic backbone of the clan system was the *be* or hereditary corporation. The members of the *be* usually followed the same occupation or occupations which were a hereditary monopoly of the *be*. The function of the *be* seemed to vary with the size and influence of the clan. In some clans there may have been as few as one or two *be* which might be charged with such basic occupations as farming or hunting or fishing. However, the range of functions of *be* mentioned in early Japanese records was much greater. Some were basically economic, being concerned with such occupations as weaving, pottery, hunting, and fishing. Others were in charge of religious functions and military affairs. The latter groups apparently existed only in the larger and more influential clans. Certain *be* attained a position of influence as great as that of some of the more powerful clans.

The members of the *be* were really a caste of hereditary workers, apparently serfs rather than slaves. The leaders of the *be* seem to have been, at least in some instances, clansmen. In other cases, they were men who were treated as if they were on the same level as the clansmen. As far as can be determined, the members of the *be* were usually people captured in warfare with other clans, non-clansmen who in some way became connected with the clan, or clansmen who were deprived of their privileges because of some crime. One thing is clearly apparent, the *be* were under the control of the clan and formed its economic foundation.

Although the members of the *be* were in actuality no more than slaves in status, there was also a group of slaves within the organization of the clans. The slaves apparently were few in number and played no significant rôle in the life of the clan. They seem to have served as household servants or agricultural labourers for the important members of the clan. The members of the *be* and the slaves were numerically in a majority in the clans, as far as can be determined. It was the products of their labour that formed the wealth of the clans and that were the economic foundation on which the power of the clansmen was based.

The economic aspects of the Taikwa Reform were no less spectacular than the political aspects. They brought about a change in Japanese economy as great as that in Japanese politics. But at the same time the change was apparent rather than real, for the controllers of economic wealth were no more dispossessed by the Taikwa Reform than were the politically powerful within the clans.

On New Year's Day of 646 an imperial edict of four articles was promulgated. This edict contained the major elements of the Taikwa Reform, although, as was pointed out earlier, the Reform continued to unfold for more than half a century. Article I of this edict was concerned primarily with the sweeping away of old economic forms; Article II involved administration and defense; and Articles III and IV covered local administration and taxation.

The *be* were the target of the provisions of Article I. Not only imperial *be,* but also those connected with lesser clans were abolished. Thus, the clans, with their economic foundation swept away, were virtually eliminated. In addition, so-called imperial granaries and certain farmsteads were abolished, but without the confiscation of the imperial wealth, because the effect of this article was to concentrate in the hands of the emperor control over all the land of the country in accordance with the idea that the emperor owned both the land and the people. It should also be noted that it was in the name of the emperor that all grants of land and commodities were made. Since control over land and people was now theoretically in the hands of the emperor alone, this article had the effect of nationalizing the land. Although the terms of this article seem to be revolutionary, the total effect on Japan's economy was not large. These moves merely confirmed control of the land in the hands of the vested interests which had existed under the clan system. The form and the theory of land holding were radically changed by the Taikwa Reform, but the actual control of the land remained unchanged. The new system will be described in detail later.

Governors for the home provinces, those around the capital,

and all other areas were to be appointed according to Article II. Men who enjoyed positions of some trust under the clan system were made governors. Again it is to be noted that the old ruling class was not dispossessed. It simply gave up its old rights and prerogatives for new ones. Regulations were also set up for the control of the capital. Provision was also made in this article for the improvement of communications, a vital factor if the new administrative system was to function smoothly.

The third article of the edict was primarily concerned with economic matters. A census was ordered, and methods for the receipt and distribution of land were set down. A system of taxation was also outlined. It was just, at least in theory, as the amount of tax rice to be collected varied according to the population of the different areas and according to the arability of the land. The final article was concerned solely with taxation. Silk and other textiles were to be contributed in place of the old demands for forced labour. Also provided for were a commuted tax on houses, and the contribution of horses, weapons, and coolies.

The edict, in effect, set up a system of public land and made the people the subjects of a central authority. Also established was a system of provincial administration, accountable to the central authorities. In other words, this edict set out to confirm and establish firmly the power of the imperial family, to subordinate the clans to a central authority, and to stabilize the livelihood of the people, at least in form.

The key economic idea of the Taikwa Reform was the new thesis that the emperor was the owner of all the land, and consequently the master of all people. The imperial clan, victor in the struggle with the Soga family, thus established its political power on a firm economic foundation. Yet this new theory was not implemented by the outright expropriation of the land holdings of all the clans. The political reforms were so integrated into the economic reforms that no one in a position of power under the clan system was relieved of either political prestige or economic holdings.

Since ownership of the land was centred in the hands of the emperor, he bestowed on all his subjects what was known as *kubunden* (literally, "mouth share rice-fields"). This *kubunden* consisted of rice-land. Every man, woman, and child in the land was to receive as his own a parcel of this land. Thus, the loyalty of the people to the absolute ruler of the country was made firmer by making them realize that their very existence depended on their sovereign.

Each male Japanese received an area approximately one-half acre in size, and females received two-thirds of the male share. These allotments were determined, of course, after surveys of the amount of land available had been made. The size of the allotment varied with the population of a given area and the amount of land under cultivation. Public slaves, that is, those engaged in labour for the benefit of the central administration, were given a share the same size as that of a free man. Private slaves were allotted one-third of a free man's share if the land was available for distribution. In addition to the *kubunden,* people were granted lands not suitable for rice culture as sites for their houses, and for the raising of mulberry and lacquer trees. This land, unlike the *kubunden,* could be bought and sold.

When the *kubunden* were granted, the boundaries were marked out carefully. Theoretically a new distribution of *kubunden* was to be held every six years. This would make the adjustments necessitated by births, deaths, reclamation, and other factors affecting either the size of the population or the amount of cultivable land. Whenever possible the recipients were to be granted land near their place of residence. When land was unproductive twice the usual amount was to be bestowed. Although this rather elaborate system was evolved, it was followed more in the breach than in the observance. The difficulties of travel and of accounting, and the clumsiness of the system itself guaranteed that adjustments would not often be carried out.

Although the theory that the emperor owned all the land went unchallenged, in practice it was understood that subjects could retain possession of *kubunden* for life. On the subject's death the land was to revert to the emperor. Generally the family was allowed to retain possession of the land until the succeeding distribution year. If deaths were even roughly balanced by births the family stood neither to lose nor to gain much by the redistribution.

Both in theory and in practice the *kubunden* was the principal source of taxes. Every share of land was to pay in to the central administration a certain percentage of its yield. Individuals were also expected to labour on public projects for a stated number of days each year and were to contribute to the central government certain other types of goods or products which were also regarded as taxes. Theoretically, the tax burden was as equitably distributed as the land. Actually, there were great inequalities in both.

Every Japanese had his share of *kubunden,* but other grants were made to those who had had greater stakes in the clan system which had been destroyed. The three types of land which were reserved for only the rich and the powerful were rank-land, salary-land, and merit-land. These three types of holdings preserved the economic inequalities of the clan system and were the formal basis for the economic oligarchy which was characteristic of the new Japanese society.

Rank-land was granted only to persons holding rank in the new imperial court. Since rank was granted in accordance with the importance of the individual's rôle in the clan system, and since the latter depended in part on the extent of the clan's estates, the grants of rank-land served to confirm the economic position of the men of the old order in the new Japan. Persons of imperial rank received the largest parcels of rank-land, although the first three of the ranks immediately below them enjoyed grants almost as great. For individuals of imperial rank the amount of rank-land varied from one hundred to two hundred acres. The officials who were named to the twelve different ranks in the bureaucratic hierarchy received from twenty to two hundred acres. Women of rank received two-thirds of the male share. Holders of rank-land could also possess other types of land. Rank-land was usually tax-exempt. Although the size of these tracts is not large by Western standards, it should be noted that even the smallest of these rank-lands was some forty times the size of the holdings of an ordinary person.

For the cultivation of these lands the holders were granted *fu* or "sustenance households," i.e., the men and women who lived on the land and were responsible for tilling it. Their labour and what they produced belonged to the holder of the rank-land and not to the government.

On a lower level, but also directly connected with the bureaucracy was the salary-land. The produce of this land went to the holders as recompense for carrying out the duties of their offices. The hundred acres that went to the prime minister were the largest holding in this category. The salary-land holders were also granted sustenance households.

The third type of land was merit-land, which was granted for outstanding public service. Deeds of the highest merit were rewarded by the granting of land in perpetuity to the recipient and his family. Deeds of high merit were rewarded with lands which could be held until the third generation; deeds of medium merit with land which could be held to the second generation. The lowest grant on this scale could be passed on only to sons or daughters. This land was given to a man only in the place where he lived, if there was a sufficient quantity available there. So-called "merit households" similar to the sustenance households accompanied these grants.

It is to be noted that these three types of land went only to members of the bureaucracy. Since the government, i.e. the bureaucrats, controlled the granting of land, it meant that the bureaucrats, already given a dominant economic position, were in a position to increase their holdings at will. There was no check, other than the jealousy of their rivals, on the amount of rank, merit, or salary-land that the bureaucrats could grant themselves or their families. They were in a position both to maintain and to increase the wide economic gap that separated them from the common people. Because of the abuses that were an inseparable part of the system, the wealthy simply became wealthier and the poor poorer. There was no chance for the people to break into this closed corporation.

The benefits to the people of the Taikwa economic reforms were illusory. On the surface, at least, their position was made more secure. Instead of being simply a labourer completely dependent on the whim of his lord for his existence, as under the clan system, the commoner now had control of a piece of land which was to be his for life, granted him by the emperor himself. But the commoner actually had to bear almost the entire burden of taxation under the new system. He was responsible either to the central administration or to his lord for the paying of taxes, either in goods or in labour or in produce. The wealthy, because they were also the government, could evade the few taxes imposed on them. They could declare their lands tax-exempt or they could simply fail to pay. There was no disinterested group, there was no law that could force them to pay their share of maintaining the new government. Since they were the government, there was no reason why the bureaucrats should force themselves to give up what they had granted themselves.

The system was elaborate, yet it probably resulted in no net change in the distribution of wealth. The leaders of the more powerful clans were rewarded with the higher positions in the bureaucracy, and although theoretically they turned their lands over to the emperor, what they received in the form of salary-land, rank-land and merit-land probably only confirmed them in their previous holdings. Those with the larger holdings as clans also had more people under their control, and this in turn meant that they were able to supply the necessary *kubunden* for all those living on their fiefs. The members of the minor clans in the provinces, if they were affected at all by these changes, were given provincial positions which confirmed them in their holdings. It is clear that the Taikwa Reform was not a revolution in any sense of the term. The old balances, economic and political, were not disturbed by the great innovations that were introduced into the country. The face of the nation, as was the case with Meiji Japan centuries later, underwent a tremendous change, but the main currents of economic and political life continued in the old channels.

Yet these qualifications should not obscure the basic significance of Taikwa economic reforms. The aristocracy was established definitely as a privileged class rather than as a collection of individuals with a common economic stake in society. The people became the group which bore the principal burden of financing the new central government. In other words the Taikwa Reform set up the structure of economic relationships that was to endure in Japan down to the present day. Japan's economy has undergone many changes, but the basic nature of the economic oligarchy has remained unchanged, with the mass of the people producing the wealth for the enjoyment of the few.

The *shoen,* or manor system, was a logical development of the economic reforms of the Taikwa period. Though it rose out of the Taikwa reforms, the system was also the expression of their failure. The *shoen* was the most important economic development of the Heian period. Although the manors were the wealth of the court nobles, they also paved the way for the shift of economic and political power from their hands to the warrior class, for they were a transitional form between the theoretically centralized control of the land of the Taikwa system and the decentralization of feudalism.

A *shoen* was a privately owned, tax-exempt estate, or in other words, a politically and economically independent unit. Economically, the *shoen* meant the denial of the Taikwa principle of public ownership of the land. Land was withdrawn from the theoretical ownership of the emperor and placed under the private control of the aristocrats. Politically, the *shoen* meant a growth of decentralization. The withdrawal of land from the control of the central administration weakened its authority and set up a number of competing units which steadily sapped its economic strength and political authority. Thus, the growth of the manors was an expression of the failure of the centralization that had been attempted by the Taikwa Reform.

The development of the *shoen* strengthened the position of the aristocrats as individuals while it undermined their position as a class. For example, while tax exemption meant wealth to the individual because it allowed him to enjoy sole control of the produce of the land under his control, it also drained the national treasury of funds which might have enabled the central bureaucracy to carry out its functions more efficiently and thus protect the interests of the bureaucrats.

The decentralization of the manorial system opened the way for the advent to power of the warrior class. Both by accident and by design what were to become most powerful warrior families found themselves in control of the manors, at the expense of the real owners, at the critical time when the struggle for power between the civil bureaucrats and the new warrior group broke out. Economic power, gained through control of the *shoen,* formed the foundation for the political power of the warriors.

The three basic reasons for the development of the manorial system are: the fundamental weakness of the central government, the practice of government grants of lands to persons and institutions, and the desire of land-owners to escape taxation. As has already been pointed out, the central government had neither the strength nor the desire to enforce to the letter the economic reforms of the Taikwa period. It commanded no effective police force that could keep down abuses, and what is more, the bureaucrats would be working against their own interests if they checked private manipulation of grants of land and tax exemptions.

The bureaucracy's power to grant land to individuals either in the form of rewards or for services rendered enabled individuals to fatten themselves at public expense. But the more they did so the less land there was to maintain the bureaucracy. In addition, the bureaucracy and the bureaucrats could bestow land on temples and shrines as a demonstration of their piety. These grants from their very nature were tax-exempt. They were what might be termed "institutional *shoen*" as compared with the privately-owned manors. Thus, manors held by both private citizens and institutions grew steadily in size as the bureaucrats granted themselves and their beneficiaries more land and more exemptions from taxation.

The most powerful of the land-holders were already tax-exempt because no tax was due on their holdings of rank- or merit-land. It would have been indeed short-sighted and ungrateful had the bureaucrats not exempted themselves from taxation or had continued to demand taxes from religious institutions. The increasing grants of land with their consequent exemption from taxation meant a steadily growing burden of taxation on those lands which were still taxable. Consequently the system of commendation of land grew steadily. The smaller land-holder, who was forced to pay staggering taxes to the central government, could escape only if he turned his holdings over to a powerful lord or to a religious institution. He would still have to till his land or turn over its produce, but he could also rest assured that he would be permitted to retain a greater percentage of his produce. It was only by such desperate means that some of the smaller land-holders could continue to exist. But the landlord to whom he commended his land had additional benefits to bestow. The lord could grant the peasant the right to bequeath his land to his descendants and could also protect the peasant against the demands of the provincial officials.

The lords did not aid the peasants for purely altruistic reasons. They enjoyed all the economic returns of the labour of the peasant that the central administration lost, that is, the tax-rice, tribute in other produce, and the *corvée*. In addition the lords held title to the land that the peasant had commended to him. Although commendation was declared illegal, the powerful could not be expected to force themselves to stop accepting these profitable gifts of land. Indeed, the practice of commendation grew at a constantly accelerating pace because the more land that was withdrawn from taxation the greater would be the burden on the remaining tax-payers and the more eager they would be to commend their holdings.

The methods by which the *shoen* grew have been outlined above, but how did the manors originate? Some *shoen* were simply old clan estates. Not all of the clans were touched by the Taikwa Reform. Hence, they simply remained in full control of their lands without surrendering their rights even nominally, as had many of the other clans. For many years before the Taikwa period grants of land in perpetuity had been made to great temples and shrines, and these grants were another source of *shoen*.

Merit-lands became privately owned, first, because some were actually granted in perpetuity, and, second, because the holders of other types simply never bothered to return them to the government when the period of tenure elapsed. Rank-land was for the most part to be held only during the life of the individual granted it, but was frequently kept in the family after the death of the holder, sometimes because the rank was made hereditary, and sometimes simply because it was not turned back to the government. Salary-land and lands given for the maintenance of serving-women in the imperial court were held for long periods, or were tax-free, and as a result became privately held. Even *kubunden*, because of the break-down of the distribution system, was held for long periods without being returned to the central government. Long tenure of the land amounted in the long run to outright ownership.

The problem of bringing new lands under cultivation in order to keep pace with the growing population of the country also played an important rôle in the development of the *shoen*. The central government was almost powerless to act alone in the work of increasing the amount of arable land. The bureaucracy had no engineering office that could carry out the work of reclaiming land. The interests of the bureaucrats were such that they could scarcely be expected to devote themselves to such mundane affairs. Consequently, the government could do nothing more than to issue orders to provincial officials and to farmers, to increase the amount of land under cultivation. Of course, the private owners of land would not be interested in carrying out such work unless they were guaranteed something in return. The most tangible reward that could be given them was tax exemption or a very low rate of taxation.

In an attempt to encourage the farmers themselves to expand their holdings, the government issued regulations concerning possession of land that had been reclaimed. It was decided that farmers would be allowed to hold for three generations any land that they reclaimed, and to hold for life any abandoned fields that they brought back into production. Finally, they were granted permanent possession, because farmers would simply desert fields when it came time to hand them back.

Similar provisions were set up regarding taxes. At first reclaimed lands were to be tax-free for a certain number of years, but this number was extended from time to time. As an attempt to limit the extent of holdings of men reclaiming fields, a limitation was placed on the amount that could be reclaimed by one individual, but it apparently was never observed.

In actual practice only large landholders were able to attempt reclamation work. The peasants had neither the time, the capital, nor the labour at their command to carry it out. The result was that reclamation was undertaken by individuals and institutions which already had under their control extensive tracts of land. Temples and shrines, provincial and central officials, wealthy local landholders, all were in a position to increase their holdings by reclamation work. All had at their command considerable labour forces. Priests, because of their function, could play on the superstition of the people, telling them, for instance, that the gods demanded that certain areas be tilled so that they could be given greater offerings. Officials, either district or provincial, had the right to demand *corvée* from the peasants under their jurisdiction. If there was no land to be parcelled out, the common people were forced to go to great landholders for employment so that they could continue to exist.

Under this system of reclamation the power of the great landholders grew apace, for they and they alone were in a position to bring new lands into cultivation. As a consequence, their power continued to grow steadily at the expense of the central government, for they not only had great tracts of land under their private control but could also mobilize their serfs to act as soldiers in emergencies.

Another development that undermined the position of the central government was the formation of alliances between certain lords who were not members of the court nobility, and the more powerful and influential of the bureaucracy. This alliance was mutually beneficial. The lords in return for payment to the bureaucrats would be exempted from the taxes that they should have paid to the provincial officials. The bureaucrats in turn would enjoy the income from such transactions. Again they were working for their selfish interests at the expense of their public duties, thus paving the way for the disaster which was eventually to overtake them.

Finally, outright corruption among the provincial officials responsible for tax collection contributed to the undermining of the central government. Provincial officials were almost completely free of control by the central authorities. The police power of the central administration was almost nil, communications with provincial offices were poor, and in addition the central bureaucrats had no real interest in the affairs of the provinces. Hence, it was perfectly natural for lords of *shoen* whose estates had not been declared tax-exempt to bribe the provincial officials in order to escape from paying taxes.

Other devices were also used to escape taxes. Manors would be reported to be smaller than they actually were. Crops would be reported as much smaller than was actually the case. The number of people on a manor would be reported as less than it was. Inspectors sent out by the central government to check on such matters would often be either outwitted or bribed. In an attempt to check such corrupt practices the government ruled that provincial officials had to submit their books for inspection at the end of their terms. But this regulation was easily evaded. The incoming official could be bribed to make a false report. Fires conveniently broke out in the provincial offices and destroyed the books. The officials exerted pressure in the capital to get their term of office extended so that they would not have to submit reports.

For a major land-holder there was an even more effective method than bribery for winning tax exemption. He could obtain a decree from the central administration which would declare his *shoen* an "imperially-exempted manor." Since most of the large landowners were high officials, it is easy to see that the bureaucrats were in an ideal place to have their private holdings exempted from taxes. The Fujiwara family who dominated the bureaucracy was very active in winning such exemptions for its members.

Thus, through corruption, the enjoyment of special rights, gifts and special grants, and the creation of incentives for the reclamation of land, the *shoen* gradually became tax-exempt and to all intents and purposes privately owned.

In its freedom from control on the part of the central administration, its exemption from taxation and its own independent administration, the *shoen* was practically a state-within-a-state. Strong enough to protect its interests against outside interference and enjoying the protection of influential individuals or institutions, the *shoen* was truly a politically and economically independent unit.

The growth of the *shoen* dealt a powerful blow to the economic and political structures of Japan as they had been set up by the architects of the Taikwa Reform. The winning of tax exemption only served to increase the tax burden on those who still had to pay their taxes, for the government had no other recourse but to raise the rate of taxation if it wished to keep its income at the necessary level. The exercise of the right of exemption by the court bureaucrats caused not only a decrease in government revenue, but also encouraged bribery which in turn accelerated the economic breakdown of the system. The private ownership of the *shoen* meant a continued decentralization of authority, as the system became more widespread. With the breakdown of the system of public domain, the ties of the estates to the central authority became more and more tenuous; and the increase of the power of the local lords meant inevitably a decline in the power of the central authorities.

The Economic Oligarchy

The court nobles who were the beneficiaries of the Taikwa Reform, because of the fact that it confirmed their grasp of political and economic power, enriched themselves as individuals by encouraging the development of the *shoen* system. It operated in favour of the nobles as long as they took a serious interest in their affairs and maintained close touch with the men whom they had delegated to manage their estates. But the concentration of their attention on the frivolous pursuits and the petty rivalries and intrigues of the imperial court gradually robbed them of the strength and the decision that they needed in order to protect their interests. When the provincial governors who broke away from the control of the central administrators, the more able administrators who were managing the *shoen,* and the provincial nobility challenged their supremacy, they had neither the men nor the resources at their command that might have enabled them to withstand the attacks of these interlopers.

When the *shoen* had shaken loose from the control of the nobility they were the foundation for the feudalism that was to develop in Japan under the newly risen warrior class. They were, as a matter of fact, fiefs in everything but name. They were independent units which, when they were cut away from their absentee owners, were under the control of local lords, many of whom had formerly served as *shoen* officials. These local lords were all-powerful in their regions, with their own armed forces and with economic holdings sufficient to maintain them and their men. When the formal control of the government passed from the nobles to the warriors Japan quickly and easily slipped into an out-and-out feudal system.

The political power of the warriors was erected on the agricultural economy which derived its strength from the peasants. This was simply the continuation of the old economic oligarchy that had grown out of the clan system. Control of agriculture was one of the foundation stones of the Tokugawa system.

The outstanding economic development of the Tokugawa period was the gradual shift away from an agricultural economy based on rice to a primitive money economy. The process was really the expression of a decline of the feudal economy of Japan with a gradual emergence of a nascent capitalism.

Through the first part of the Tokugawa period, rice, as it had been for centuries, was the basis of Japan's economy. The restoration of normal conditions of peace and order, and the return of relative prosperity, stabilized Japanese agriculture. Rice was the principal food of the nation, although many peasants were forced to barter or to sell the rice they grew for cheaper cereals, a situation that has not been unknown in modern Japan. But the rôle of rice in Japan's economy was even more basic. It was the standard of value and the most important medium of exchange. Wealth was measured in terms of the amount of rice that was produced by the lands under one's control, and most goods were obtained by barter of rice. One Japanese scholar, writing in English, has said: "The foundation of the economic life of the country lay, therefore, in the production and distribution of rice."

The rice production of Japan at the beginning of the Tokugawa period was estimated to have been 28,000,000 *koku* (one *koku* being equal to slightly less than five bushels). Of this, 8,000,000, or more than a quarter, was produced from lands under the direct control of the Tokugawa family and their retainers. By way of contrast, the whole imperial court was granted what amounted to about one-half of one per cent of the national production. By the time that this meagre income was divided among the members of the imperial court, it was nothing more than a pittance. This deliberate policy of inflicting poverty on the imperial court was eventually to drive some of the more intelligent and forceful courtiers into the arms of those who were plotting against the Tokugawa régime.

As has been pointed out, Toyotomi Hideyoshi originated many of the oppressive measures that enabled the Tokugawa régime to keep the peasants under strict control. The ultimate source of Japan's wealth was, of course, the peasant. The peasant, as under the *shoen* system, owned his land in common law if he tilled it for a certain number of years and if he kept up his taxes. The feudal lords and the Tokugawa *bakufu* were not concerned with the problem of the actual ownership of the land. What they wanted was not the mere title to land, but the produce of the land, namely, rice. It was through the villages and the "five-men groups" that they were able to exact what they considered was their due.

The village was a type of legal entity. It was regarded as a kind of corporation that could act as a person in various legal matters.

It could enter into contracts with neighbouring villages and could own property such as forests or hill land, types of land which were not as directly productive as rice fields. In addition, the village often suffered communal punishment for failure to discharge its responsibilities. Economically, the village was responsible for the amount of tax-rice assessed against it by the authorities, either local or central. The village was forced to contribute a flat amount, and if any members failed to attain their quotas their fellows were compelled to make up the difference.

But there was a still smaller unit of control, the *gonin-gumi* or "five-men groups." The members of these associations were mutually responsible for their conduct and for their own welfare. If one fell sick and could not till his field, the rest had to do his work for him. If one or more members failed to pay their taxes, the remainder had to make up the deficit. If one member ran away, the others had to hunt for him and if they failed to find him to pay a fine. They were expected to check on each other's industry. The mutual responsibility was so heavy that the members of the *gonin-gumi* had a voice in the family succession of its members. If the heir of a member seemed, in their opinion, not likely to become a good worker, they had the right to demand that he should not be allowed to succeed to the headship of the family.

It is to be noted that this village and group responsibility was unilateral, that of the peasant to his lord. Though they were given some latitude in the management of their affairs, the basic idea was not to give the people a voice in government, but to see to it that they performed their duties more efficiently and fulfilled without fail their responsibilities to their masters. There was no place in this system for the people to exert pressure on the lords for lower taxes or for better treatment. Their only means of expression were rioting and an occasional petition which might or might not be recognized. The police powers of the warrior ruling class were too great, and rule by oligarchy too firmly entrenched, to permit the development of forms of democratic expression which would undermine the basic philosophy and the basic relationships on which the power of the warriors rested.

There was a sharp distinction between the functions of production and of tax collection. Generally speaking, the peasant's task was to produce and the lord's to collect taxes. Only a few of the more progressive lords had any real interest in the problems of increased agricultural production. The lords were interested only in the collection of the finished product.

Some care was taken to set up and to compute the rates of taxation. Land was divided into different grades according to its productivity and taxes were scaled to match the amount that the land could produce. The quality of the land, its distance from the residence of those who had to work it, its accessibility to water, its exposure to the sun, and other items were taken into consideration in computing the tax rate on it. Land surveys were made at fairly frequent, though not at yearly, periods. The survey was taken to determine the total productivity of a village. Hidden fields were hunted out and every care was taken to discourage the farmers from concealing parcels of land for their own use. In some cases the punishment for hiding fields was crucifixion. The surveying instruments were crude, consisting only of bamboo sticks and pieces of rope. If errors were made, they would favour the lord whose men were in charge of the operation. A plot six feet square was arbitrarily selected as giving the average yield of a village's entire holding. It would be against human nature for the lord's officials to pick out a plot that obviously produced little.

Another device that added to the lord's income was the rule that the peasants had to bear the burden of the expense of both the survey of the land and the collection and delivery of the tax-rice. In the long run this meant that the lord's income was pure velvet, for it was free of all production costs.

The general condition of the village when the tax was computed might also be taken into account. The rate of taxation was usually at the ratio of four to the lord and six to the village. This ratio, however, varied greatly from fief to fief and from year to year. It was, however, used frequently enough to become a common expression among the people. One device that served to keep up the lord's income during seasons of short crops was to compute the tax on the basis of a yearly average. This juggling forced the peasant to pay a much higher proportion of his crop than he should, in years of short crops. It seems to have been a widely accepted practice not to reduce the tax rate unless the crop was at least one-third less than normal. Computation of the expected yield was also bound to result in a figure favourable to the lord.

Though taxes were paid in to the feudal lord, he could not reserve them for his exclusive use. Much of the lord's income had to be paid out to his retainers in the form of salaries. Each warrior member of a lord's sometimes extensive retinue was given an income of a certain number of *koku* of rice per year. Keeping their retainers supplied with rice became one of the most pressing economic problems of the lords in the later Tokugawa period.

Rice was the foundation stone of the economy of the early part of the Tokugawa period, but as time went on its economic position was increasingly challenged by the development of money as a medium of exchange. The first coins were minted in Japan before the Nara period, but they never circulated widely. Before the Tokugawa period many feudal lords had set up their own primitive monetary systems, but there was no uniformity among them. However, money came into increasingly wide use during the first part of the Tokugawa period, and by 1700 it had become firmly established as an integral part of Japan's economic system. It had important social, economic, and political effects. The main impact was felt by the peasants, the warriors, and the merchants. The nobility was too far removed from ordinary affairs to be affected as a class.

The introduction of money as an economic factor was an additional blow to the peasants. They continued to bear the heavy burden of the rice tax, but their masters began to demand taxes in the form of money as they felt the need for more cash. From early times the peasants had paid taxes in kind as well as in rice, but the lords began to demand money instead of produce. They heaped extra taxes on the peasants, levying on almost everything that they could think of. The peasants could turn to the growing of other income crops, but the very limitations of time prevented them from devoting too much time to them, for rice was still the main crop for which they were responsible.

To relieve the economic pressure on themselves the peasants had to resort to such means as infanticide and abortion to keep starvation at arm's length. Rioting was the most frequent means of expressing discontent with the system which barely allowed them to continue to exist. Another trend was the movement from the land to the cities, which was one of the main reasons for the growth of the cities during the latter part of the Tokugawa period.

With the cities becoming increasingly the commercial centres of the nation, with merchants and warriors demanding more consumers' goods, there was work in the cities which would enable men and women to earn enough to make a better living than the bitter existence they were forced to lead on farms.

The fate of the peasant, never a happy one, became even worse, and the unrest that was expressed in the form of riots continued to undermine the authority of the Tokugawa régime. This peasant movement was never decisive, either economically or politically, but it did loosen the hold of the Tokugawa régime on the nation. Had the peasants been able to band together for a common expression of their common grievances and to take action against all that the Tokugawa system stood for, the history of modern Japan might have developed along far different lines.

The trend toward a money economy also weakened the economic position of both the feudal lords and their retainers, but in different ways. The *sankin kotai* system was closely connected with the lords' need for money. In their travels to the capital they needed money as soon as they left the limits of their own domains, for lords through whose fiefs they had to pass demanded money in payment for goods. The enforced residence in Edo also meant that the lords required money; for in the capital the merchants sold for money, and in addition it was in the cities that money was in widest use. The ceremonial visits of the *shogun* to the lords' mansions in Edo also wrung more cash out of them, for they had to pay for the elaborate entertainment that was expected of them.

This need for ready cash forced the lords more and more to sell their rice in the open market. This in turn led to the further development of a system of rice brokerage. The merchants advanced money to the lords against their coming crop of rice. This practice over a long period of time meant that the warriors as a class became indebted to the merchants. The economic pressure that the merchants were thus able to exert resulted in a gradual, if informal and quasi-illegal, relaxation of some of the restrictions that the *bakufu* had placed on them. The merchants were also able to strengthen their economic position still more by forcing extra concessions from the Tokugawa government in the form of monopoly rights and a lessening of other restrictions. But it must be repeated that the merchants as a group were not able to mold their newly won economic power into a political weapon. They were able to force a relaxation of the restrictions on them, but they could not dominate the warrior class.

But the economic burden on the common warrior weighed as heavily as it did on his master, for he was forced to carry some of the new burden that was heaped on the lords. The warriors could not escape their lords' demand for money any more than the more harassed peasant, and they had as little defense, although the methods used by the lords against their retainers were a little less harsh and a little less direct than those used against the peasants. The most direct method of reducing the income of the *samurai* was simply to lower the amount of stipend rice that was his due. Another less formal method was for the lord simply to give his retainers part payment of what was due them, with no assurance that they would receive the remainder. Feudal lords became more and more sensitive to violations of regulations by their followers, for if a *samurai* were caught in such a violation he could be dropped from the rolls of his master, and one less warrior meant an increase in the lord's income. The result of these measures was that the *samurai* were driven to the money lenders even as their masters had been.

The Tokugawa *bakufu* made desperate efforts to help the warriors. It issued edicts reducing or cancelling the interest on debts owed by the lords and their retainers. It set the limit on payments of debts at a low level. It even cancelled debts. But these measures did not solve the basic difficulties, for they only made the merchants reluctant to risk their capital in loans to the warriors.

The *bakufu,* as time went on, was forced to embark on a policy of currency debasement. This, of course, drove much good money out of circulation and its beneficial effects, if any, were of a purely temporary nature. The problem of the currency was additionally complicated by the fact that Japan's economy was still largely based on rice; hence the value of the currency and the price of rice became closely related, which only made the position of the *bakufu* increasingly difficult.

The growth of cities during the Tokugawa period resulted in the creation of an increasingly large group in the population which could neither live directly off the land nor depend on barter to supply the daily necessities of life. They were forced to use money to purchase the things that they needed. This made the money price of rice, their staple food, of vital importance to them. The Tokugawa *bakufu* was caught between two currents. Cheap rice meant difficulties for the feudal lords and those dependent on them; expensive rice meant distress in the cities, with consequent unrest. The Tokugawa policy of currency debasement helped the warriors, for the higher the price of rice, the greater would be their money income. In turn, this adversely affected the lives of the city-dwellers who had to pay for their rice. But a reduction in the rice price, while helping the urban dwellers, squeezed the warriors.

The instability of the currency affected the price of rice, but in addition, rice, like all agricultural crops, was at the mercy of the elements. Currency could be controlled, but the elements could not. Crop failures forced the price up and bumper harvests forced it down.

The government was finally forced to adopt a policy of price control. The authorities urged the citizens of Edo and Osaka to buy huge quantities of rice and to store it. This was designed to stabilize the market, and hence to maintain prices. The government also encouraged the consumption of *sake*, which is brewed from rice. Certain monopoly rights were granted to guilds of rice merchants as an additional step to check price fluctuations.

Naturally the only group to profit from this new economic development was the merchants. They became the bankers, the brokers, the shippers, and the wholesalers and retailers in Japan's new economy. They understood the function of money and they were willing to deal in it. They thus had a great advantage over the warriors, who were the only other group in a position to gain from the new economic developments. The warriors did not understand financial transactions and, as has already been pointed out, believed that money was something contaminating, that no warrior should touch it if he wished to remain true to his profession. Thus, the merchants became the bankers in Japan's new economy.

Their capital and their knowledge of markets equipped them to become rice brokers. They purchased the warriors' rice for cash. They formed guilds for buying, selling, and storing rice; they speculated in the rice market; their position as bankers enabled them to advance loans to the warriors against the rice harvest. Thus, their control of money and their knowledge of the rice market placed them in an extremely strategic economic position.

The merchants also gained control of the new and highly important business of shipping. The growth of cities, which naturally created a supply problem — the necessity for transporting rice and other products to market — stable conditions in the country, which encouraged normal internal trade — all demanded the development of shipping guilds. The guilds virtually monopolized this new business.

The development of large cities, such as Edo and Osaka, furnished wider opportunities for buying and selling; and the large populations of these cities created a demand for various types of goods and services which could be supplied only by this new class.

It is small wonder, then, that the merchants gained the dominant economic position in Tokugawa Japan. The authorities adopted many methods in an attempt to control their growing economic power. The merchants were forced to make loans to the government, which were never repaid. They were made the object of special exactions by the authorities. The *bakufu* even confiscated the wealth of men whose ostentation grew too galling or whose wealth seemed to give them a dangerous amount of power. Sumptuary laws were also used to control the merchants.

But the wealth and economic position of the merchants were too great to be seriously curtailed by such methods. Though individuals may have suffered as a result of the *bakufu's* repressive measures, the merchants as a class continued to flourish through the Tokugawa period, although they were unable to get their hands on political power.

Perhaps the most important consequence of the rise of the merchant class was the fact that it placed them in a position to play a key rôle in the development of the new Japan that was to appear after the abolition of the Tokugawa-dominated feudalism. The sweeping away of the old class distinctions left them free to participate as equals in the construction of modern Japan. While it is true that men from the warrior class dominated the political development of Japan in the modern period, the merchants co-operated fully with them, first by supporting them financially in their struggle against the Tokugawa clan, and second by placing at their disposal their talents and their knowledge of the workings of commerce and finance. Thus, the more powerful of the old merchant class paved the way for their appearance as the great monopoly capitalists in modern Japan.

The economic pressures that contributed to the political downfall of the Tokugawa régime have already been described. The economic changes that swept over Japan as a result of the Tokugawa collapse were great, but the rulers of the country took care that these changes did not produce sufficient dislocation to create active resentment against their rule. After the original surrender of the fiefs in 1869, it was decreed that the government would pay each *daimyo* one-half of his normal income from the lands that he had surrendered. Thus, by giving them economic security the new government guarded against political unrest on the part of the lords. This was soon found to be much too great an economic burden on the new government.

To escape the crushing weight of these payments the government decreed in 1873 that anyone who wished could voluntarily commute his pension into a lump sum, one-half of which was to be paid in cash and one-half in government bonds. It was decided that those having hereditary pensions should get the equivalent of six years' payments, while those holding pensions good only for life would be paid a sum equivalent to four years of pension payments. But there were few who would voluntarily give up what was at least a life income in return for an almost picayunish payment.

In 1876 a compulsory commutation scheme was set up under which all persons receiving pensions from the government would have to give them up in return for lump sum payments. The government took care to cushion the effects of this step as much as possible, particularly as it affected those with smaller pensions. Interest payments were higher on the smaller pensions, and the period of payments was longer. But the net effect of this move was to guarantee the financial position of the *daimyo,* while bringing about virtual ruin for the lower *samurai.*

The *daimyo* emerged from the death of feudalism with an improved financial status. They no longer had to support large retinues of *samurai* from their income, as was the case during the feudal period. Their economic well-being was no longer at the mercy of the elements; they no longer had to fear the effects of the weather on the rice harvest. In addition, their power and influence made them the natural appointees to important positions within the new government. None of the leaders of the old feudal order was sufficiently discontented because of financial hardships wrought on him to lead an attack on the new régime.

Some of the more important *daimyo,* because of the handsome settlement that the government made on them, were able to become members of the new capitalist class and to take their places alongside the once-despised merchants as the new financial overlords of Japan.

The *samurai,* on the other hand, were hard hit by the settlement. Most of them received very small sums in return for the surrender of their pension rights. These men speedily lost what little they had, because of their inexperience in financial and business affairs. On the other hand, minor government positions were open to them, and so they were able to become policemen, army officers, naval officers, or minor bureaucrats.

The position of the peasants, as in the days of the Taikwa Reform, was greatly improved in theory. They were freed from their allegiance to a feudal lord, and the wilful and arbitrary feudal system of taxation was brought to an end .They were allowed to own their own land outright for the first time in Japanese history. The illusion of change was great, but again the position of the peasant was improved very little.

Although the farmers no longer had to fear the arbitrary acts of a feudal lord, they were subjected to the impersonal demands of the state in the form of money taxes. Their living standard may have been raised, but only in comparison with the past and their less fortunate neighbours. Their poverty was great by Occidental standards. From the beginning of the Meiji period until to-day the Japanese peasant has been forced to pay a disproportionate share of the expense of being governed. As in the past, the peasants have had to bear the burden of paying for a government in which they are not allowed to participate.

The farm problem in Japan was not solved by the destruction of the economic feudal order and the establishment of a theoretically more just system; the lot of the peasants has remained one of the major concerns of the Japanese government and one of the most pressing problems in Japan's economy.

Japan's modern economy, like her feudal economy, has been dominated by an oligarchy, although economic power was no longer concentrated in the hands of those who were also politically dominant. The core of the new economic oligarchy was the monopoly capitalists, the lineal descendants of the merchant class; but the imperial family, the government, and former feudal lords who were made wealthy by the feudal settlement, were also represented. In modern Japan, as in ancient Japan, the people were the foundation of the economic order. Earlier their labour was only in agriculture, but now they were the labour pool for both agriculture and industry, and their share in the wealth that they produced was destined to be no greater than before.

The pattern of economic development in Japan prevented the appearance of a strong middle class. The peasant carried the economic burden in pre-modern Japan, and the system and philosophy of Japanese politics and economics kept him from getting his hands on political power or enjoying what he produced. The strict control maintained over the members of the merchant class, who might logically have been Japan's bourgeoisie, prevented them from acquiring the political power that came into the hands of their counterparts in the Western world. The policy of seclusion which eliminated the possibility of foreign trade thus closed off a source of income that might have contributed to the development of a substantial middle class. Thus, economically as well as politically, power was concentrated in the hands of the few at the top.

Japan's economy did not go through a period of *laissez faire.* Close ties between the Tokugawa *bakufu* and the merchant class had already established a tradition of government control over private enterprise. It was a type of control, however, that yielded benefits to both parties. It was only natural that this control be continued, because the political change that brought down the Tokugawa régime did not alter the basic relationship between the governing and the governed. Although the merchant class had chafed under the restrictions placed on it by the *bakufu,* it had never been able to acquire political power of its own. Both control and co-operation marked the relationship between government and business in modern Japan.

A community of interest between business and government developed out of this relationship. Government itself was in business. Shipyards, steel mills, arsenals, rail transportation, the salt monopoly, state-controlled banks, and other enterprises gave the Japanese government the same type of business interests that the monopoly capitalists possessed. Private industry turned out many of the implements of war needed by Japan's Army and Navy. Government subsidies helped not only to start but also to develop and expand private enterprises. Government allowed private business to enjoy huge profits. Business was interested in a docile labour supply. Government was interested in furthering political passivity among the Japanese people. Thus, in many respects their interests were either identical or complementary.

Japan's burning desire to build up her defenses and to arm and equip a modern army brought government and business close together. The government had the plans and the policies. Business had the capital, the personnel trained in finance if not in technical matters, and the desire to help the government if it could turn a profit thereby. Close teamwork between the two explains in part the rapidity with which Japan built up her industrial structure. They both knew what they wanted, and consequently were able to go to the West and import exactly the sort of techniques and technicians that they needed. Thus, they were able to take advantage of Western technical advances which had been worked out over a long period, without going through a similar process of trial and error.

The close alliance between the government and business is undoubtedly one reason why big business did not and could not effectively stand in the way of the expansionist policies of the militarists who controlled the government. By the time that Japan struck at Pearl Harbor the fate of the businessmen was so bound up with that of Japan itself that they could not and would not stand in the way of war. Japan's big business was no more a force for moderation than big business had been in Germany and Italy.

Although it is possible that in the early 1930's certain elements among big business in Japan may have stood for expansion by peaceful rather than war-like means, they were forced both by outside pressure and by inner conviction to go along with the extremists. It would be a mistake to consider business in pre-war Japan as distinct from government. The alliance was too close. There might have been minor differences, but business was never in a position to control the policies of the government. Had the policy of the government been peaceful, business most certainly would have followed. But once the government was committed to aggression, business did nothing to alter that policy. Intimidation from the outside and profits from aggression, at least as great as those from peaceful trade, kept business in step with the government.

Japan's chauvinists virtually forced any reluctant businessmen into accepting their expansionist policies. The assassinations of 1932 and 1936 included prominent businessmen and their political sympathizers. The assassins were completely outspoken in revealing their motives. They were out to eliminate capitalists, who, they said, were extremely unpatriotic because they were harbouring ideas which had no place in Japanese life, and were also making profits in munitions, an utterly unthinkable thing when Japan was in such a state of crisis. The ostentation of wealth became dangerous, and it is said that the number of limousines in Tokyo took a decided drop after the 1936 assassinations. At this time army pamphlets also took up the same line of criticism. Business took the hint. There is no evidence, however, that big business lost any army contracts.

The profits from foreign markets were lost to Japan's great trading companies when the militarists' policies isolated Japan from the rest of the world, but aggression in China had meanwhile opened new areas for exploitation. Also, the interests of the great monopoly capitalists, those who were regarded as a "moderating" influence in Japan, were so wide that whatever they might lose from a shrinkage of their foreign markets could be more than made up in the increased business of their heavy industries. Had their interests been less multifarious, they might have taken a stand against the militarists in order to protect their stake in peaceful trade. The small manufacturers whose businesses were particularly hard hit through the curtailment of the export trade were also able to convert their facilities to the production of war materials. The profits from war were as acceptable as those of peace, and also continued to flow in regularly.

By far the most powerful economic group in Japan is the Imperial Family. By giving the throne wealth, the creators of modern Japan took an additional step toward the goal of making the emperor absolutely dominant in Japanese life. As we have seen earlier, the emperor did not always enjoy prosperity. During the Tokugawa period the emperor and all his court lived on a microscopic allowance. But to-day the Imperial Household is certainly one of the greatest financial powers in all Japan. The makers of Japan appreciated the importance of wealth to the position of the emperor. The centre of the new state was given the prestige that accrues to wealth.

According to the latest available statistics, the wealth of the Imperial Family flows from almost every section of Japan's economic structure. Forests, farm lands, building sites, buildings, livestock, estates, palaces, villas, hunting preserves, shares in all types of companies, all contribute to the wealth of the Imperial Family. For example, the Imperial Family holds 141,000 shares of stock in the Bank of Japan, 10,000 in the Hypothec Bank, an unstated but undoubtedly large number in both the Yokohama Specie Bank and the Industrial Bank of Japan, 54,000 shares in the Mitsui Bank, 161,000 shares in the great Oji Paper Company, 38,000 shares in the South Manchuria Railway, 24,000 shares in the Tokyo Electric Light Company, and 40,000 shares in the Taiwan Sugar Manufacturing Company. These shares alone must total well into the hundreds of millions of yen. The real estate holdings mentioned above must add many more millions to the wealth of the Imperial Family.

The Japanese people formed the ideal foundation for the new authoritarian state that was being constructed in Japan. They had all the "right" attitudes that made them willing workers and docile subjects, bowing to the will of both government and capital. They had behind them a long tradition of grinding toil. They expected nothing more from life than the right to continue to exist. They had never participated in government or enjoyed profits. They had always lived under control. They were isolated from the dangerous streams of thought that had awakened the ambitions of workers in the Western world. They lived under and accepted a régime which did not allow them the freedom to think their own thoughts or to demand a change in their lot.

Their very numbers made them even better fitted to be subjects of the totalitarian state. The size of the labour market almost automatically kept discontent at a minimum. There was too much competition for jobs. No worker was going to risk what little he had in order to grab at something he might not get. Strikers knew that they could be replaced almost immediately by others, who needed work so badly that they had no scruples about taking jobs of those who were attempting to improve their position. The tremendous growth of Japan's population will be reviewed briefly here in its relation to the problem of Japan's modern economy.

Before the middle of the nineteenth century Japan seems to have had a remarkably stable population. From 1721 to 1846 censuses were taken about every six years. Although it is impossible to determine the accuracy of these figures, the population varied only a few million from a base figure of around 27,000,000. For all practical purposes the population was stationary during this period, a startling contrast to the tremendous growth during the past few decades.

Attempts have been made to explain this remarkable stability. The generally depressed level of living of the peasants who made up the great majority of the population is one of the reasons that is most frequently stressed. Both abortion and infanticide were widely practiced by the Japanese peasantry in order to lessen the number of mouths dependent on the limited food supply. As has already been described, the Japanese peasant during the Tokugawa period led an unenviable existence, and it is not surprising that he made every effort to keep the size of his family as small as possible.

The upper level of Japanese society during this period, the warrior class, looked with disfavour on large families. The warrior believed that sons were important because they maintained the continuity of the family, but that large families were slightly indecent because they were more animal than human. The latter is very likely a rationalization rather than a true reason. The warrior, like the peasant, was hard pressed economically, and was also undoubtedly anxious to stretch his income as far as possible.

Undoubtedly one of the major factors in the stagnation of the population was the fact that Japan's economy was a static one during the Tokugawa period. Although she enjoyed a long period of peace, her economy was almost completely an agricultural one. The size of the population, therefore, was controlled by the yield from agriculture. There was no industry, no foreign trade, not even an extensive internal trade which would supply livelihood to the margin of population which could not live directly off the land. Although the urban population grew considerably during this period, the growth was occasioned in large part by the fact that those who could no longer win a living from the soil were forced to flee the cities, where they might eke out a bare existence as labourers of one sort or another. Japan's policy of seclusion had retarded her domestic economy. A rigid balance had to be maintained between agricultural production and the number of people who could live directly from it. This factor was changed with the industrialization of Japan.

The greatest rate of growth of the Japanese population has taken place during the past two decades. From 1872 until 1920 the population increased by about 21,000,000, from about 35,000,000 to about 56,000,000. From 1872 to 1920 the average yearly rate of increase was about 437,000, while during the past two decades it has been around 800,000. This is reflected in pre-war Japanese population statistics, which place a large proportion of the total population in the one to fourteen-year age group.

This spectacular growth of the Japanese population is not a phenomenon peculiar to Japan. A tremendous growth in population has been observed in all sections of the world where industrialization has taken place. It will be recalled that the populations of Europe and of the United States grew tremendously during the nineteenth century, when the full impact of the Industrial Revolution began to make itself felt. Japan's case is the more conspicuous because it came when the population curves of the rest of the world were beginning to level off.

The industrialization of Japan was undoubtedly one of the major factors in Japanese population growth. It is possible to plot a definite correlation between the speed of the growth of the Japanese population and the intensity of her drive toward industrialization. The population grew at a fairly steady but relatively unspectacular rate through the first World War, but as the impact of that war began to make itself felt on Japan's industrial structure the population figures immediately show a sharp rise. The pace has continued with the intensification of Japan's industrial program as a result of her imperialistic ambitions during the past decade. As Japan's industry has grown, there have been more and more jobs to absorb the surplus that the land could not support directly; and as the number of jobs grew so did the demand for workers. This phenomenon follows exactly the same pattern as that observable in the industrial nations of the West. In the last half of the nineteenth century Japan's economy ceased to be a static one, and became a rapidly expanding one, with the result that the old checks on her population growth were destroyed.

Japan's numbers supplied the soldiers for the armies and the labour for the plants that armed them. They were ideal for both rôles. The men of Japan made good, obedient soldiers who did what they were told without question. The men, women and children of Japan worked long hours for little wages, happy to get only enough to exist, and did not wonder about their condition. They were the perfect tools for the rulers of modern Japan.

Chapter IV

THE EMPEROR IDEA

The emperor idea has been one of the key concepts of the thirteen hundred years of recorded Japanese political history. Although the emperor has wielded real political power on only a few occasions, he has consistently been maintained as the repository of the right to rule and as the only person in Japan who could bestow authority to administer the country. He has been the tool of the oligarchy for those who have controlled the body of the emperor have controlled the government. They have wrung from him the authority to rule and have operated behind the protection of his sacredness. Consequently, the oligarchy has surrounded the institution with sanctity while depriving the individual emperors of all semblance of real political power. The oligarchy has preserved the emperor as the unassailable source of authority in order that it could obtain from him the legitimization of its exercise of power. With this backing the oligarchs enjoyed the additional advantage of being able to charge those who actively opposed them with being rebels against the highest authority.

The religious and political aspects of the emperor's position have been inextricably woven together. The basis of his political power lies in the fact that he has been considered not only the chief priest of the nation, but also the divine representative on earth of the gods who watch over the destinies of the country. His political powers have flowed from and have been confirmed by his alleged divinity. The sanctity that has surrounded his position has been used as an excuse, by those who manipulated him, to remove from his hands the mundane work of handling the affairs of the nation. Had the religious rôle of the emperor been less exalted it is extremely likely that early in Japanese history the imperial family would have been reduced to the position of only one of a number of ruling dynasties. As it was, his religious rôle gave him a prestige far beyond that which would have risen from political leadership alone.

Distinguishing between the person of the emperor and his rôle as an institution will also clarify his rôle in history. It has been the institution that has been revered and that has played a pivotal rôle in Japanese history. The emperor's person has been relatively unimportant. The emperor as an institution has gone serenely on through Japanese history, untouchable and untouched. The threats to the institution in historical times can be counted on the fingers of one hand. But individual emperors have been deposed. They have been wilfully kept, as is the present incumbent, in a position of political impotence. They have been neglected in poverty. Children and mere boys have been set on the throne and deposed at will. If political authority were actually allowed the emperor, he would be in a position to exercise the prerogatives of the throne and thus seriously circumscribe the ambitions of those who wished to monopolize the exercise of political power. Hence the aim was to preserve the institution, but to control it by reducing individual emperors to the status of easily manipulated puppets.

The position of the Japanese emperors has been unique in world history, but there is nothing mysterious about it. As has just been outlined, the emperor has been simply a force in Japanese politics, given certain divine attributes and maintained in a position of theoretical omnipotence, because it served the political ambitions of the oligarchy, both civil and military, to do so.

The roots of the emperor idea extend back to Japanese prehistory. Much of its strength to-day springs from the haziness that surrounds its beginnings, thus making it a matter of faith rather than of cold logic.

The Japanese myths on which is based the account of the alleged divine descent of the emperors and of the Japanese people were undoubtedly handed down for generations by word of mouth, as all myths have been, long before they were set down in writing. No trace of an early Japanese written language has yet been discovered, and there is no reason to believe that Chinese was not the first written language known in Japan. The myths were recorded at a fairly late date in Japanese history, and were set down with definite political aims in mind. Although the myths were originally unsophisticated, it must be remembered that they were recorded for the first time, not as an exercise in literature, but with the aim of strengthening the hold of the court aristocrats on the power they had gained, by giving them the sanction of divine or semi-divine descent.

The mythological account has become crystallized into historical dogma because it has furthered certain political aims of those who have controlled Japan. It was to the interest of the ruling groups in early Japan to trace the descent of the emperor from the gods because of the prestige that it gave the newly-created imperial family. It is to the interest of the present rulers of Japan to stress the divine descent of the emperors because it gives the Japanese people a feeling of uniqueness and superiority that is part of the foundation of their dangerous nationalism.

The two earliest extant Japanese histories, the *Kojiki,* compiled in 712, and the *Nihongi,* compiled in 720, were the first written after the Taikwa Reform had established the court bureaucracy. These two books mention still earlier records, but all were destroyed during the political strife of the mid-seventh century. The great emphasis on genealogical tables and the care taken to associate the ancestors of the politically powerful families with the gods clearly reveal the political intent of the compilers, who, incidentally, were under the direction of the victorious imperial faction that was interested in building up an unshakable foundation for its power.

These books describe the relationship of the imperial family and the other powerful families to the gods who were supposed to be the ancestors of Japan. This gave the new ruling group a prestige that reinforced its political power, and also made the imperial family divine. They are the foundation on which Japanese chauvinism rests. It is one of the tragic ironies of the history of Japan that the scientific facts on which our knowledge of early Japan is based are obscure and indefinite, while the myths which have no true reality have been made to appear to the Japanese as absolute and incontrovertible fact.

A careful examination of Japanese mythology will reveal that it is made up of several different cycles which have been welded together in a rather haphazard fashion. This accounts for the numerous contradictions, conflicts, and general lack of continuity. The dominant stream, the so-called Yamato cycle, belongs to the tribe to which the imperial family traces its descent. The central figure in this cycle is Amaterasu O-Mikami, the Sun Goddess. Another group seems to have come from the old Idzumo region of Japan on the northern shore of the western end of Honshu. Susanoo-no-mikoto, the brother of Amaterasu, is the key figure in this series. The final group, the Kyushu cycle, centring around sea myths bears a marked resemblance to myths of peoples in the South Pacific.

The world, according to the Japanese version of the creation, appeared out of the vast formlessness that existed before the appearance of man and most of the gods. Izanagi, the male, and Izanami, the female, appear as the first two of the gods with personalities, although others are described briefly but obscurely. These two stood on the "Bridge of High Heaven," and Izanagi dipped his spear into the vast sea that covered the world, worked it around and withdrew it. The mud on the tip fell back into the water and formed a tiny island which is identified with Awaji in the eastern end of the Inland Sea. The two then descended to this speck of land where Izanami gave birth, in due time, not only to a multitude of gods, but also to all the other islands making up the Japanese archipelago. This accounts for the divine origin of Japanese soil which has long been stressed by Japanese chauvinists.

As a result of giving birth to the god of fire, Izanami was so severely burned that she died. She departed for the underworld, followed by the grief-stricken Izanagi who failed to bring her back to the land of the living. On his return to the upper world Izanagi felt that he was polluted. He then purified himself by bathing in a stream. As he cleansed the various parts of his body, gods sprang forth from them, and finally when he cleansed his left eye the Sun Goddess was born.

After the passage of a long period of time, the Sun Goddess, who dwelt in a sort of heaven, decided that the land should be pacified by her descendants. She first decided to send one of her sons, but the gods whom she sent out as scouts either deserted her or found the task of pacifying the land too difficult. She finally sent her grandson to the earth, and he set foot on Japanese soil, on a mountain in the southern part of the island of Kyushu. She had bestowed upon him the so-called Three Sacred Treasures the possession of which guarantees the legitimacy of the emperor's claim to the throne. These Sacred Treasures are the Mirror, which represents the spirit of the Sun Goddess—the Jewels (curious comma-shaped stones rather than jewels)—and the Sword.

The Heavenly Grandson succeeded in winning over the inhabitants of the land to his side. In the third generation from the Heavenly Grandson was descended the Emperor Jimmu, the first to sit on the throne of Japan.

When Jimmu ascended the throne he was given the Three Sacred Treasures. The Mirror and the Jewels were connected with one of the most famous incidents in Japanese mythology. The Sun Goddess became angry, it is said, when her brother, Susanoo-no-mikoto, performed a number of wild pranks. She withdrew into a cave, causing darkness to descend on the world. In order to entice her out of the cave the other gods set up a sacred tree and hung on it the Mirror and the Jewels, and then began to sing and dance. Her attention being attracted by the noise of the carefully planned merriment of the gods outside the cave, the Sun Goddess peeked out and saw her reflection in the Mirror. Fascinated, she remained gazing at it until one of the stronger of the gods seized her and pulled her out of the cave. Japanese mythology says that the sword was simply found in the tail of a dragon slain by the above-mentioned Susanoo-no-mikoto.

The Three Sacred Treasures have played an important rôle in Japanese history because they have been the insignia of office without which no emperor could legitimately occupy the throne. The Mirror is in the Grand Shrine at Ise, the Sword in a shrine at Atsuta near Nagoya, and the Jewels at the Imperial Palace in Tokyo. Replicas of the Sword and Mirror are also kept at the Imperial Palace.

According to Japanese chronology, Jimmu Tenno ascended the throne on a date corresponding to February 11, 660 B.C., the year 1 in Japanese chronology. The present emperor, Hirohito, is the 124th occupant of the throne and is descended in an unbroken line from Jimmu and hence from the Sun Goddess, says Japanese pseudo-history. The year 660 B.C. was apparently arbitrarily selected, about 600 A.D., as the year of Jimmu's enthronement. Since even according to Japanese mythology there were only thirty-eight emperors until 600 A.D., their reigns had to be stretched out over a period of 1300 years. This meant that some were credited with extraordinarily long tenures of the throne.

In 667 B.C., seven years before his enthronement, Jimmu is supposed to have set out on a career of conquest from southern Kyushu, where the first gods set foot in Japan. He went north along the east coast of Kyushu, east through the Inland Sea, and eventually arrived in the Yamato country, which lies to the south of Kyoto. There he completed his subjugation of the land and was enthroned at a place called Kashiwabara. The account of Jimmu's conquests is quite possibly the reflection of an actual historical movement of a tribe or clan. It is also to be noted that according to this mythological account he established his rule by force of arms.

Jimmu reigned for seventy-five years and died at the ripe old age of 127, according to Japanese history. During the seventy-four years of his reign following his accession to the throne Japanese chronology lists only four events. Following Jimmu's reign the entries in Japanese history for many centuries are few and far between.

This, then, is the mythological account of the origin of the Japanese soil, the emperors, and the Japanese people, who, according to Japanese orthodoxy, also descended from the common ancestor, the Sun Goddess. This mythology is taught as actual history in the schools of Japan and absolutely cannot be challenged by anyone. To challenge the authenticity of this story is to be guilty of *lèse majesté*.

The account of the divine origin of the Japanese people has been one of the corner stones of the development of Japanese super-nationalism. It has served as the most effective agent for the creation of a strong feeling of national unity and it has also provided the ideological basis for the Japanese belief that the Japanese are the "chosen people," who are destined to rule over the world because of their divine descent. The divinity of the emperor as the direct descendant of the Sun Goddess, the divinity of the Japanese people as descendants of the gods, and the sacredness of

Japanese soil are three of the basic ideological components of Japanese chauvinism.

Although Japanese history treats him as an "emperor," Jimmu was probably nothing more than a tribal chief, if he existed at all. Indeed, the thirty-sixth emperor, Kotoku, who came to the throne in 645 A.D., is the first one who can properly be regarded as having been an "emperor," if we mean by the term one who was in a position to rule as something more than a local chief. Before the Taikwa Reform the emperors were, properly speaking, only the heads of the imperial clan, which was only one of many. However, in Japanese history the heads of the imperial clan are regarded as having been "emperors" even though their rule was purely local and even though the very existence of many of them is doubtful.

The chief of the imperial clan and those of the others, like similar individuals in other primitive societies, exercised the dual function of chief priest and of ruler of the clan. Each clan apparently had its own pantheon at the apex of which stood the clan deity, who controlled the clan's earthly affairs. The members of the clan apparently felt that they were the direct descendants of their gods. The clan chief and his immediate family seem to have been regarded as the clan members most closely related to the clan god. This belief, of course, has been revived and applied to the Japanese nation as a whole, so that now all Japanese claim descent from the Sun Goddess. It is thus one of the foundation stones of Japanese racial theories.

The closeness of the relationship believed to exist between the chief and the clan god gave rise to the idea that of all clan members the chief was in a position to know what was in the mind of the god, and hence was best qualified to rule the clan. In this supposed kinship can be seen the genesis of the dual nature of the clan chief, for the religious ceremonies were designed to enable him to commune with the clan god in order to receive the divine orders which he would carry out in regulating clan affairs. The clan god was consulted on all important matters concerning the clan. Much of this rigmarole is still preserved in rites performed by the emperor. It was believed that the chief's powers to commune with the god were inherited, and that marriage outside the immediate family of the chief would dissipate his powers. Consequently, consanguineous marriages were frequent.

Control of the clan lands seems also to have been vested in the chief, probably because of the importance of religious rites in agriculture. He was thus regarded as having absolute control over both the land and the people.

As time went on, the imperial clan seems to have become more powerful and more respected than the others, but its position seems still to have been only *primus inter pares,* as one noted Japanese scholar put it some years ago. There was nothing to indicate that the chief of this clan had any more of the divine in him than the heads of other clans. This clan probably possessed more efficient fighting men, and perhaps through the accident of favourable geographical location gained a position of power and prestige in the Yamato region. We do not know how extensive its holdings were, but we do know that by the early seventh century it definitely enjoyed a position of ascendancy over the other clans.

The chief of the imperial clan was transformed into the emperor of Japan by the Taikwa Reform in the seventh century. The immediate political cause of the Reform was an internal struggle revolving around the attempt by the Soga clan to supplant the imperial clan. The land holdings of the latter and its prestige were prizes to be coveted by any group that felt that it could challenge its position.

The Soga family traced its descent back to a famous legendary statesman, Takeshiuchi-no-Sukune, who, according to the unreliable early chronology of Japanese history, died in 367 A.D. The family was powerful and held a position of trust *vis-à-vis* the imperial clan. Through the last years of the sixth century and the first half of the seventh century the Sogas made definite attempts to become the dominant ruling group. They failed because they attempted to rule not by controlling the emperor, as was done so successfully later on, but by supplanting him.

In 592 Soga Umako caused the assassination of the Emperor Sushun who was his nephew. Apparently there was bitter hatred between the two men and Umako merely prevented his own murder by having the Emperor assassinated. As the successor to Sushun the Empress Suiko was brought to the throne. She was a niece of Umako, and the standard interpretation of her enthronement is that, being a woman, she could be more easily controlled by the ambitious Umako. Suiko died in 628 and was succeeded by the Emperor Jomei, one of whose wives was a sister of Soga Emishi. The Sogas were using family ties to manage the emperor, a method that was later to be formalized as a regular technique in emperor control.

Thirteen years later Jomei died and was succeeded by his wife, the Empress Kokyoku, another puppet. In 643 Soga Iruka caused the murder of an imperial prince, who was the logical candidate to the throne. Those who recorded these events after the Soga bid for power had been ended, declared that his move was in preparation for the placing of a male Soga on the throne. Meanwhile the Soga family had, so later historians declared, infringed on imperial rights by constructing imperial tombs for their own use and by building a palace which rivaled the emperor's. A Soga scion was also granted the right to wear a purple cap, an honour reserved for imperial princes.

In 645 the Soga family's ambitious bid for supreme power was ended by the assassination of the two principal members of the family, though members of another branch of the family continued to hold relatively high office. Iruka was slain at an imperial reception for a group of envoys from a Korean kingdom and his father, Emishi, was slain the next day. The family's property was burned or confiscated. Japanese historians regard the burning of the main family mansion as one of the great tragedies of Japanese historiography, as many of the so-called national histories which had been compiled to that time were destroyed. Had these documents been saved we might have a more accurate picture of the early years of Japanese history.

The near-success of the Soga attempt to supplant the imperial clan prompted the clan and its advisers to set in train the Taikwa Reform. The clan's position had to be strengthened, so that possible later attempts to dispossess it could not succeed. The imperial clan emerged from the Taikwa Reform as the new imperial family, in whose hands all political power was concentrated, at least theoretically. A firm economic foundation for this new political power was laid by placing the ownership of all land in the emperor's hands. His control of the land was absolute, and the manner in which land reforms were carried through made it clear that all subjects should consider the emperor as having graciously bestowed on them the means for livelihood.

The gods of the imperial clan became the national gods and were henceforth to be worshipped not only as the ancestors of the emperors, but as the creators of the nation. This reinforced the emperor's position as spiritual head of the new nation. A special government department was also established in order to help him carry out his religious duties. Other important families retained their own clan gods, but these were ranged in a hierarchy that corresponded to the importance of the families' positions within the newly established political bureaucracy. Thus, the leading political figure in the new state was backed by the most important gods.

Although the new Japanese state, as established by the Taikwa Reform, was shot through and through with Chinese influences, the position of the emperor was untouched by Chinese political theories. No part of the Chinese theory of the "Mandate of Heaven" was imported into Japan. The emperor reigned and ruled simply because of his descent from the gods. He could not be held accountable, as could Chinese emperors in Chinese political thought, for poor administration. The Japanese emperor was the embodiment of the mandate of heaven and hence it could not be bestowed or withdrawn, as in China.

Control of the person of the emperor was one of the devices most effectively used by the Fujiwara family to maintain its dominance over the aristocratic oligarchy. The leaders of the family developed emperor control into a formal political technique, one which has been followed, with variations, until the present. That control was to guarantee the security of their political power. Marriage, religion, social activities, elaborate court ceremonies, and aestheticism were used by the Fujiwara leaders to control the lives of the emperors and to divert their minds from the serious affairs of state.

But the Fujiwara leaders never took the logical step which would have given them complete domination over Japan, in name as well as in fact. They did not usurp the throne. They continued to maintain the fiction that the emperor was the source of all political power. Perhaps the fact that the imperial blood was as much Fujiwara as imperial was enough for them. The technique of control operated so well that there was no necessity to take the final step, which might have awakened a considerable amount of opposition.

Though the elimination of the Soga clan marked the advent of the Fujiwara to a position of power, that family, under a different name, had apparently long enjoyed great prestige, for it traced its descent back to a god that ranked only a little below the Sun Goddess herself. Utilizing the distinction of its blood, the family gained the position where it supplied the consorts for all emperors. The wife of every emperor, and many of his concubines, came from the Fujiwara family. This meant that the father-in-law and the grandfather of every emperor was a Fujiwara. The political advantages of this situation are obvious.

Religion became a means of distracting the emperor's attention from politics. Emperors were encouraged to study the complicated Buddhist scriptures, a task which had no political implications and which involved enough to occupy much of their time. A refinement of this tactic was to encourage emperors to abdicate in order that they might concentrate their full attention on Buddhism. This move, of course, would prevent any emperor from building up a powerful political faction of his own, because it would limit his tenure of the throne.

The development of the civilization of the court nobles, which in many respects was the highest flowering of Japanese literary and aesthetic sensibilities, proved to be another means of centring the emperor's attention on considerations other than politics. Social life, according to the detailed accounts of court life contained in the literature of the period, was highly developed. The cultured individual of the court, and this meant everyone, had to have many accomplishments: brilliant conversation, poetic talent, musical ability, and a knowledge of many pastimes with little meaning, but with a high aesthetic content. Mastery of these obviously demanded a tremendous amount of time. Whoever set out to make himself a cultured gentleman also had to possess a considerable degree of will-power, if he wanted to continue any activities connected with affairs of the world.

The elaborate rituals of court life also demanded a great deal of the time of the sovereign. The court calendar was filled with religious observances and ceremonial occasions that had to be carried out with the greatest attention to every detail. The schooling required to attain perfection in these court rituals also concentrated the ruler's attention on problems not connected with the realities of political administration.

All these techniques had the result of separating the emperor not only from proximity to political power, but also from the world around him. The emphasis on religious rites and on court rituals removed the emperor more and more from all contact with the outside world. He was not and could not have been the object of wide national worship, as he has been made in recent years, for the simple reason that he lived and moved and had his being on a plane completely removed from the knowledge and understanding of the mass of the people who were his subjects. He became simply the repository of the divine power to bestow the right to rule. He continued to bestow that right on the Fujiwara family because it had him completely under control. He was fulfilling a political function which worked to the advantage of those who controlled him. That is the key to the understanding of his position both then and in later centuries. Had it served the purposes of the Fujiwara family, or of any succeeding ruling clique, to have made him the ruler of the masses, he would have been made such a ruler as he has been in the modern period.

In the latter part of the eleventh century there developed a peculiar political manifestation known as *insei* or "government (or administration) by retired emperor" which was an attempt by the emperors to regain some of their political power. The retired emperors referred to in the phrase were of two classes, *jōkō,* or "retired sovereigns," and *hoo* or "priestly retired sovereigns," i.e., abdicated emperors who entered Buddhist orders, a step which did not preclude taking part in political affairs.

The institution of *insei* continued, though with gaps, until 1840, when it came to an end with the death of the retired sovereign Kokaku. However, the institution retained its vitality as a factor in Japanese political life only through the first three men who practiced it, the ex-emperors Shirakawa, Toba, and Go Shirakawa. These three men exercised their power through *insei* during the stormy years that saw the collapse of the court nobility and the accession to political dominance of the warrior class.

The idea of *insei* seems to have originated with the emperor Go Sanjo, who was one of the rare emperors with political vision and the ability to carry out his ideas. He was the first emperor in many years to escape Fujiwara domination. Through a combination of lucky circumstances he was the only one eligible for the throne whose mother was not a Fujiwara. A whole series of imperial consorts of Fujiwara blood had either died childless or had only female children. Not only was Go Sanjo free of Fujiwara domination, and a mature man of thirty-five, but also he was able to perceive and to understand the Fujiwara methods of political control. He attempted to break the Fujiwara economic power by a series of reforms, but his moves were blocked by the still powerful Fujiwara factions. He abdicated with the intention of ruling from retirement. His death, shortly after, prevented this, and it remained for his successor to become the first practitioner of *insei*.

Shirakawa succeeded to the throne in 1073 at the age of twenty, and remained on the throne until 1087 when he retired and established the first true *insei*. He continued to rule in this manner until his death in 1129 at the age of seventy-seven. He was strong-minded and capable, and succeeded in keeping a fairly firm rein on the ambitions of the Fujiwara family. On the threshold of maturity when he ascended the throne, he had the ability to understand what was going on around him and to perceive clearly that he could not hope to rule as long as the throne was surrounded with so many restrictions. He realized that it was only by escaping from the onerous trivialities of the court that he would have the opportunity and the relative leisure necessary for the actual exercise of power. Neither he nor any of his predecessors could have ruled effectively, because their exalted rank kept them isolated from all but those of high court rank, and these were all members of the Fujiwara family, the very group that was most interested in keeping political power away from them.

What the *insei* amounted to was simply an administrative system, independent of that already established, for the operation of the government. It could scarcely, and did not as a matter of fact, develop into an effective instrument of administration. It was a duplicate system, which did nothing but inject an additional element of confusion into the political disorder that was rapidly overtaking Japan. It was a device that permitted political action on the part of a few capable individuals for a relatively short period of time. It could have been made to function as an effective administrative unit only if Shirakawa had had enough military force at his command to sweep away Fujiwara control. That force was lacking, and during the administration of Shirakawa's immediate successors the new ruling group in Japanese history, the warrior class, appeared with the military strength and organization that enabled it to sweep away the disintegrating court nobility.

Under the warriors, the emperor was even more powerless than before. Not only were his political powers taken from him, but he was removed from association with those who governed. Under the court nobility, the emperor at least lived in the same city as the rulers of the land and his court was the centre of the social, if not administrative, activities of the ruling group. But with the establishment of the warrior régime the administrative capital was removed to the town of Kamakura, not far from Tokyo, in what was then remote frontier land as far as the imperial capital was concerned. The great leader of the Minamoto family, Yoritomo, realized the advantages of setting up his government in Kamakura. He wanted to escape the enervating and distracting intrigues of the imperial court, and the purposeless social life of the courtiers, both of which were hindrances to good administration.

Yoritomo and his immediate successors established the system of rule by *shogun,* as has been described. Though the right to administer the affairs of the nation was given to the *shogun,* the emperor continued to reign over the land. Theoretically the emperor remained the repository of all political power and bestowed it on the *shogun* who ruled only as his deputy.

Though the institution of the *shogun* knew its vicissitudes just as the institution of the emperor had known and was to continue to know its own, one of the remarkable facts of Japanese history is that not one of the many *shoguns* attempted to dispossess the emperor and occupy the imperial throne, even at the times when the authority of the *shogun* was complete and absolute, and he had at his command military forces so formidable that no one could have stood in his way had he attempted actually to usurp the throne.

The complete domination of the emperor by the *shogun* (and

those who controlled them in turn) can be simply and dramatically expressed by listing, in the period between 1198 and 1318, the emperors and their ages at the time of accession and abdication.

Emperor	*Age*	*Year of Accession*	*Year of Abdication*	*Age at Abdication*
Tsuchimikado	4	1198	1210	16
Juntoku	14	1210	1221	25
Chukyo	3	1221	1221	3
Go Horikawa	10	1221	1232	21
Shijo	2	1232	1242	12
Go Saga	23	1242	1246	27
Go Fukakusa	4	1246	1259	17
Kameyama	11	1259	1274	26
Go Uda	8	1274	1287	21
Fushimi	23	1287	1298	34
Go Fushimi	11	1298	1301	14
Go Nijo	17	1301	1308	24
Hanazono	12	1308	1318	22
Go Daigo	32	1318	1339	53

Thus, in a period of one hundred and forty-one years, twenty-one of which were covered by the reign of one man, only three emperors had attained their majority when they came to the throne, and only two were more than thirty when they left it. Such adolescents were perfectly safe politically. They could not have the maturity or the judgment that ruling would normally require. It is significant that the last in this group, Go Daigo, a mature man, played a major rôle in the events that brought one line of *shogun* to an end and established a new family in power.

The emperor Go Daigo (Daigo II) came to the throne in 1318 at the age of thirty-two. He was fully aware of the prerogatives that were his in theory, and determined to render them into reality so that he could rule as was his right. Japanese historians credit him with being a student of history and consequently fully cognizant of the fact that for generations the emperors had been denied the political power that should have been theirs. His struggle to regain the power and prestige that he was firmly convinced belonged to the throne, his short-lived triumph, his betrayal and eventual defeat, form not only one of the most interesting chapters in all Japanese history, but also one of the best examples of the manipulation of the throne.

In 1331, Go Daigo set in motion a plot designed to bring to an end the power of the Hojo family, which had gained control of the *shogun*. This scheme proved abortive. Go Daigo's forces were not powerful enough to defeat the Hojo forces on the field of battle. The result was that he was forced to abdicate, and Kogon was made emperor by the Hojo family. These two events, the abdication of Go Daigo and the enthronement of Kogon, are not recognized in Japanese history as being legitimate, undoubtedly because the power of the Hojo clan was not equal, in the long run, to the task of maintaining it in control of the situation.

Go Daigo was ordered to hand over the Three Sacred Treasures to Kogon. He first refused, and then presented a spurious set. After his capture at Kasagi-yama near Kyoto he was exiled to the island of Oki in the Sea of Japan, about forty miles off the coast of Western Japan. But loyal retainers, chief of whom was Kusunoki Masashige, who has been made into one of the outstanding symbols of loyalty to the throne, remained behind and worked steadily to prepare for his return. In 1333 he escaped from exile and returned to the capital. The Hojo raised an army to crush him and his forces once and for all. But the imperial army received invaluable assistance in the desertion of two of the principal Hojo generals, Ashikaga Takauji and Nitta Yoshisada. The latter captured the Hojo capital, Kamakura, put it to the torch, and exterminated the major opposition in the Hojo family.

Go Daigo was restored to his rightful position on the throne, and succeeded in rehabilitating, at least for a period, the position of the emperor. But he apparently was not as able an administrator as he was a political plotter. History records that he rewarded, not those who were mainly responsible for his return to power, but those who were his favourites. His control over his new government was never strong, and complex political intrigues multiplied.

Ashikaga Takauji, who had served his new sovereign by deserting to his colours at an opportune moment, now proceeded to betray Go Daigo himself. He was almost crushed when he first turned against his ruler, but rallied and succeeded in capturing Kyoto, causing Go Daigo to flee from there to Mount Yoshino, some miles to the south. Takauji at this juncture was supreme, and could have taken over the government and even ascended the throne had he so desired. But having once been declared a rebel for having attacked Go Daigo he apparently felt that his position would be insecure unless he received divine sanction for his rule from the hands of the emperor. He solved the question easily. He simply sought out a member of another branch of the imperial family, placed him on the throne as the legitimate heir to Go Daigo, and received from him the right to rule the land as *shogun*.

Takauji had at his command all the force that he required to establish himself at the head of the state. That he did not usurp the throne is probably due to his political astuteness. There is no doubt that the throne still had much prestige, and no one would deny that the imperial family was still closest to the gods who were supposed to guard the nation's destiny. Had he simply usurped the throne the opposition might have been in a position to gain tremendously and perhaps decisively in strength, by raising the cry that he had traitorously deposed the emperor. As indicated above, he showed quite clearly that he realized the necessity of having someone on the throne to legitimize his rule.

His action in setting up a rival line of emperors set off one of the major dynastic struggles in Japanese history, between the North and South Courts or *Namboku Cho*. The struggle lasted for almost sixty years, from 1336, when Takauji put his candidate, Komyo, on the throne, until 1393, when it was resolved. The North Court was located in Kyoto and was the line of the imperial family favoured by Takauji. The South Court was based at Mount Yoshino whence Go Daigo had fled. It remained there, in exile, during the course of the dynastic dispute.

It was the possession of the Three Sacred Treasures which determined the legitimacy of the contending lines. Japanese history treats the five emperors of the Southern Dynasty as the legitimate rulers during this period, even though they were in exile and completely without political power, because they did possess the insignia of office; that is what has counted through all of Japanese history.

In 1392 it was agreed that the Southern Court would return the imperial insignia to Kyoto. This was done, and the emperor of the Northern Court, Go Komatsu, was legitimized on the throne and became the legitimate ruler. Apparently the members of the Southern Court were under the mistaken impression that the emperor would be chosen alternately between the two lines. But they were soon disabused of that idea. The Northern line was in possession of the imperial insignia and was therefore the line of legitimate succession. Naturally when Go Komatsu abdicated in 1412, his successor was chosen from the same line, to the exclusion of the Southern Dynasty.

The ensuing two centuries saw the emperor reach the lowest ebb of his power. It is recorded that one emperor had to sell specimens of his calligraphy in order to obtain funds to buy rice; and that one even had to remain unburied after his death, because of a lack of resources to provide him with a proper funeral. The plight of the court nobility was no happier. Indeed all Japan was plunged into one of its unhappiest periods. There was no strong centralized authority. Civil wars and clan struggles swept through the land, bringing all the economic dislocation and suffering that inevitably follow in the wake of such strife. Yet the emperor continued to reign. Completely powerless, poverty-stricken, and ignored, the imperial family remained on the throne.

When the next great period of centralization began in Japan in the early seventeenth century under the great Tokugawa Iyeyasu, it soon became apparent that the emperor was to retain his rôle of the repository of the supreme authority to rule the land. Iyeyasu and his advisers had apparently read the lessons of Japanese history well, for they took special care to set up regulations concerning the activities of the court nobility and the imperial family. They retained control of the person of the emperor, and made certain that no one would have an opportunity to wrest that control from them. In a series of regulations issued by the Tokugawa government in 1613, it was ordered that court nobles were to spend their time in study. Needless to say, this study was impractical, covering such fields as poetry, literature, and ancient customs. They were to take part in symbolic guard duties and to serve in court ceremonies, but these duties, though impressive-sounding, were in reality insignificant. Courtiers were specifically enjoined not to wander around in the streets "in places where they have no business." Those closest to the emperor were not to be allowed to develop any dangerous political tendencies.

The emperors, too, were to spend their time in the same sort of study. Orders of court precedence were established, unimportant in themselves, but useful in eliminating court intrigues which might develop into dangerous political manœuvring around the throne.

Military men were permitted to hold honorary court rank, but were forbidden to "go near the court or have anything to do with it." The Tokugawa authorities understood all too clearly the danger of allowing feudal lords to have access to the imperial court, where they might succeed in winning imperial permission to carry out an attack on the ruling group with the aim of restoring the rightful prerogatives of the court. The foresightedness of these early Tokugawa administrators was amply proved when Tokugawa power was crushed two and a half centuries later, for it was in the name of the emperor that the attacks against the Tokugawa family were carried out by other feudal lords jealous of its position.

The imperial court depended completely on the Tokugawa authorities for its existence. The Tokugawa *bakufu* understood the political implications of economic power. Control of the land and its produce was the basis for building up large armed forces. That is the technique that they had followed, and they were keen enough to know that their potential enemies would do the same thing if given the chance. Where the Tokugawa authorities erred, however, was in keeping the allowance of the imperial court too low. Discontent, fomented by the inability to provide adequately for themselves because of Tokugawa restrictions, was to drive many court nobles to intrigue with the rivals of the Tokugawa.

An important official of the Tokugawa government was stationed in Kyoto to keep a strict watch on all affairs there. One of the families most closely associated with the Tokugawa was given hereditary charge of this highly responsible position. It was his duty to see that no plots were hatched against the *bakufu,* and to report all significant developments.

But in spite of the numerous restrictions with which the throne was hedged by the *bakufu,* the Tokugawa carefully maintained the fiction that the emperor was the ultimate source of all political power. Each Tokugawa *shogun* solemnly received his investiture in office from the emperor.

Though the Tokugawa authorities kept the emperor under strict control, a movement was gaining impetus among the Japanese intelligentsia to restore him to his rightful position. The Tokugawa government adopted as one of its policies the fostering of learning among the members of the warrior class, but unfortunately for it this revival of learning took the direction of research into ancient Japanese history, with the result that scholar-warriors made the discovery that in ancient times the emperor exercised personal, direct rule, and actually enjoyed political power.

This discovery provided the major ideological basis for the attack on Tokugawa authority. The Tokugawa family was charged with being usurpers of the imperial prerogatives. Their answer, of course, was to charge the opposition with being rebels against the throne, but they were unable to retain control of the person of the emperor, and when their opponents received the imperial sanction the Tokugawa family soon bowed to the inevitable.

With the end of Tokugawa feudalism and the dawn of the modern age, a sudden and dramatic change came over the position of the emperor in Japan. He was given wealth such as his ancestors had never enjoyed. He was made the object of national worship. He was given more prestige than any of his predecessors had ever known. He was made the absolute ruler of the nation. Yet he was given no more personal power than before. The foundations of his new position were still in the past, and his old rôle as the honoured, but powerless, source of all political power was to remain unchanged.

The late Emperor Meiji occupied the throne from 1867 to 1912. This was the crucial transitional period in modern Japanese history. It was really in his reign that the process of emperor deification took place, and the Japanese emperor was changed from an interesting and harmless historical and political phenomenon into the activating force of a dangerous chauvinism.

That the emperor's position in the new Japan was not going to differ markedly from that of earlier centuries can be seen in the fact that Meiji (his personal name was Mutsuhito) was only fourteen years old when he came to the throne. As in past centuries, the real ruling was to be done by the small group of men who acted as his "advisers," and in whose hands was the power to make all the decisions affecting the new nation. The same familiar pattern is apparent: the emperor was revered, while the actual business of government was carried out by men who were nominally only his advisers but who were in fact the rulers of the nation.

Not only did the modern oligarchy cloak its actions with imperial sanctions, but it also set out deliberately to make the emperor the centre of a nation-wide cult of emperor-worship. The leaders realized that their positions would be secure as long as they controlled the emperor's person and that the emperor would provide Japan with a spiritual basis for a strong political unity.

The emperor was used as the centre of a new national unity which Japan had to possess if she were to retain her independence in the face of threatened Occidental encroachment, and if she were to attain the destiny that her leaders were envisaging. The idea of loyalty was firmly ingrained in the patterns of Japanese behaviour, but it was centred on the local feudal lord. The problem was to shift this loyalty from a local, a provincial basis, to a broad national one. The emperor was the ideal focal point for this new loyalty. By utilizing a political concept already firmly rooted in Japan the creators of the new state prevented the injection of ideological dislocation into Japan. This native concept had an aura of sanctity and venerableness that could not be matched by alien concepts from the Western world.

As the basis for an understanding of the nature of the process of the shift of political loyalty from the feudal lord to the emperor, the genesis of the concept of personal loyalty as a part of Japan's political psychology will be traced briefly here.

The Japanese are by nature no more loyal than any other people. Betrayal of one's master or allies has played an extremely important rôle in Japanese political history. The example of Ashikaga Takauji has been described at some length. Particularly during the fifteenth and sixteenth century, betrayal became the normal pattern of political behaviour. Betrayal of master, ally, friend, father, children characterized the political life of that period. It is to be noted that this was a period of utter political chaos, a period of almost constant warfare during which no one individual or combination of individuals was able to create a strong centralized government. Amidst such disorder expediency was the rule of the day.

With the creation of a centralized state under the Tokugawa, a deliberate attempt was made to develop the sense of personal loyalty to the highest degree. It was on the concept of loyalty, more than on any other principle, that the Tokugawa based their theory of government. They reasoned that if it were firmly established in Japan, the foundation for a stable political order would be laid. Such loyalty would imply, at least, an acceptance of the established order and would inhibit the development of political movements designed to destroy any part of the structure. Loyalty of peasant to feudal lord was the lowest level in the hierarchy of loyalties. This would act to eliminate widespread discontent with political and economic conditions. Loyalty of retainer to lord lessened the possibility of internal betrayal instigated by rival lords. Loyalty of the feudal lords to the *bakufu* would reduce the danger of political intrigue directed at the ruling group itself. The Tokugawa themselves pretended that they were loyal to the emperor.

A deliberate campaign was carried out to exalt the virtue of loyalty. Stories were written and circulated on the theme of loyalty of retainer to master. The newly arisen popular theatre was encouraged to produce dramas that would emphasize the martial virtues and portray classical examples of loyalty. The state philosophy was based on a Confucianism that stressed the idea of the maintenance of the proper relationship between ruler and ruled.

The idea of mass loyalty to the emperor did not appear, for the reason that there was no need for it. Political solidarity was maintained by concentrating loyalty on a lower plane. As a matter of fact it is highly doubtful that even a knowledge of the existence of the emperor was widely spread among the Japanese people. Since the Tokugawa authorities served their political purpose admirably by keeping the emperor and his court under their complete domination, there was no need to develop mass emperor worship.

When the founders of the new Japan destroyed Tokugawa power, they also swept away the feudal economic and political structure on which Tokugawa rule was based. This eliminated the basis for the loyalty of most of the people of Japan, for the feudal lords, the old focal point of loyalty of the masses, were gone. But the new rulers did not permit the destruction of the concept of loyalty. They simply shifted that loyalty from the feudal lords to the emperor. A narrow local loyalty to a feudal lord was replaced by an allegiance to the emperor as the head of a nation, in the modern sense of the term.

The Meiji Restoration had been carried out in the name of the emperor and with the announced intention of restoring the emperor to his rightful place as the ruler of all Japan. Every effort was made to rehabilitate the emperor both as a ruler and as an institution. In modern Japan, for the first time in Japanese history, the emperor became the object of national worship. That worship is founded on centuries of history and of mythology that must be treated as if it were history.

During Meiji's reign there centred around his person a curious dual process, one part of which brought him close to his people, the other removing him from all contact with them. It is a safe statement that the great Meiji was seen by more Japanese than any other emperor in all of Japanese history to that time. Both foreign and Japanese observers testify that he was intensely interested in the problems of Japanese government, and often attended important conferences. In addition, he made tours of inspection to many sections of the country. This was a far cry from the old times when the emperor dwelt in isolation in the old imperial capital, completely cut off from all contact with the people. But at the same time the rulers of Japan set in motion the process of deification, which was to result in the creation of an even wider gulf between the ruler and his subjects.

They utilized several methods in setting up the emperor as the core of the new state. His supreme political position was guaranteed by the Constitution; a theory of government was gradually built up which placed all government officials in the position of mere advisers to the emperor; he was made the object of worship in Japan's new nationalist religion, Shinto; anything that might possibly be interpreted as being *lèse majesté* was quickly and ruthlessly punished, either legally or extra-legally; the Japanese people were thoroughly indoctrinated with the belief that the emperor is "divine"; and, finally, his economic position was completely rehabilitated.

For centuries the position of the emperor, exalted as it was, had not been defined in law. There had been no necessity for it, tradition and religious sanctity having given him all the sanction he needed. With the modernization of Japan, it was deemed necessary to give Japan a constitution. This political innovation was used to formalize the paramount political position of the emperor. The highest law of the land firmly established him as the capstone of the new authoritarian state.

Prince Ito Hirobumi, certainly one of the greatest politicians and statesmen in all Japan's history, is credited with being the father of the Japanese Constitution. He clearly recognized the tremendous political importance of the emperor, and built the Constitution around him. In 1884 he was instrumental in creating a special government office, the Bureau for Investigation of Constitutional Systems, which was part of the Imperial Household Department. The reason for this strategy is not difficult to discover. By placing the drafting of the Constitution under the control of the Imperial Household Department, Ito removed it from all possibility of criticism, for it was regarded as being under the direct supervision of the emperor himself. The Constitution will be discussed in some detail in a later chapter. Here only the section dealing with the emperor will be analyzed.

The preamble to the Constitution, because of the light it sheds not only on the position of the emperor, but also on the political theories of the founders of modern Japan, is worth repeating here.

"Having, by virtue of the glories of Our ancestors, ascended the Throne of a lineal succession unbroken for ages eternal; desiring to promote the welfare of, and to give development to the moral and intellectual faculties of Our beloved subjects, the very same that have been favoured with the benevolent care and affectionate vigilance of Our ancestors; and hoping to maintain the prosperity of the State, in concert with Our people and with their support, We hereby promulgate, in pursuance of Our Imperial Rescript of the 12th day of the 10th month of the 14th year of Meiji, a fundamental law of State, to exhibit the principles, by which We are to be guided in Our conduct, and to point out to what Our descendants and Our subjects and their descendants are forever to conform.

"The rights of sovereignty of the State, We have inherited from Our ancestors, and We shall bequeath them to Our descendants.

Neither We nor they shall in future fail to wield them in accordance with the provisions of the Constitution hereby granted.

"We now declare to respect and protect the security of the rights and of the property of Our people, and to secure to them the complete enjoyment of the same, within the extent of the provisions of the present Constitution and of the law.

"The Imperial Diet shall first be convoked for the 23rd year of Meiji, and the time of its opening shall be the date, when the present Constitution comes into force.

"When in the future it may become necessary to amend any of the provisions of the present Constitution, We or Our successors shall assume the initiative right, and submit a project for the same to the Imperial Diet. The Imperial Diet shall pass its vote upon it, according to the conditions imposed by the present Constitution, and in no otherwise shall Our descendants or Our subjects be permitted to attempt any alteration thereof.

"Our Ministers of State, on Our behalf, shall be held responsible for the carrying out of the present Constitution, and Our present and future subjects shall forever assume the duty of allegiance to the present Constitution."

The points to be noted particularly in the preamble are: (1) the Constitution is promulgated by the emperor himself; (2) "the rights of sovereignty of the State" have been handed down from emperor to emperor; (3) all amendments must be initiated by the throne; and (4) the ministers of state are to be held responsible to the throne for the carrying out of the Constitution. Those four points indicate quite clearly that the founders of the new Japan understood the value of the emperor in the game of Japanese politics.

By creating the impression that the Constitution was a gracious gift from the emperor to his people, the actual drafters were removing their handiwork from the possibility of any tampering whatsoever. No matter how dissatisfied their political opponents might be with the nature of the Constitution, they could not criticize it, for to do so would be to express dissatisfaction with the work of the emperor himself. The point that all amendments must be initiated by the throne further confirmed those individuals in power who were closest to the throne. Whoever controlled the emperor controlled the Constitution. Furthermore, this point indicates the desire on the part of the drafters to keep their work unaltered. They had created what they believed to be the perfect document for their purposes and had no wish to see it altered in directions which might give the people a greater voice in the government. If the oligarchy that was creating modern Japan was to be self-perpetuating, and that was apparently its aim, then it would always control the person of the emperor, which meant that it would likewise control the power to amend. The declaration that the ministers of state are to be held responsible to the throne is another indication that ministers were to be responsible to the oligarchy and not to the people. In the eyes of the actual drafters it was only natural that the emperor who "drafted" the Constitution should also be the one to whom the ministers were responsible for carrying out the provisions of the Constitution. The final point, that the rights of sovereignty were handed down from emperor to emperor, is designed to give the throne additional sanctity.

The first section of the Constitution, consisting of seventeen articles, is devoted to the emperor. Article I, *"The Empire of Japan shall be reigned over and governed by a line of Emperors unbroken for ages eternal,"* is the constitutional expression of Japan's proudest boast, one that has been consistently used to demonstrate the "superiority" of the Japanese system of government.

Article III, *"The Emperor is sacred and inviolable,"* is designed to bolster his unassailable position in Japan's political system. Prince Ito's comment on this article is well worth repeating. "The Emperor," he says, "is Heaven-descended, divine and sacred; He is pre-eminent above His subjects. He must be reverenced and is inviolable. He has indeed to pay due respect to the law, but the law has no power to hold Him accountable to it. Not only shall there be no irreverence for the Emperor's person, but also shall He not be made a topic of derogatory comment nor one of discussion."

The remaining fifteen articles of this section deal with various powers of the emperor, the questions of succession, and the regency. Among other powers the emperor "convokes the Imperial Diet, opens, closes and prorogues it, and dissolves the House of

Representatives." The power that this gives the throne over the legislature is obvious. Article VIII vests the emperor with the right to issue "Imperial Ordinances in the place of law" in consequence of an urgent necessity to maintain public safety or to avert public calamities. Even though these ordinances are subject to review by the Imperial Diet, it is clear that in time of emergency whoever controls the emperor controls the destiny of the nation.

From the standpoint of the development of modern Japan, Articles XI and XII are of the utmost importance. Article XI reads: *"The Emperor has the supreme command of the Army and Navy,"* and Article XII: *"The Emperor determines the organization and peace standing of the Army and Navy."* These articles have, in effect, given the leaders of the Army and Navy freedom from the control of civilian elements in the government, for they have taken the position that only they, as trained technical experts, had access to the emperor on military and naval matters. In his comments on Article XII, Ito says: "The present article points out, that the organization and peace standing of the Army and Navy are to be determined by the Emperor. It is true, that this power is to be exercised with the advice of responsible Ministers of State; still like the Imperial military command, it nevertheless belongs to the sovereign power of the Emperor, and no interference in it by the Diet should be allowed." Given the paramount position of the military in Japanese affairs and the key rôle of the emperor in Japanese politics, it is little wonder that Ito and his fellow drafters took care that command of the imperial forces be placed in the hands of the emperor himself. It is obvious that the emperor as an individual could have no determining voice in military affairs; on the other hand, since he is supreme commander, his advisers are given an unassailable constitutional position.

Promulgated at the same time as the Constitution was the Imperial House Law, the articles of which regulate the conduct of the Imperial Family, and deal with such problems as succession, regency, coronation, marriage, the management of estates, and court etiquette. The primary concern of the Imperial House Law is to prevent disputes over succession, a most fruitful source of political intrigue in early Japanese history.

Affairs of the emperor and of the imperial family are under

the control of the Imperial Household Department, which is supervised by the Minister of the Imperial Household. The latter minister, although of ministerial rank, is independent of the cabinet; he continues in office regardless of its fate. The department "controls and conducts affairs relating to Imperial Household, members of the Imperial Family, peers and others." The minister supervises the affairs of the department, controls all peers, and advises the emperor on all matters relating to the Imperial Household. From this catalogue of his duties, his importance is clearly apparent. It is significant that in the wave of political assassinations during the 1930's, Imperial Household ministers were on the assassins' lists. Superficially, attacks on individuals so close to the emperor might be regarded as a form of *lèse majesté,* but the assassins cloaked their acts in righteousness by declaring that these officials were "guilty of advising the emperor wrongly," hence, according to their reasoning it was their duty as patriotic Japanese to remove the men who were misleading the emperor.

With the emperor firmly established as the absolute ruler of Japan under the provisions of the Constitution, and with the drafters of the Constitution being motivated by a desire to create an authoritarian state, it was only natural that the next step be taken and a theory of ministerial responsibility be worked out, which would make the ministers of state responsible to no one save the emperor. This made it doubly sure that the Japanese people would not be allowed a voice in their government. The main points in the constitutional struggle concerning ministerial responsibility will be sketched later. It is sufficient to point out here that the establishment of this theory meant the continuation of the control of the government, and of the person of the emperor, by an oligarchy. The modern theory of rule by the emperor has been, as a matter of fact, based on the idea that the emperor rules only on the advice of his ministers. This, though it may appear so on the surface, is not a limitation on the powers of the emperor. His ministers are "appointed" by him and simply act as his agents in the business of government. In effect, according to this view, when the emperor rules only on the advice of his ministers, he is acting solely on the advice of his own agents, therefore, he is being self-advised, for his ministers have all been appointed by him.

If a theory of ministerial responsibility had been developed which made ministers responsible to the people, then the whole foundation of oligarchic government would have been shaken.

The creators of the new Japan were careful not to neglect the sacred aspects of the new position of the emperor. They were aware that the emperor, if established simply as a political institution, would in time become the object of purely political attacks by men who wished to participate more widely in the government of Japan. They realized fully the usefulness of the same technique that had been used before in controlling the person of the emperor, namely, to place him on such a high religious plane that to attack him would be sacrilege.

The new sacred position of the emperor was not manufactured out of whole cloth. There was sound historical tradition behind it, but the aims of the new rulers were far more ambitious than those of their predecessors. What they wanted was to make the emperor the basis of worship on the part of the entire Japanese nation. They were motivated by a two-fold desire: to create a focal point for political unity which would prevent the widespread dissemination of foreign concepts of government, and to cloak the throne in a sanctity which would prevent criticism of the established political order as operated by the oligarchy itself. The institution of the emperor was ideally suited to their purposes.

Following well-tried Japanese political practice, the founders of the modern Japanese state were intensely interested in building up the sacred aspect of the ruler in order, at the same time, to strengthen his secular position. The Constitution had insured that the person of the emperor could be controlled by the oligarchy, and now it was necessary to make his position absolutely unassailable, and, incidentally, its own. The method was simple: the emperor was made into the central figure of Japan's new national religion, Shinto.

The materials for this cult, the Sun Goddess, the direct descent of the emperors from the Sun Goddess, the uniqueness of the imperial line, the emperor as the father of the people, the Sun Goddess as the ancestress of all Japanese, all lay ready at hand, sanctified by tradition and awaiting only the appearance of a few purposeful men to be wrought into an ingenious and powerful machine for molding the loyalties of the Japanese people into a unified whole. The introduction of a system of mass education meant literacy, the instrument necessary for the indoctrination of the people with the belief that the emperor was divine and that in some way they, as his people, shared in that divinity and were responsible for the spread of the "divine way" throughout the world.

Mass propaganda by means of carefully prepared schoolbooks, the contents of which masqueraded as history, was undoubtedly one of the major factors for the establishment of the emperor as the living godhead of Japanese nationalism. Not only were school children from the first grade on (they were, of course, exposed to the idea long before they entered school) carefully indoctrinated in the belief that the emperor was divine and that he and all Japanese were divinely descended from the Sun Goddess, but all criticism of this official "history" was forbidden. Many scholars would not, and those who wished to, could not criticize these fairy tales.

Mere passive acceptance of the idea by the masses was not enough. The few intelligent, questioning Japanese who might cast doubt on the whole tissue of the mythology on which the cult was based also had to be controlled. Against such people the weapon of *lèse majesté* was used. This permitted the use of methods directly by the state police to handle anyone who might challenge the official history. The Constitution itself guaranteed the emperor against too much criticism, but the oligarchy had the power to see to it that no one could criticize the emperor or anything else connected with him. Individuals were thrown into prison if they were only suspected of having criticized the emperor. Not only that, but *lèse majesté* was an extremely handy weapon to use in order to discredit anyone who was suspected of harbouring wrong ideas. Publications ranging all the way from fairy tales to serious treatises were suppressed if the censor detected anything even remotely resembling a slur on any emperor or any aspect of the imperial family. Besides these direct methods of suppressing any tendency toward what they regarded as *lèse majesté,* the oligarchy adopted another effective course of action, that of treating with extreme leniency all private citizens who used violence against persons suspected of *lèse majesté.* In this way, official Japan condoned the actions of extremist groups and individuals if they were directed against any anti-emperor, anti-imperial family activity. This official and unofficial terrorism soon had the desired effect of stifling all criticism.

Besides the techniques of propaganda and terrorism directed against critics or doubting Thomases, a few other simple, but extremely effective devices have been utilized to make the Japanese people supremely aware of the divinity of the emperor. The idea of remoteness is used to create in the minds of the people the idea that the emperor is a creature apart. He does not mingle with his people. Streets are cleared by police before the Emperor passes. This is done both to keep the plebeian eyes from resting on the imperial person, and to prevent attempts on the imperial life, several of which have been made.

The imperial palace itself in the centre of Tokyo is surrounded with the same aura of divinity. Ringed by wide and deep moats, the banks of which are shored up by gracefully curving stone embankments over which swoop the ancient boughs of large pines, the palace grounds are one of the most beautiful spots in all Japan, but their beauty is to be seen only by the human eye itself. Photographing and sketching are absolutely prohibited, except for one small section at the principal entrance to the grounds. Passers-by, on foot, on bicycle, on street-car, in bus, or private automobile, must remove their hats and bow respectfully toward the palace when they pass the main gates. Visitors to the capital must go to the palace and bow before it. Soldiers, sailors, or others leaving the country do the same if it is at all possible. Processions celebrating victories go to the great plaza in front of the palace, and cheer the Emperor. Rarely does the Emperor appear. Bows and cheers are directed not at the imperial person, but at the imperial dwelling.

Though the Emperor does not appear among the people the royal features, or reasonable facsimiles thereof, are well known to the Japanese. Cheap photographs, which belong to the same genre as the early twentieth-century calendar art of the United States, are to be found in most homes. The imperial portraits are treasured in every schoolhouse. Because of the flimsy construction and the extremely combustible nature of the average Japanese school building, the imperial portraits are usually placed in a small fire-proof shrine at the entrance to the school, and each student doffs his hat and bows toward the shrine as he leaves or enters the school grounds. Before the practice of building these little fire-proof receptacles became standard, a regularly recurring story in the Japanese press concerned the principal who dashed into the burning schoolhouse to save the imperial photographs — sometimes emerging slightly singed and sometimes going up in smoke with the imperial pictures. These incidents were always played up to the credit of the principal's patriotism.

Another extremely effective device is that of the ceremony of the national bow in the direction of the imperial palace. On New Years' Day, the Emperor's birthday, April 29, and February 11, the date when the first emperor is supposed to have ascended the throne, all Japan pauses in what it is doing, and bows respectfully in the direction of the imperial palace. On the face of it the procedure is absurd, but it is extremely effective in making all Japanese feel that they are not only joined together in the worship of the emperor, but that there is a great spiritual bond uniting them all.

The result of all these moves has been to transform the emperor, not into an effective ruler of his nation, but into the dangerous symbol of the Japanese chauvinism that has brought death and suffering to millions of non-Japanese, and which has led the Japanese themselves to the most dangerous position they, as a people, have ever known. The Japanese Army and Navy will suffer a crushing defeat at the hands of the United Nations. We do not yet know what the fate of their Commander-in-Chief, the Emperor, will be. His future rôle in Japan is a problem concerning the welfare not only of the Japanese people, but of the rest of the world.

Chapter V

FOREIGN INFLUENCES AND ANTI-FOREIGNISM

At every decisive period in her history Japan has turned avidly to China or the West for inspiration, but she has also revealed the opposite tendency of resolutely rejecting any foreign influence whenever her leaders deemed it necessary. Japan has eagerly accepted materials and institutions which could be fitted to Japanese requirements, but has not allowed the entry of ideas that would undermine the basic attitudes of the people toward the Japanese political, economic, and social systems.

This selectivity has been possible because foreign influences have come into the country only on Japan's terms. Foreign invasion has never flooded Japan with unwanted ideas, customs, and institutions which might have left their mark on Japanese society. In addition, during each period when the flood of foreign things was the greatest, in the seventh, sixteenth, and nineteenth centuries, Japan was under the control of strong men newly come to power. They had succeeded by force of arms and political adroitness in gaining control of the government, and were interested in building up the power and prestige of their new régimes. To consolidate their positions they turned to China or the West for institutions and materials that would provide even more effective methods of internal control. They neither needed nor desired foreign theories or philosophies of government, because their power was firmly based on Japanese ideas and needed no additional bolstering.

The purely geographical factor of the distance between Japan and the continent has helped to determine the extent of the inflow of foreign ideas. The relative nearness of the continent to Japan has permitted the importation of ideas and institutions from the continent. But at a time when efficient means of communication and transportation were lacking, the hundred-odd miles from Western Japan to Korea, to say nothing of the longer distance to China, served as a moat which protected Japan from being overwhelmed by military invasion. A few men could bring ideas of major importance into Japan, but it would have taken a great army to conquer the country. Japan was thus in a position to enjoy the benefits of the continent, but was protected from the disaster of military conquest.

Japan, moreover, lay on the perimeter of Chinese experience. Japan had nothing that appealed to China. She had no great wealth. There were no strange products which would appeal to the Chinese. There were no ideas that would attract the interest of the Chinese scholars. China knew that most of what lay beyond the ocean in Japan had originally come from China itself. Consequently, the one time Japan was threatened by invasion from the continent was when a Chinese "foreign" dynasty, the Mongol, attempted unsuccessfully to mount an invasion across the Korean straits.

China has had her periods of expansion, but they have been directed to the west and to the south. A periodic pulsation has characterized Chinese expansion to the west, into the vast reaches of Central Asia. In spite of the great distances involved it was relatively easy for Chinese forces to be sent to that area. Besides, in that direction lay the Occident, from whence came many of the exotic things that China wanted and used. And in the Occident was a demand for the goods of Cathay.

China absorbed the main impact of the coming of the West to the Far East, and protected and sheltered Japan from many of its more serious dangers. China, of course, was known to the West centuries before Japan was. Chinese goods, especially silks, found their way into the Roman Empire. Christianity was known in China long before it reached Japan. The great traveller, Marco Polo, knew China intimately, yet the only mention he has of Japan is a fantastic account of a semi-mythical country where "they have gold in the greatest abundance," where there were many pearls and precious stones, and where the inhabitants practiced cannibalism, "asserting that human flesh surpasses every other in the excellence of its flavour."

When Japan was first discovered by the West about A.D. 1550,

China had already had some 1600 years of intermittent communication with Europe. Japan owes its greatest debt to China for the manner in which she absorbed the impact of Western imperialism in the eighteenth and nineteenth centuries. Indeed, had it not been for China, Japan might well have been reduced to the status of a colonial power during the nineteenth century. But Europe and America first established contact with China, and succeeded in establishing large interests there, with the result that Japan was never more than of secondary importance in the eyes of those who might have brought her under their domination.

Japan's early relations with the continent were mainly through Korea. Korean influence on early Japan was of a secondary rather than a primary nature, but that does not detract from its importance. Korea was a cultural bridge between China and Japan, a middleman between the two nations, rather than a source of direct inspiration to Japan. For example, in the field of art Korea sent both art objects and artists to Japan, but these had either come from China or had been inspired by the Chinese. R. K. Reischauer, in his excellent study of early Japanese history, declares that Japan was interested in Korea only as a means of obtaining Chinese culture. This statement might tend to be extreme, but it does point up well Korea's rôle in the cultural relations between China and Japan.

Early Japan had both cultural and political relations with Korea, but her interest in the peninsula died out by the middle of the seventh century. Except for the last decade of the sixteenth century, Japan's relations with Korea were minor until the latter part of the nineteenth century, when the chain of events was set in motion that eventually ended in the absorption of the peninsula into the Japanese empire. Korea's greatest single early contribution to Japan was undoubtedly the transmission of the Buddhist religion. Japan's relations with the peninsula at that time have provided Japan's nationalists with the basis for a tradition of expansion on the continent.

There is a Japanese legendary account of an invasion of Korea by forces under the command of the redoubtable Empress Jingo. This story is fanciful in almost every detail, but it has formed one of the corner-stones of the Japanese tradition of continental conquest.

According to this legend Jingo was divinely inspired, and one of the Japanese deities, speaking through her, said: "There is a land to the westward, and in that land is abundance of various treasure dazzling to the eye, from gold and silver downwards. I will now bestow this land upon thee." This was duly reported to the emperor, but he, obviously a skeptic and not imbued with the spirit of conquest, declared that if one ascended a high place and looked to the west, there was no land to be seen. Consequently he was not interested in the statement of the gods, and simply continued to play his lute. The gods, angered by such lack of vision, proceeded to strike him dead.

Jingo, so the legend tells us, thereupon prepared to take full advantage of the offer of the gods. She made the proper offerings to the divinities, equipped an army, and marshalled vessels to transport it to the peninsula. Confirming the divine nature of the mission, the gods sent to her point of embarkation the fishes of the sea, which bore her fleet on their backs. The gods also sent a favouring wind which speeded her expedition even more. She conquered the kingdom of Shiragi without a struggle and the neighbouring kingdom of Kudara also gave in. According to the exceedingly unreliable chronology of the early Japanese histories, this expedition took place sometime in the early part of the third century A.D. The story is not confirmed in any way by materials in Chinese or Korean histories; however, the Japanese attacks on Korea which are mentioned in early Korean annals may be reflected in this account of the Empress Jingo's expedition.

The traditional Japanese historical interpretation of this invasion is that it had an extremely important effect on the development of national feeling among the Japanese. The view is that this overseas expedition gave the Japanese a feeling of power and strength toward those on the continent with whom they were in contact.

In modern Japanese nationalistic thought, the rôle of this story is not difficult to perceive. This early adventure in imperialism, it is to be noted, was undertaken on the specific instructions of the gods who watch over Japan's destiny. In addition, they contributed to the success of the mission by providing the divine aid of fishes and the wind. It is also significant that the legend reports that the expedition was carried out by a member of the imperial family.

The introduction of Buddhism into Japan in the middle of the sixth century A.D. was one of the key events in Japanese history. Like all great religious movements, its effects extended far beyond the realm of the spiritual. The actual introduction of Buddhism was more a political than a religious event in its immediate consequences. A Korean kingdom desired to create an interest in Buddhism in Japan because it hoped to receive military aid in return, not because of missionary zeal. Immediately on its introduction into Japan, it played a major rôle in Japanese internal politics.

Buddhism was a tremendous stimulus to the development of Japanese culture. It provided new elements of artistic sophistication and of aestheticism that had been lacking in earlier native Japanese civilization. Buddhism has a large number of holy books, consequently the importation of these scriptures into Japan proved to be a major factor in the spread of reading and writing among the Japanese aristocracy. The use of images and pictures in Buddhism was a great stimulus to the development of painting and sculpture in Japan. Buddhist thought and Buddhist attitudes also molded Japanese literature along new lines.

As a religion Buddhism supplied new concepts and new ideas on a level much more sophisticated than that of the native Japanese religion of Shinto, which was based mainly on the worship of nature and of superior beings. The new religion gave Japan a more philosophic approach than it had ever had before, to many of the problems of man and nature.

A little more than half a century after Buddhism became firmly rooted in Japan the Taikwa Reform was instituted. The Reform was shot through with Chinese influences. At this crucial period in her history Japan was as greatly indebted to China as she was to be to the West twelve centuries later, during the Meiji Restoration.

Now as well as later the leaders of Japan did not allow themselves to be overwhelmed by the flood from beyond their shores. They knew exactly what they wanted from China and they utilized only those things which would guarantee the construction of a political and economic structure which would perpetuate their power.

It was inevitable that Japan would turn to China for inspiration at this crucial period in her history. The brilliant T'ang Dynasty had just been established in China, and the nation was entering into one of its most glorious periods. China undoubtedly was the greatest nation of the world at that time. The Japanese embassies, composed of priests, scholars, and important officials, could not but be impressed by what they saw in their great neighbour. Consequently, as Japan was to do in the nineteenth century when she turned so avidly to the West, she feverishly imported institutions, customs, city plans, literature, art, and almost everything else connected with human activity, as long as it did not challenge the supremacy of the ruling oligarchy.

One of the best examples of the extent with which Chinese thought invaded Japan is the fact that Chinese literature, from that time until the present, has been one of the principal fields of interest for Japanese men of letters. They have not only studied the history of Chinese literature, but they have also slavishly imitated both form and content of Chinese literary works. Needless to say, most of their product has been sterile and lacking in inspiration because they had no contact with the social and cultural milieu out of which Chinese literature grew. For several centuries the study and production of Chinese literature were the principal preoccupations of the Japanese men of letters. Almost to the exclusion of their native language, the men of the Japanese court wrote Chinese poems and Chinese essays. It remained for the women of the court, to whom the study of Chinese literature was barred, to create the masterpieces of Japanese literature of this period.

The sending of Japanese embassies to China was continued until the end of the ninth century, when it was obvious that the T'ang Dynasty was crumbling, and that Japan had attained a point in its development when outside inspiration was no longer necessary. The great flood of Chinese influences came to an end at this time, but not before China had placed an indelible and ineradicable imprint on Japanese customs, institutions, and thought.

In the succeeding centuries Japan was to continue intermittently its contact with China. These contacts ranged from piratical Japanese raids on the Chinese coast to the importation from China of philosophical concepts used to bolster the Japanese social order. In the fourteenth and fifteenth centuries a relatively flourishing trade was built up between China and Japan, mainly on the initiative of Japanese merchants, feudal lords, and Buddhist temples.

Fifteen hundred years after China had established contacts with the Western world, Japan had its first relations with European nations. China had reached out across the great Asiatic land mass and had met the West. Over the long, difficult routes contacts had been maintained intermittently through the long centuries, but no Europeans had had the curiosity or the hardihood to push on to Japan. Even the great Marco Polo had only hearsay knowledge of the land of "Zipangu."

The great era of voyage and discovery in the fifteenth and sixteenth centuries finally brought Japan into the ken of the non-Asiatic world. The development of sea routes circumnavigating the globe for the first time in the history of man inevitably brought Japan into contact with the West. Spain, Portugal, Holland, and Great Britain were reaching out in search of new routes across the seas to the fabled lands of treasure in Asia. The Portuguese succeeded in reaching China by sea in the early sixteenth century, some years before Japan was discovered.

Although the nations of the West would certainly have sought out Japan, the first discovery was by accident rather than by design. In 1543 three Portuguese on board a Chinese pirate junk were blown off their course by a gale and wrecked on the shores of the island of Tanegashima, just south of Kyushu. Ironically, they bore with them the first firearms known in Japan.

Probably in 1548, a Japanese by the name of Yajiro fled from Japan aboard a Portuguese vessel. He reached the city of Malacca in Malaya and there he met the great missionary, St. Francis Xavier. Yajiro became a Christian and as a result of his conversations with St. Francis the latter determined to push on to Japan.

St. Francis Xavier (1506–52) was one of the greatest of the early Jesuit missionaries. Having made his decision to proceed to Japan, he arrived in Kagoshima in southern Kyushu in 1549. It is recorded that in ten months he had more than a hundred converts.

He succeeeded in mastering the Japanese language by the simple means of being granted the gift of tongues, tradition says. A year later he went farther north to the town of Hirado. From there he intended to start on his self-appointed task of converting all of Japan to Christianity. He went to Kyoto, but it was practically in ruins, having been the scene of many of the battles in the civil wars that were shaking Japan at the time. He soon left there and went to the city of Yamaguchi. On his arrival he presented gifts, brought from the Portuguese possession of Goa, to the local feudal lord. The gifts included such objects as clocks, firearms, cloth, and mirrors. In return he received commissions to evangelize the district. He remained in the vicinity of Yamaguchi and in northern Kyushu until 1551. He left Japan in that year *en route* to India, but died in Canton in the following year.

Christianity was moderately successful in Japan. This religion, completely foreign to Japanese attitudes, became firmly established in the western part of the country, and was later destined to play an important political rôle. However, it did not strike deep root in Japan. A number of factors contributed to the establishment of the religion. It came to Japan at a time when society was in a state of great turmoil. The established religion of Buddhism offered the people no solace or escape from the brutal realities of the times. The Buddhist priests constituted one of the most unruly elements in Japanese society, and worldly rather than spiritual considerations guided them. It took no great degree of penetration for the people to see that such priests could offer nothing in the form of religious comfort. Most of the true converts to Christianity undoubtedly turned to it in an effort to find spiritual comfort in the midst of turmoil.

In addition to the spiritual factors, political considerations contributed to the early success of Christianity. In the mid-sixteenth century Japan was the battleground of a number of feudal lords fighting among themselves for political supremacy. Casting about for any available aid, they turned to the Christian missionaries. They knew that relations between missionaries and merchants were close, and realized that by becoming Christians they might be in a strategic position to acquire the new weapons that were being introduced into Japan. Moreover, many missionaries had a knowledge of European weapons and tactics. Consequently the lords felt that the possible political returns from conversion to Christianity would more than balance any conflicts they might have with their consciences. It was easy for a lord, after conversion, to order all his retainers and serfs to embrace the new faith, which they doubtless did with as little zeal and sincerity as their master. This accounts, in part, for the spectacular increase in the number of Japanese Christians at this time.

The missionaries received great aid from Oda Nobunaga, who was rapidly asserting his supremacy as the most powerful political figure in Japan. One of his accomplishments was the final crushing of the power of the Buddhist monasteries, that had proved to be such a disrupting force in Japanese politics. He was astute enough to realize that patronage of this new and foreign religion might undermine still farther the power of the Buddhist temples. He himself did not become a convert, but he did aid the missionaries in many ways.

On the other hand the missionaries themselves were responsible for much of the success of their work. Their excellent organization — especially that of the Jesuits, which was practically military in nature — aided them to carry out their work with great efficiency. They studied the language and they studied their rival, Buddhism, in order to be able to combat it more efficiently.

There were other non-religious reasons for the early success of Christianity. The early missionaries were much concerned with medicine and relief work. They also brought with them the material objects of a new civilization. They introduced Western medicine, maps, and firearms. Besides the purely material objects they brought such intellectual accomplishments as astronomy, geography, and mathematics. There is no evidence that they were as successful in Japan as they were in China in utilizing these intellectual devices in propagating their religion, but they did win some converts by these means. Christianity's association with trade also benefited it. Many lords became interested in protecting Christianity because it brought trade in its wake. Japanese merchants were also willing to contribute at least financial aid to the church for the same reason. It was this close relation with trade that contributed in the long run to the collapse of Christianity.

It is estimated that the number of Christians in Japan grew from 150 in 1549 to 150,000 in 1582. In the next two decades, according to one Japanese authority, the number leaped to 700,000. But there were already indications that Christianity was approaching difficult days. By the second decade of the seventeenth century persecution was in full swing, and it was soon to equal if not to surpass all the fury of religious persecution at its worst in the Western world.

In 1587, the great Toyotomi Hideyoshi issued the first ban on Christianity, although previously he had regarded it with some favour. Under the terms of this prohibition all missionaries were to be expelled from Japan within three weeks and no more were to follow them. However, trade with the Western merchants was to continue to be permitted. It is not known why Hideyoshi issued this ban, but it is popularly believed that it was because missionaries attempted to interfere with his acquisition of a new mistress. But whatever his immediate reasons might have been, there were other more fundamental causes for the opposition to Christianity.

Christianity and its material appurtenances were something novel and strange to most Japanese, and, as is the case in all such situations, there was a strong, conservative opposition to the new religion and the civilization that it brought with it. The intolerance of the missionaries only encouraged the development of still greater opposition from the existing religions, Buddhism and Shinto. Another factor was the attitude of the missionaries toward the morals, or lack thereof, of the feudal lords. The missionaries criticized the conduct of the lords from the standpoint of their own moral standards, without making allowances for differences in customs.

The above considerations were minor when compared with the political implications of Christianity, as they were seen by the rulers of Japan. In the first place, there was a conflict between Christiantiy and the traditional morality of Japan. One of the ideals of Japanese political conduct was the willingness to die for one's master. Christianity substituted for this the concept of dying for an impersonal faith. Religion therefore was made greater than the ties of loyalty that bound retainer and lord, and on which the basis of political order was established.

The missionaries also threatened to be a factor contributing to disorder in the country. They were taking sides in political affairs, and were particularly strong in Kyushu, where Hideyoshi had had trouble in subduing the lords. As a matter of fact, his first ban on Christianity came when he was in Kyushu reducing the last opposition to his rule.

An even greater political danger, in the eyes of the rulers of Japan, was the close alliance between Christianity and the rulers of the European nations from which the missionaries came. The famous *San Felipe* incident, whether true or not, confirmed in Hideyoshi's mind the dangers of the religion. According to the story that has been handed down, the *San Felipe,* a Spanish ship, was deliberately wrecked by the Japanese for the treasure that it contained. The captain, after his rescue, boasted that his nation always followed a certain pattern of conquest. First of all came the missionaries, then the traders, and finally the army. The Japanese had had experience of the first two and there was nothing to indicate that the third might not follow according to the plan as outlined by the captain. When this story was reported to Hideyoshi, he immediately ordered the death of all Christian missionaries.

Although the Japanese must have felt that there was little likelihood that they would be invaded, they saw no need of "appeasing" the foreign governments of whom the missionaries and merchants might be the forerunners. The long period of civil war had toughened the government. The country had just been unified by force, and the leaders of Japan, particularly Hideyoshi, had no reason to fear the possible wrath of the governments of distant lands.

Hideyoshi, moreover, had adopted a policy of reconstructing Buddhist temples. This contributed to the anti-Christian movement among the Buddhist priests, and reinforced their attitude toward the missionaries. The Portuguese slave trade also helped to discredit the Christian religion. The Japanese could not, as was natural, reconcile the practice of slaving with the principles of Christianity. It took no very great sophistication to see that there was a fundamental contradiction between the two, and that consequently it could be reasoned that there was probably something inherently weak in the Christian attitude. Inter-denominational strife also undermined the position of the missionaries.

In the early years of the seventeenth century the attack on Christians took on an increasingly vicious aspect. In 1603 all missionaries were ordered expelled from Japan, but this edict, like previous ones, apparently was not rigidly enforced. But in 1609 twenty-eight Japanese were reported to have been killed in Macao in a brawl with Portuguese. The result was that Tokugawa Iyeyasu ordered all Portuguese missionaries in Japan put to death. In 1612 and 1613 other edicts were issued banning missionaries, Christianity, and missionary work. In the following year a period of fierce persecution, lasting about twenty-five years, began, culminating in the famous Shimabara Rebellion.

Shimabara, not far from Nagasaki in Kyushu, was the scene of the rebellion, which lasted from October, 1637, to April, 1638. Though the rebellion has often been characterized as a struggle against religious persecution, there is also evidence that it had its roots in economic problems as well. The local feudal lord oppressed the people and imposed extremely heavy taxes on them.

It took an army of 100,000 men to put down the rebellion. The rebels numbered only 20,000 fighting men who were encumbered by the presence of some 17,000 women and children. All but 105 of the rebels were slain in battle before the rebellion was put down. Although the reasons for the rebellion were probably economic as well as religious, the fighting soon took on a religious aspect. The rebels used the words "Jesus" and "Mary" as battle cries. Religious banners served as battle flags. Mass was held regularly twice a week.

The Shimabara Rebellion was the last open attempt by Christian elements to reassert their faith. Thereafter, the religion was driven completely underground. Persecution was relentlessly maintained. One curious practice was the test of *fumi-e* (literally, "picture treading") . Anyone suspected of being a Christian was required to tread on a holy picture; if he refused to do so, he was regarded guilty. All Christians were ruthlessly hunted down and men and women were encouraged to report any of their neighbours whom they suspected of being Christians. Terrible tortures were devised to force confessions from Christians.

It is difficult to determine to what extent the persecutions of the Christians were religious, and to what extent political. While the Buddhists and Shintoists were no doubt anxious to see their religious competitors removed from the scene, there is no evidence that the persecutions were based on sectarian grounds. The primary causes were undoubtedly political. All in all, Japanese history has been singularly free from religious strife, but religions have been persecuted for political reasons. The fight over the introduction of Buddhism was, in its final elements, a struggle over an issue of domestic political nature. The persecution of Christianity at the period under discussion was based primarily on the threat to internal political order and the threat of external interference in Japanese affairs. The crushing of the power of the Buddhist priests by Oda Nobunaga was carried out for political considerations primarily. The constant piling of restrictions on Christianity in recent years was due to the fear on the part of the government that allegiance to God would undermine the allegiance of the Japanese people to the emperor.

Christianity is one foreign influence that did not leave an imprint on Japanese life and thought. The basic tenets of the religion were completely foreign to Japanese thought, and, unlike Buddhism some centuries earlier, it did not become the property of the privileged group within Japanese society. But the ruthless persecution to which the religion and all its believers were subjected is the primary reason for its failure to influence Japan.

The closing of Japan was a deliberate act inspired by a desire to increase domestic political control and to break off apparently dangerous relations with the Occidental powers. As has already been pointed out, the rulers of Japan feared both the ideological aspects of Christianity and the possible imperialistic ambitions of the Occidental powers.

The process of closing the country was a gradual one and it is impossible to determine when it ceased to be a series of unrelated acts and hardened into a definite policy. The political implications of Christianity which have been pointed out above, and the failure of Occidental merchants to prove that they were indispensable to the future well-being of Japan, led the rulers of Japan to the conclusion that Japan had to be closed. Christianity and the Christian missionaries were the first to feel the displeasure of Japan's leaders, and then the merchants were excluded in spite of the profits they brought in their wake.

The progressive intensification of the laws against Christianity is a fair barometer of the progress of the development of the policy of seclusion. The implications of the Shimabara Rebellion were not lost on the Tokugawa *shogun,* and that event perhaps was the main precipitating element. At first, the policy had been either to eject or to bar foreigners from Japan, but by the late 1630's edicts were being issued which were designed to prevent the outflow of Japanese from their own shores. The edicts against Japanese travel set forth that no Japanese was to leave Japanese shores, that no seaworthy ships were to be built in Japan, and that any Japanese, forced for any reason to leave the country, could return only on pain of death. The result was that, from the middle of the seventeenth century until the second half of the nineteenth century, Japan, except for what little the Dutch were allowed to bring in through their tiny colony on Deshima in Nagasaki, was completely isolated from the Western world. The Dutch, the only Europeans allowed in Japan, were virtual prisoners hedged about with many humiliating restrictions.

From the standpoint of the political policy of the ruling Tokugawa family the closing of the country was a good thing. Indeed, about its only favourable aspect in terms of the historical development of Japan is that it helped to solidify the nation's social structure at a time when the country was regaining its feet after decades of political and economic dislocation. The barring of Christianity, and the check on the inflow of other Occidental ideas, prevented the undermining of the principles of authoritarian government on which the rule of the Tokugawa was based. The prohibition on the departure of Japanese from the home islands eliminated the possibility of the return of "contaminated" Japanese, who might have become the nucleus for anti-Tokugawa movements. The elimination of all foreigners except the Dutch from the Japanese scene prevented the development of a "fifth column" which might lay the foundation for a foreign invasion of the country, as the *San Felipe* incident had hinted. All these insured the Tokugawa structure against the development of undermining influences originating outside the country. Yet the gains to Japan of this policy were more than cancelled by its negative effects.

It is impossible to determine the extent to which the seclusion policy retarded the development of the Japanese nation. Yet the effects have been great, for it removed Japan from contact with an Occident that was in a stage of tremendous development. A few of the results of Renaissance thought percolated into Japan, but the flow of those ideas was just beginning when the country was closed. But what is more important is the fact that Japan had no experience with the ideas or philosophies underlying liberalism, capitalism, democracy, the Industrial Revolution, and all the other great currents of thought and action that swept through eighteenth- and nineteenth-century Europe and America.

The result was that, when the time came for Japan to emerge again, she took the material aspects of the advancing West without grasping the philosophies of government and economics newly developed by the Occident. Consequently, the material developments of the West were superimposed on the feudal mentality of the Japanese. The authoritarian ideas of the Japanese oligarchy inspired the men who were manipulating the new machines and the new technologies that had been developed in the Occident.

Isolation from the rest of the world did much to intensify the insularity of thought of the Japanese. Given the beliefs in the divine descent of the emperor and of the Japanese people, the isolated development of the people and a general lack of knowledge of the outside world, it is little wonder that the Japanese people and their leaders have harboured delusions of grandeur about themselves and about their mission in the world. American and European rationalism of the eighteenth century had no chance to sweep away the mystic cobwebs that clutter up the mind of the Japanese nationalist.

All in all, Japan's deliberate turning away from foreign influences in the seventeenth century had almost as important an effect on the development of her history as her intense interest in them at other periods in her history. This negative rôle is comparable in many respects to the wave of anti-Western sentiment that has swept through Japan since the early 1930's. Indeed, the motives of the rulers of Japan were similar in both cases. Both the Tokugawa feudal authorities and the modern militarists feared the effect on their political security of foreign ideas, ideas that would undermine the philosophies on which they based their rule.

Japan could not forever keep her doors closed to the West. She had decided on the policy of seclusion on her own initiative, but she could neither prevent nor hold at arm's length political and economic developments in the Western world which inevitably broke down the barriers with which she had surrounded herself. The invention of the steamboat in the early nineteenth century shrank the vast spaces of the Pacific Ocean, which had guarded Japan against the coming from the East of unwanted visitors. The crossing of the Pacific by sailing vessels was possible, and frequently carried out, but such ships were completely at the mercy of the elements. The famed Yankee clippers made the run to China, and adventurous whalers were appearing off Japanese shores with increasing frequency in the first part of the nineteenth century; but the steamship was opening new vistas of commercial possibilities in the Pacific. The steamship, although it was more the master of winds and currents than the sailing ship, required fuel, and fuel meant coaling stations at strategic points along the Pacific route. Indeed, the desire for coaling stations was one of the principal factors behind American interest in Japan.

In addition to making the technological contribution of the steamship, the United States was becoming more and more interested in the Pacific. As indicated above, the clipper and whaling ships from New England were not only making this country more and more Pacific-conscious, but also the westward continental expansion of the country was awakening the nation to the fact that it had an extensive coast-line on the Pacific. Explorers, fur traders, and gold prospectors, during the first half of the nineteenth century, were making Americans conscious of the vast possibilities of the Pacific and what might lie beyond.

Russia, too, was developing Pacific interests. Russian expansion eastward over Siberia began in the latter part of the sixteenth century, and Russians reached Kamchatka by the overland route just before 1700. After the limits of eastward expansion by land had been reached, the Russians began to turn southward. This move, of course, brought them into contact with Japan. From the end of the eighteenth century onward, contacts between the Russians and the Japanese became increasingly frequent, with a consequent development of fear in the minds of the Tokugawa authorities that Russia had designs on Japanese territory.

Great Britain was also slowly and surely extending her interests toward the Far East from still another direction. She had become entrenched in India during the eighteenth century, and had also begun the development of extensive trade with China during the same period. It was logical that Britain should begin to probe northward, from her trade bases in China, in search of new markets in unknown Japan.

Behind these new interests in the Far East lay the tremendous pressure of the Industrial Revolution, and the resulting search for new markets for the products that were beginning to stream from the factories of Britain and the United States. Thus, the incipient conquest of space and the development of new types of economic interests were focusing Western attention more and more in the direction of the little-known island kingdom.

The opening of Japan to commerce with the nations of the Occident was an epoch-making event in the history of Japan's foreign relations, but it also played a major rôle in the unfolding of Japan's internal political history at the crucial time when the Tokugawa régime was crumbling and the whole feudal structure of Japanese society was being undermined. The coming of the West exerted so much pressure on Japan's internal affairs that it is misleading to consider it as only a development in Japan's foreign affairs. Although the issue in itself was directly concerned with Japan's foreign relations, it was utilized by the anti-Tokugawa forces as an extremely effective weapon in bringing about a change in the internal political structure of the country.

The coming of Commodore Matthew Calbraith Perry to the shores of Japan, and the tortuous path of his negotiations with the Japanese, are so dramatic in themselves that they tend to overshadow the long period of contacts that Japan had with foreigners, American and otherwise, before Perry's appearance. The Japanese had had more than ample warning that serious attempts would be made to force her doors. Russians, Englishmen, Frenchmen, Dutchmen, and Americans had all made unsuccessful attempts to reverse Japan's policy of seclusion. They nibbled vainly at the Japanese policy and failed, but their work laid the foundation for Perry's subsequent success. The pressure on Japan's shores was becoming greater and greater, and Commodore Perry provided only the final weight that broke down Japan's gates.

All the attempts to open Japan before Perry's coming conformed to a single pattern. All asked for something; all had no backing of force; and all permitted the Japanese to retain the initiative in the negotiations. Not one of the petitioning countries offered anything that would impress the Japanese. They were all asking either for special favours, or for a relaxation of Japanese laws that the Japanese had found satisfactory for many decades. The lack of success of these weak petitions tended only to confirm in Japanese minds the idea that the Japanese were strong and that they could flout with impunity any foreign overtures. The foreigners allowed themselves to be put off again and again by the authorities with whom they hoped to deal. They came to Japan with few ships and with no impressive armaments. They suffered indignities at the hands of high and low officials alike, and took no steps to wipe out the blot of the insults. They permitted themselves to be disarmed. There was nothing about them that would frighten or impress the men who were ruling Japan at the time. The Japanese at all times retained the initiative in the negotiations, the foreigners allowing them to make their own terms at their own free will. No firm stand was taken against the positions arbitrarily assumed by the Japanese authorities.

In 1849 Commodore James Glynn, commanding the *Preble,* was sent to Japan in order to obtain the release of American sailors who had been cast away on Japanese shores and had been imprisoned in Nagasaki. Glynn accomplished his mission, and on his return submitted a report which was to have an important influence on the Perry expedition. He declared that a commercial treaty with Japan was absolutely necessary. If the United States was to open a steamship line to China, coaling stations would have to be opened in Japan. He also pointed out the need for American naval bases in or near Japan if this country was to develop its Far Eastern interests. Although believing that goodwill between the United States and Japan was necessary, he felt that the treaty with Japan should be negotiated peaceably if possible, but if not, then by force. He recommended that in the next communication sent to Japan, it should be pointed out that the United States did not wish to interfere with Japan's internal affairs, or to interfere in any way with Japanese religion. Glynn also thought that the United States might make more headway in its efforts to open Japan, if the attitude of European nations were taken into consideration. Consequently, he recommended that the

United States should seek no exclusive privileges in Japan, that the government should get on good terms with the Dutch, who were still in possession of the exclusive rights to station traders in Japan, and that the bearer of the American note to Japan should go to the Far East via Europe. Finally, he recommended that a first-rate man be selected for the mission.

The United States, soon after his return in 1852, moved to act on Glynn's recommendations. Commodore John H. Aulick was appointed commander of the United States East India squadron, and was given full power to negotiate a treaty of amity and commerce with Japan. He was instructed to get coaling stations in Japan, to obtain a guarantee of safety for American sailors and property that might be wrecked on Japanese shores, and to open Japanese ports to trade. But Aulick's mission was dogged with misfortune. Dissension broke out on the ships under his command, and baseless rumours were circulated through his ships, with the result that Aulick was removed from his command when the small squadron touched in South America. The glory that might have been his went to Commodore Matthew Calbraith Perry, who was appointed to succeed him.

Commodore Perry was sent to Japan with definite instructions to bring about a final resolution of the problem of Japan's relations with the United States. That he was the ideal man for the job is attested not only by the results of his expedition, but also by the manner in which he attained them. He negotiated on his own terms, forced the Japanese to abandon their policy of evasion and dallying, and accomplished his mission without the use of force.

He made two visits to Japan, the first in the summer of 1853 and the second in the early months of 1854. His first visit laid the foundation for his negotiations, and his second brought final success in the form of the Treaty of Kanagawa, signed on March 31, 1854. This was the first treaty negotiated between Japan and a Western power on a footing of equality. It was the last blow that knocked down the barriers that Japan had set up between herself and the world more than two centuries before. It was not finally to open Japan to free intercourse with the world; there was still to be a stormy period of transition before Japan could truly be said to be open to the world.

Briefly, this is what the Treaty of Kanagawa provided: the opening of the ports of Shimoda and Hakodate to American ships for coaling and provisioning; the protection of the property and persons of American citizens cast away on Japanese shores, who were to be taken to one of the above ports; the freedom of American citizens in Japan as in other countries—but they were to be "amenable to just laws"; the freedom of movement of American citizens in the above ports, within certain limits, but without the restrictions placed on the Dutch at Deshima; the guarantee of careful deliberation to settle matters involving any business between the Americans and Japanese; the right to trade under Japanese regulations; the obtaining of wood, water, and provisions only through the agency of Japanese officials appointed for the purpose; a most-favoured-nation clause; the ban on the entry of American ships into other ports unless forced to do so by the stress of weather; and the right to station consuls or agents in Shimoda, "at any time after the expiration of eighteen months from the date of the signing of this treaty; provided that either of the two governments deem such arrangement necessary." There was no extraterritoriality clause.

Perry obtained everything that he had been instructed to obtain from the Japanese government, and a little more besides. But he also succeeded in reversing a policy held by the Tokugawa government for more than two hundred years. The negotiations were, moreover, carried out on a basis of complete equality. He attained his ends without recourse to war, and succeeded without bringing humiliation to the Japanese government, and without causing widespread enmity among the Japanese people. His judicious use of a show of force succeeded where the exercise of force might have had disastrous results. His work is one of the minor diplomatic triumphs in the history of American foreign relations. Japan soon negotiated treaties with Great Britain, Russia, and The Netherlands.

Townsend Harris, the first United States consul in Japan, negotiated the first American commercial treaty with Japan. Harris arrived at Shimoda, via the European route, in August of 1856, but it was not until November, 1857, that he was allowed to proceed to Edo. The Japanese threw every possible obstacle in his way. When he first appeared, the officials who greeted him told him that according to the terms of the Treaty of Kanagawa, no consuls were to be sent to Japan unless both nations desired it, and that since Japan did not there was no legal basis for his coming to Japan. He was surrounded by spies and police. He was kept in complete isolation from those around him. Officials lied to him on every possible occasion. As if that were not enough, his own government seemed to have forgotten his existence completely. After he had been put ashore and established after a fashion, he received no instructions from his government and no news of any kind from home. Besides the mental torture of not knowing whether his government had abandoned him or not, he suffered from physical ailments. But in spite of all these obstacles he persevered at his task, gradually won the Japanese officials over to his side, and was finally accorded the honour of an interview with the *shogun* in the capital, after the government had agreed that he should make the journey from Shimoda to Edo as if he were a great feudal lord. A lesser man would have succumbed before the seeming impossibility of his task. But even after arriving in Edo, he still had almost eight months of long, tedious negotiations before he finally negotiated the commercial treaty of July 29, 1858.

The treaty threw open many other ports to American merchants. American citizens were granted the right to lease ground, buy buildings, and erect dwellings and warehouses. Importation of opium was prohibited. Americans who were convicted of felony, or of misdemeanour twice, were to be deported; and the Japanese government was to co-operate with the American consul, at his request, in the enforcement of law and order among the American population. The Japanese government, according to the terms of the treaty, could purchase American ships of war, steamers, merchant ships, cannon, munitions, arms of all kinds, and any other things that it might require. It could also hire American scientific, naval, and military men, artisans, or mariners with the sole proviso that such experts could not be used by the Japanese in a war against a power friendly to the United States. This was to throw Japan open to the flood of foreign experts that she wanted and required, if she was to reconstruct the country so that it would be safe against the foreign aggression that was so greatly feared.

Thus, after more than two hundred years of haughty isolation, when their only contacts with the West had been through the

Dutch, whom they had kept in complete and humiliating subjugation, the Japanese were now legally forced to treat foreign nations and foreigners as their equals. The treaties, from Perry's on, had been negotiated on a footing of equality. Foreigners were again allowed to tread freely on the "sacred" soil of Japan. In addition, Japan's sovereignty had definitely been impaired by the treaties. Tariff autonomy had been removed from Japanese hands and the Japanese were deprived, by extraterritoriality, from controlling men who were allowed to dwell on their soil. Much of Japan's efforts in political, economic, and judicial reforms, and in foreign relations, were to be devoted for the next four decades to the task of attaining complete sovereignty over her affairs and attaining a position of equality with other nations. Japanese eyes were also definitely turned toward the West. The most dramatic expression of this new orientation came, of course, in the Harris treaty, which provided for the employment of American experts by the Japanese.

No amount of negotiation and treaty-making between representatives of the West and the Japanese authorities could break down the attitudes toward all foreigners that had been built up over so many years. The despised foreigner was still hated. The right to enter Japan with more or less freedom simply placed the foreigners in a position where more of them could be attacked by the xenophobic Japanese. The negotiation of the treaties was taken by the enemies of the Tokugawa régime as a sign of its weakness and decay, and the presence of foreigners in the country created a situation in which its power and prestige were even more seriously undermined.

The Tokugawa *bakufu* now found itself caught in a difficult position between the governments of foreign lands and its political enemies at home. If it allowed foreigners to enter in accordance with the treaties it signed, it only became more embroiled with its domestic political opponents. If it attempted to stem the flood of foreigners as a result of domestic pressure, it found itself either actually or potentially opposed by the armed might of the Western powers which it could not successfully counter with the meagre resources at its command. The fifteen years between the coming of Perry and the final fall of the Tokugawa régime saw the *bakufu* constantly harassed by the problem of attempting to balance the forces that were being applied to it from within by its political opponents, against those applied from without by the foreign nations with which it had been forced to negotiate.

The burst of anti-foreignism that broke out following the establishment of treaty relations arose out of a complex of factors. Foreigners as well as Japanese were responsible. The utility to the anti-*bakufu* forces of the presence of "barbarians" in Japan has already been pointed out. Continued attacks on foreigners in Japan served the useful purpose, from the standpoint of the anti-Tokugawa forces, of continuously embroiling the Japanese government with foreign governments. Thus a part of the anti-foreign feeling was the result of a deliberate plan on the part of those wishing to gain control of Japan's government. On the other hand many *samurai* who owed allegiance to no lord were traditionally swaggerers, and had long vented their nastiness on the defenseless peasants and virtually defenseless merchants. The foreigners who came into Japan were an even better target for their spleen, because they were outlanders and interlopers. The violation of the ancient traditions of Japan furnished additional cause for resentment against foreigners, because they had been excluded from Japan's soil for more than two centuries.

Economic reasons also contributed to the resentment against the foreigners. The introduction of this new foreign trade brought with it an intensification of the economic dislocation that had been steadily developing in Japan. The demand for articles for export by the foreign merchants disturbed the Japanese price scale. The outflow of Japanese gold also intensified economic disturbances. The rise in prices and the scarcity of money were particularly felt by the *samurai,* whose fixed incomes had already been under great strain because of the changes in Japan's economy. The added economic distress served to intensify the dislike already felt toward the outlanders.

The foreigners themselves were responsible for a good deal of the anti-foreign feeling. Many of the merchants who came to Japan had already been doing business in China, where they had shown no respect for the rights and feelings of the Chinese. Naturally, they took this attitude with them when they went on to Japan. They were also not interested in the niceties of establishing smooth and friendly relations with people whom they regarded as being simply the source of the profits that they were so eagerly pursuing. Law violations did not tend to endear the foreigners to the officials, or to develop respect for them among the common people. They frequently sold firearms to the Japanese in violation of the treaty agreements, and they also frequently went out on hunting excursions beyond the bounds set up by treaty. Most of the Occidentals were merchants, and this was precisely the class of people that was held in lowest esteem by Japan's warrior class. The influx of merchant vessels meant that sailors set foot on Japanese soil in fairly large numbers. Their conduct ashore was not likely to endear them to any part of the population. They frequently attacked Japanese in the streets and broke into Japanese homes and shops.

Thus, irresponsible elements among both the foreigners and the Japanese contributed to a worsening of a situation that would have been difficult even without the additional complication of acts of individuals. The burst of anti-foreign incidents fell just short of open warfare between Japan and the Western powers. On at least one crucial occasion Townsend Harris probably prevented the outbreak of war. On other occasions "acts of war" occurred without resulting in the formal declaration of hostilities between the governments involved.

The bombardments of Kagoshima and of the Choshu forts at Shimonoseki grew out of anti-foreign agitation, and taught Japan two lessons: first, that anti-foreignism had to be kept within bounds; and second, that Japan did not have the strength successfully to withstand direct foreign attacks. The bombardment of Kagoshima was a British affair, but the attack on the Choshu forts was a joint enterprise.

The Kagoshima bombardment grew out of the murder of an Englishman by the name of Richardson, in September of 1862. Richardson was a member of a group riding on the highway near Kanagawa when the procession of Shimadzu Saburo, the great lord of the Satsuma clan in southern Kyushu, passed by. The Japanese claimed that Richardson and his party were disrespectful to the Satsuma lord, first, by failing to dismount when he passed by, and second, by cutting in front of the procession. At any rate the Satsuma men cut Richardson down. The British government immediately seized on the incident to bring both the *bakufu* and one of the most powerful of the feudal lords to account. The *bakufu* immediately moved to make amends, for here it was caught between the Satsuma clan, one of its most dangerous rivals, and the British, who were the most aggressive of the foreign powers in Japan. The *bakufu* promised that it would build a new road for the use of the *daimyo,* and establish more blockhouses on the old one for the protection of foreigners. Also they promised to provide guards for foreigners who might wish to use the roads while *daimyo* were passing.

But the British government was not satisfied. It held both the *bakufu* and the Satsuma clan responsible for the murder. They demanded that the Tokugawa régime make ample and formal apology and pay a penalty of £100,000. From the Satsuma clan they demanded execution of those responsible for the Richardson murder, and the payment of £25,000 indemnity. Both were threatened with punishment if they did not meet the British demands. The *bakufu* speedily gave in, but the Satsuma clan was defiant. A British squadron proceeded to Kagoshima, the Satsuma capital, subjected the city to bombardment and leveled at least half of it. The Satsuma representatives in Edo thereupon promised to pay the indemnity. The victims of this British retaliation were the men who were later to become a dominant group in the new government in Japan. They saw before their eyes a demonstration of the might of weapons which Japan did not yet possess, and realized the extent of the task before Japan if she wanted to rival the power of the Occident.

In 1863, the forts of Choshu on the straits of Shimonoseki fired on American, French, and Dutch boats passing through the straits. American and French gunboats retaliated, but the straits remained closed for more than a year. In September of 1864, an allied fleet of seventeen ships, nine of which were British, reduced the Choshu forts and opened the straits. The so-called Shimonoseki Convention was signed in October of 1864 by the British, Americans, French, Dutch, and Japanese. Both the Mori clan, which controlled the forts, and the *bakufu,* were held responsible. A three-million dollar indemnity was levied against Japan, but the alternative was that Japan could open additional ports for trade instead, because money was no object to the foreign governments. Diplomacy being what it was in those days, the foreign governments got both the indemnity and the additional ports for trade. The United States, however, refunded her share later.

Through the period from 1862 to 1864 the imperial court in Kyoto and its political allies attempted to reverse the policy forced on the *bakufu,* and to close the country, by announcing that the negotiation of the original treaties had been an error and had been carried out without imperial approval. However, the court was unable to make its decisions stick, particularly in the face of the convincing demonstrations of foreign might at Kagoshima and Choshu. Finally, in 1865, after a virtual ultimatum from an allied fleet gathered off the present Kobe, the imperial ratification of the treaties previously negotiated by the *bakufu* was granted. This solved the problem of the treaty status of the foreigners once and for all, with both contending parties in Japan's internal politics having set their seals to the foreign agreements.

In 1868 and 1869 additional attacks on foreigners took place, but both these were speedily and ruthlessly punished by the new government which had replaced the *bakufu.* One of the first acts of the new government had been to arrange an imperial audience for the ministers stationed in Japan, and an imperial rescript was issued on the question of foreign intercourse. It ordered the nation to "obey His Majesty's Will in the fulfillment of the Treaties with Foreign Countries in accordance with the rules of International Law." In addition the rescript said: "All persons in the future guilty of murdering foreigners or of committing acts of violence towards them will be acting in opposition to His Majesty's express orders and be the cause of national misfortune. They will therefore be punished in proportion to the gravity of their offense, and their names, if *samurai,* will be erased from the roll." It was no longer patriotic to murder foreigners, because in the face of the words of the Emperor it would be *lèse majesté* to act violently toward any foreigner.

The pressure of the West on Japan during this crucial period, when Japan was in the midst of internal political changes, was great and in a sense decisive; but Japan was able to withstand the impact of the West, whereas China was almost dragged down by it. Indeed the very extent of Western interests in China served to protect Japan. The Western powers were firmly entrenched in China long before they became interested in Japan. China, as was pointed out earlier, really absorbed the principal shock of the coming of the West to the Far East.

Conditions in Europe and America also tended to distract Occidental attention from Japan at a crucial period. In the two decades of the opening of relations with the West, Europe and America witnessed the Crimean War, the American Civil War, and the Franco-Prussian War. These absorbed Occidental attention, energies, and resources at a time when slightly more of them might have meant an even greater blow to Japan's independence. For example, no foreign power became deeply involved in Japan's domestic politics. Although *bakufu* and *daimyo* both attempted to gain as much outside aid as possible in terms of arms and money, neither side was extensively backed by a foreign power. Had such strength been thrown behind any group within Japan the internal struggle might have become much more prolonged. As it happened, Japanese problems were settled by Japanese. In addition, the series of incidents involving Japanese attacks on foreigners were settled speedily in most cases, and the dangers and difficulties of foreign intervention were avoided. The attacks on Western interests might have evoked much greater reaction if Western attention had not been so centred on its own problems.

Another decisive factor was the foresight of the leaders of Japan. They saw clearly the dangers of Western intervention, and they understood the power that stood behind the nations that had come to Japan. Hence, they saw and understood the futility of opposition to the West. The leaders of the new Japan realized that the West would have to be fought with its own weapons. They had before them the example of China, and they knew that mere contempt was no defense against gunboats and rifles. The most violent anti-foreign leaders did not gain a position of supremacy in the councils of Japan, again a contrast with the situation in China.

With the problem of treaty rights finally settled, and with Japan's relations with the West established as an unavoidable diplomatic, commercial, and political fact, Japan turned immediately to the West and sought all in the way of material objects that would hasten the day when she would be able to stand on a footing of equality with the West. The floodgates were opened and the things of the West began to pour into Japan. But the floodgates were floodgates and so they could be regulated. The flood of the Occident was never allowed to threaten the basic attitudes of the Japanese toward their government and toward the social structure that had been solidified during the period of Tokugawa absolutism.

While it cannot be denied that the change that has come over the face of Japan in the short space of less than a century is little short of miraculous, it must also be kept in mind that the basic spirit that motivates the Japanese people and their leaders has remained relatively untouched by the flood of influences from the West. For virtually every aspect of the West that has been transplanted to Japan, there is a compensating native Japanese factor that has either limited or modified its influence on Japanese life. A completely new form of government administration has been set up in Japan, yet the men who control and who operate it have basically the same political philosophy that motivated the feudal Tokugawa régime. A new educational system has been set up, yet it has been used to teach the young of Japan the ideas of authority, obedience, and respect that are inherent in Japanese social relations in the wider sense of the term. New attitudes toward marriage and the family have appeared in Japan, but the old customs and attitudes have not been overwhelmed and submerged by these exotic ideas. New and foreign ideas came into Japan, but they were never allowed to get out of hand.

The control factor has been both conscious and unconscious. Its unconscious operation is best revealed in the basic conservatism of the mass of the people, their resistance to the new and strange ideas which threaten the bases of the established ways of life that Japanese tradition has approved. This is not a peculiarly Japanese trait, for every nation reveals the same strain of conservatism when confronted with new and strange ideas. Japanese superstition resisted the introduction of the railroad and the telegraph, just as Occidental superstition resisted them.

More important than the social inertia of the mass of the people was the policy of the new Japanese government toward the things of the West. The policy was two-fold: to accept and accept eagerly and rapidly all things of the West which would make Japan strong and which would raise its prestige in the eyes of the world; to reject and reject completely and ruthlessly all things of the West which would undermine the basic concepts on which Japanese society was erected. This policy explains why it was that the forms of Western government of the nineteenth century were accepted, while the philosophies out of which those forms developed were rigorously controlled if not barred.

The leaders of the new Japan accepted the West; the Tokugawa authorities rejected it. Each did so to strengthen its hold on political power. The Tokugawa régime rejected the West because they feared that it would undermine their authority. The leaders of the new Japan turned to the West because they saw that it offered them certain techniques and certain tools by means of which they could consolidate their hold on authority in the new Japan. Indeed, their motives were identical with those of the men who molded Japan at the time of the Taikwa Reform.

Japan's militarists have isolated the nation from the outside world as completely as the Tokugawa régime did three centuries ago. The new isolation is not due to the present war, for the process began years before Pearl Harbor. The process of isolation has been carried out as deliberately as the policy of welcoming certain selected aspects of the West had been. The material strength of the Occident was copied so that Japan could become as strong as the nations whose strength she envied and desired to duplicate. But the ideas of the West were never permitted to become firmly rooted, for the rulers of Japan feared that they would enervate the old ideas which were forming such an excellent foundation for the new career of aggression that was being planned for the nation.

While attacking more and more bitterly the ideas of democracy and communism during the 1930's, Japan bound herself to Germany and Italy, for she saw in them two nations whose ideas and aspirations most nearly matched her own. To praise nazism and fascism was safe, for they both stood for authoritarian and absolutist forms of government, the philosophies of which were not too different from Japan's. The Japanese people could be shown these two nations as successful examples, in the Occident, of nations who thought and acted as Japan did. But the ties among the three were never as strong as the governments tried to make them appear. If nothing else, their mutually exclusive theories of racial superiority acted to keep them apart.

On the other hand, the United States, Russia, and Great Britain stood for everything that was dangerous to the ideology on which the rulers of Japan had built their power. The ideas on which the governments of those three powers were based were almost diametrically opposed to the Japanese theories of state. Communism, the ideology of the modern Russian state, was the first great fear of the Japanese government. Japanese communists, and everything even remotely resembling communist thought or communist writings, were ruthlessly hunted down in Japan. Every precaution was taken to keep them out of Japan, and to eliminate them if by any chance they managed to percolate into the country.

Communism was triply dangerous in the eyes of the Japanese government. First, it was the ideology of a nation which Japan had long feared and distrusted; second, it opposed the ideas of political oligarchy which had been the foundation of Japanese government for centuries; third, it challenged the ideas of economic oligarchy that had formed the foundation for Japan's political oligarchy. The theories of communism recognized the right of the people to participate not only in their government, but also in the wealth which they produced. These were ideas, which, if accepted in Japan, would have swept away the ideological foundation of the Japanese state. The attitude of communism toward all monarchical institutions could not be acceptable to a ruling group which had deliberately made the emperor into the symbol of the unity and solidarity of the Japanese people.

It is little wonder that communism speedily became anathema to the rulers of Japan. The liberation of the Russian masses from a system and an ideology strikingly similar to Japan's must have warned the Japanese leaders that a similar process might also succeed in Japan. At any rate, the attacks on communism and communists succeeded in driving the movement completely underground in Japan. The methods used to stamp communism out have been compared with the attacks on Christianity in Japan in the early seventeenth century. In both cases the ruling oligarchy succeeded in eliminating an ideological threat to its supremacy.

Liberalism and democracy were attacked, but never with the viciousness and thoroughness that were used against communism, probably because they did not have behind them the organization and planning of communism. Communists were the better target because they were imbued with the desire of winning over converts and of openly propagandizing as organized groups for the ideas in which they believed. The followers of liberalism and democracy were on the other hand individuals who believed in their principles, but who were not organized to spread them. The rulers of Japan and their followers attacked liberalism and democracy through the pressure of public opinion, rather than by the means of organized terror. Anyone who followed liberal or democratic thought was stigmatized as being degenerate for having departed from the path of the true Japanese. They were accused of being as soft, as undisciplined, and as reliant on luxury and easy living as Americans and Englishmen were painted to be. The Japanese public was urged and forced to give up such things as dancing, Western-style clothes, Western hair styles, Western attitudes toward love and the family, and even Western sports, for they were predominantly of British or American origin.

Liberal and democratic political ideas were attacked vocally at every opportunity. They were a deviation from the true Japanese way, and therefore had to be shunned if Japan was to become and remain a great country as befits a land of the gods. Liberalism and democracy, like communism, were fundamentally opposed to the Japanese theories of government. They recognized the right of the individual to live his own life and to determine the form of government under which he lived. They fostered the idea that government should be responsive to the will of the governed. They encouraged criticism of the policies of the governing. A government of, for, and by the people would neither accept the unbridled exercise of power by an oligarchy nor respect the empty holiness of the institution of the emperor.

The militarist rulers of modern Japan have built their power on Japanese institutions and on Japanese theories of government. They have developed the Japanese state to its ultimate stage in terms of purely Japanese concepts of government. Power is theoretically centred in the hands of an emperor whose divinity insures him a supreme and unchallengeable position in the Japanese state. The economic structure is under the secure control of the emperor, the state, and a group of monopoly capitalists all of whom are enjoying the fruits of the labours of the mass of the Japanese people. The nation is knit into a unified whole behind the ideas and ideals of the ruling clique. The rule of authority is unchallenged.

But the results are not such as to be encouraging to any thinking Japanese. Japan is to-day standing virtually alone against the world. Its conquests in Asia have won it only the hatred and suspicion of the peoples that it has pretended to deliver from oppression. Half a century of intrigue and aggression in China has not won the Chinese over to the Japanese side, and there is no evidence that the peoples of more recently conquered territories are any more favourably disposed toward their conquerors. Her attacks on the United States and Great Britain, once friends of Japan, have turned those great powers against her. The failure of the other totalitarian powers should have brought home to Japan the basic weakness of the totalitarian philosophy of government. The Japanese people are poorer, hungrier, and less healthy than ever before. Finally, crushing military defeat will bring home to Japan and the Japanese people the bankruptcy of the ideals of the militarists.

The victorious United Nations will have to bring to Japan new influences from without, new ideas this time, rather than the forms that Japan has so carefully imported at previous periods of her history. The new ideas will have to undermine emperor worship, authoritarian rule, the economic subjugation of the people, and the ideals of militarism. They must be so firmly implanted in the Japanese soil that they will stand as a Japanese barrier to the resurgence of the ideas of the past that have determined the development of Japanese aggression abroad and of Japanese oppression at home.

Chapter VI

THE AUTHORITARIAN STATE

A ruling class, not a philosophy of government, came to an end with the collapse of the Tokugawa régime. The absolutism of the old warrior oligarchy was retained as the basis of the new government. The Tokugawa *bakufu* was a government by warriors; the new state in Japan was an oligarchy dominated by militarists. The old class lines separating the warriors from the rest of Japanese society were broken down, but the warrior psychology was a powerful motivation of the builders of the new Japan. The Meiji Restoration was organized primarily by men from the warrior class to further their own ends as members of a ruling oligarchy. As sweeping as the Restoration was, it left intact the basic political, economic, and social attitudes on which the old structure of government in Japan had rested.

The new Japan was not the child of revolution. The transition from the mediæval to the quasi-modern was carefully controlled by the oligarchy. It retained control of the process of political change as it monopolized political power itself. Modern Japan arose out of the political strife of oligarchic faction against oligarchic faction, not out of a clash of class against class and ideology against ideology.

The old feudal attitudes toward authority remained untouched. They were deliberately preserved in the face of all the changes that were being wrought in Japan, for they provided the perfect foundation for the obedience and subservience demanded of the subjects of new Japan. The old divisions between the classes were legally abolished, but the attitudes that were created by the class distinctions of the Tokugawa period continued.

Subservience to the state and obedience to its authority were sedulously cultivated by both education and indoctrination. State control of education guaranteed that the "proper" attitudes toward government would be cultivated among the young. Emperor worship and the glorification of the military ideal were constantly drummed into the ears of the people. The few who managed to gain a liberal education were stigmatized as being apostates who had deserted the true way of the Japanese subject. The great mass of the Japanese people was ready to accept Japanese totalitarianism both because it was a part of the Japanese tradition and because they were indoctrinated to accept it as the normal form of government.

The new machinery of government that was set up in Japan was authoritarian both in spirit and in form, although the dramatic contrast between it and the old Tokugawa absolutism tended to create the impression that it was both advanced and at least partially democratic. The Constitution, for example, was (and is) a political instrument created by believers in authoritarian government and designed to keep control of Japan in the hands of the few, and to exclude popular participation.

Representative government in Japan, as expressed in the creation of a House of Representatives, did not take root, for there was no tradition of popular rule in Japan. The grant of universal manhood suffrage in 1925 was deceptive. It created the impression that the Japanese people were going to have a genuine voice in government. But the vital element of democratic experience was missing. Government could not be made responsive to the will of the people, for the people had never been conscious of possessing a will of their own in matters of government.

The factor of leadership cannot be ignored in evaluating the emergence of the modern Japanese state. The new government was the creation of a group of men who designed it so that they could dominate it with a minimum of interference from the people. The creators of the modern state in Japan were reactionary in their philosophy of power, for they were as reluctant to widen the base of government as their Tokugawa predecessors had been. Unlike most reactionaries they possessed a breadth of vision, boldness of execution, and a flexible willingness to use new and exotic techniques of political control. They knew what they had and they knew what they wanted, but they also realized that political power could not be retained simply by looking back over the shoulder at the past. They were superb politicians, because they were ambitious, power-conscious, and bold in both the conception and the execution of their plans. They knew that their political power could not be built on the dry-rot that they had inherited from the Tokugawa régime, and so they deliberately went beyond Japan's borders for new materials for government.

With the deposition of the Tokugawa régime and the collapse of the feudal system, the old political structure disappeared. The centralized control of the *bakufu* over the feudal lords was swept away, and the ties between the lords and their retainers vanished. The old loyalties and the old controls were gone, and new ones had to be found to replace them without altering the basic philosophy of government.

The problem that faced the architects of the new Japan was to find a new object for the loyalties of the people without changing the traditional relationship between the governed and the governing. Japan was still to be ruled by an oligarchy, and the people were not to be given a voice in the way in which they were to be ruled. In other words, the old pattern of government was to be maintained in the new state that was being set up. The machinery of government was to be completely overhauled, but the principles on which it was built and the driving force behind it were to be unchanged. The loyalties of the people were centred on the emperor, as has already been described. But other problems remained.

The Japanese people were given certain rights under the organic law of the land. This was something that had never happened before in Japanese history, but the "rights" that were bestowed upon them were largely illusory in character. These rights were a gracious gift from the emperor, and were to be accepted as such without question. These rights had no firm rooting in the Japanese political tradition. There was in Japan no concept of "the rights of man."

The first ten amendments of the American Constitution, the "Bill of Rights," are generally regarded by Americans as its most important section. The comparable section of the Japanese Constitution, fourteen articles entitled "Rights and Duties of Subjects," forms a startling contrast. Article I of the Bill of Rights reads as follows: *"Congress shall make no law respecting an establishment of religion, or prohibiting the free exercise thereof; or abridging the freedom of speech or of the press; or the right of the people peaceably to assemble and to petition the Government for a redress of grievances."* On the other hand the comparable articles of the Japanese Constitution read as follows:

"Article XXVIII. Japanese subjects shall, within limits not prejudicial to peace and order, and not antagonistic to their duties as subjects, enjoy freedom of religious belief.

"Article XXIX. Japanese subjects shall, within the limits of law, enjoy the liberty of speech, writing, publication, public meetings and associations."

The American Constitution specifically enjoins Congress from infringing the rights of American citizens, while the Japanese Constitution places no limits at all on the power of the government to curtail the rights of Japanese subjects. Under the American Constitution the citizen is guaranteed certain rights; under the Japanese Constitution, the citizen enjoys only as much freedom as the government sees fit to grant him. These attitudes epitomize the difference between the American and the Japanese philosophies of government.

To return to the above two articles of the Japanese Constitution, Japanese citizens are allowed religious freedom as long as it is "not antagonistic to their duties as subjects." The aim of this qualification is obviously to prevent the allegiance of the Japanese subject from being weaned away from the emperor. If, for example, a Japanese became a devout Christian, he would regard the Christian God as his spiritual inspiration, and if he went that far, he might possibly relegate the emperor to a secondary position, which would certainly be antagonistic to his duties as a subject. Article XXIX creates the illusion of liberties that simply were not there. The phrase "within the limits of the law" makes mockery of all the liberties enumerated.

Needless to say, this article has permitted the Japanese authorities to stamp out anything resembling freedom. It has proved to be one of the most useful weapons in the armoury of those who attacked non-conformist political and economic tendencies in Japan. Other liberties mentioned in the Japanese Constitution, such as the liberty of abode, the conditions of arrest and trial, the sanctity of the home, the secrecy of letters, are all limited by similar phrases. It is perhaps significant that the only right to which no qualifying phrase has been attached is the right of property. Article XXVII says: "*The right of property of every Japanese subject shall remain inviolate.*" It is not surprising that the drafters of this Constitution, who were thoroughgoing authoritarians, should be interested in property rights in inverse ratio to their interest in human rights.

Although the above articles are repressive and unenlightened, by democratic standards, other sections of the Constitution granted the Japanese people certain rights and privileges which had previously been denied them. Article XIX reads: "*Japanese subjects may, according to qualifications determined in laws or ordinances, be appointed to civil or military or any other public offices equally.*" This definitely wrote into Japan's organic law the abolition of the strict class lines that had been characteristic of Tokugawa society. No longer was membership in a certain class to be the prerequisite to office. That this was inserted into the Constitution was natural, for many men, such as Prince Ito, who had played leading rôles in the Restoration, were commoners, though they had sprung from the warrior class. Article XX reads: "*Japanese subjects are amenable to service in the Army or Navy, according to the provisions of law.*" This sounded the death knell of the monopoly that the warrior class had had on the right to bear arms. Conscription was old by the time the Constitution was promulgated, but this article made the "right" of all to bear arms a part of the nation's organic law.

The people were also given the carefully delimited right to elect legislative representatives. Article XXXV of the Constitution reads as follows: "*The House of Representatives shall be composed of Members elected by the people, according to the provisions of the Law of Election.*" The Law of Election was designed to be an effective check on too wide a participation of the people in government. Prince Ito Hirobumi, the father of the Constitution, comments: "The provisions relating to elections are, as stated in the present Article, passed over to those of a special law, so as to make it easy, when the necessity for it arises in the future, to make additions or alterations in the mode of carrying out elections. It is, therefore, undesirable that the Constitution should enter into minutiæ on the subject."

With election laws under the control of the oligarchy, the latter was able to keep the people from interfering in government by restricting the right of suffrage. In the original election laws the voter must have paid "direct national taxes to the amount of not less than fifteen yen." In the case of income tax, he must have paid it for a full three years; for other taxes the limit was for one year. This qualification had a severe restricting effect on the number of electors in Japan. It must be remembered that in 1890 Japan's economy was still largely agricultural and that farm conditions were in a chronic state of depression. This property qualification was assurance that the electors would come from the class that had most at stake in the maintenance of the *status quo*. The number of electors in 1890 was less than half a million, out of a population of about forty million.

In 1900 the tax qualification was revised downward to ten yen, in 1920 to three yen, and in 1925 it was finally abolished altogether. In 1925, after a bitter debate in the Diet, the universal manhood suffrage law was passed. Under this law, all males over twenty-five years of age are eligible to vote. Only those suffering from some mental or civic disability are disqualified. The only persons barred from voting for financial reasons are those receiving public or private help or relief because of poverty. In 1925 the number of voters was slightly more than three and a quarter million, while in 1939 the number qualified to vote had risen to more than fourteen and a half million, or about one in every five of the total population.

Besides maintaining a careful watch over the electorate, the rulers of Japan have also kept elections under strict control. By placing limitations on both the electorate and on those elected there was little chance that the grasp of the oligarchs on the Japanese government could be loosened. From one point of view, the laws governing elections reduced the amount of corruption in politics, but from another they placed serious restrictions on the operation of elections as a part of normal political behaviour.

According to pre-war Japanese election laws, candidates had to deposit ¥2,000 in cash or public bonds as security; no voting was to be held if the number of candidates was less than the number of members to be returned; election expenses could not exceed forty sen for each voter residing in the district (this sets the expense of a campaign at from twelve to fifteen thousand yen) ; in the event that the expenses of a candidate exceeded the legal limit his election was to be declared void; the defraying of election expenses was to be in charge of chief election commissioners or those appointed by them; only election commissioners and election committees were permitted to take part in campaigns; house-to-house calls were illegal; and, finally, violations of the election laws were subject to a maximum fine of ¥2,000 and a maximum imprisonment of three years. The controlling and limiting effect of these laws is even more apparent when it is recalled that they were to be enforced by the state police.

Perhaps the most important consideration to keep in mind in regard to the ballot in Japan, is the fact that there has been no concerted campaign on the part of the Japanese authorities to educate the Japanese people at large in the exercise of the ballot. When the universal manhood suffrage law was passed in 1925 sanguine Japanese and foreign political observers felt that Japan had at last come of age politically, and that liberal democratic government was to be attained. But there was in Japan neither a tradition of the ballot nor a program of training as to its significance. The right to vote alone did not and could not free the people from the rule of the oligarchy.

Although the people were given the right of suffrage, the ballot even in its restricted form was not to be allowed to become a lever with which additional concessions might be pried from the oligarchy. The legislative branch of the government, the only one which was remotely responsive to the voice of the people, was severely limited in its functions and its powers.

Political parties, a major element of systems of representative government, did not become firmly established on Japan's political soil. Parties as an instrument of politics were completely foreign to the Japanese political mind, and when they were introduced into Japan, and even after, they were not natural growths, but simply devices for fighting the age-old political struggle of the ins against the outs, or for gaining or protecting certain special interests. They were, in other words, the tools of the oligarchs who were ruling Japan, not political instruments by means of which the electorate could apply pressure on the government.

The early political parties in modern Japan were created by men who were desirous of wresting from the oligarchy certain political concessions which they felt were being denied them. They were men for the most part as authoritarian in their political philosophy as their opponents were, the only difference being that they were not in power and desired to gain control of the government. In self-defense the ruling oligarchy formed rival parties. These early parties withered and died, for they served no fundamental political need.

The two most powerful parties in modern Japan, the Minseito and the Seiyukai, struggled for power during the 1920's and the early 1930's before they were finally dissolved in 1940. These two parties were scarcely more than the house organs of the most powerful Japanese business interests. The Mitsubishi interests controlled the Minseito, and the Mitsui the Seiyukai. These two parties dominated the House of Representatives, and it was through them that the great business interests were able to apply significant pressure on the government.

There were some small parties, a few of which were probably directly responsive to the will of at least a small percentage of the voters, but these parties were never able to challenge the position of the two leaders. They too fell by the wayside during the 1930's, when the Army and the chauvinists attacked political parties as being deviations from the Japanese way of politics.

Although the parties were attacked on ideological grounds, their opponents also had abundant factual evidence at their fingertips to prove that they were not ideal instruments of government. Party men were interested only in being elected to office, and political corruption was widespread. Party men were more than once convicted of accepting bribes. All in all, the records of Japan's elected representatives were no argument for their retention as a part of a genuine parliamentary system of government.

All political parties were finally dissolved in 1940, and were replaced by the Taisei Yokusan Kai (Imperial Rule Assistance Association), which is now Japan's single party. It bears no more resemblance to the party system of government than does Germany's Nazi party. The purely political aspects of the I.R.A.A.

were taken over in the spring of 1942 by the Taisei Yokusan Seiji Kai (Imperial Rule Assistance Political Society), a group completely subservient to its parent.

With their "rights" severely circumscribed by the Constitution, their power to be represented in the government limited by law and the inertia of tradition, it would seem that the Japanese people would be powerless to interfere with the oligarchy. But the latter took no chances. Two branches of the new government, the Home Ministry and the Education Ministry, were used to keep the people from developing ideas that might make them discontented with government by oligarchy. The former was used to suppress the wrong ideas and the latter to cultivate the right ones. In other words, they carried out the functions of "thought control."

Among its other duties the Home Ministry is charged with both police and censorship functions. Japan has a system of state, not local, police, with the result that the nation's entire police force is at the disposal of the government. It is not only charged with the duty of maintaining law and order, but also with the task of making the people adhere strictly to whatever way of life is laid down for them. The police, for example, are charged with the administration of the election law. Consequently, in the past they have been in a position to disqualify or at least seriously circumscribe the activities of candidates not favoured by the government. They can arrest and detain for questioning, without the embarrassment of habeas corpus proceedings, anyone who is suspected of being a spy, a communist, a free-lance plotter against the established order, a spreader of the "wrong" ideas, or in any way suspected of threatening peace and order.

This suppressive function of the police is carried out under the "Peace Preservation Law," first instituted in 1887 and since revised a number of times, which permits the suppression of anything that threatens the "peace and order" of the nation. The definition of "peace and order" is such that almost anything can be interpreted as threatening the safety and security of the state. Any ideas which are not according to the standards set down by the oligarchy have been and can be ruthlessly suppressed by the Japanese police. The record of unreasonable arrest, unjustified detention and torture, that the Japanese police have compiled, is as black as anything of its kind in the rest of the world.

The censorship function of the police has given them absolute control over every type of literature not only imported from abroad but also produced in Japan. Probably more editions of daily newspapers, and more books and magazines, have been suppressed in Japan by the police than in any other country. Japan is one of the shining examples of what an irresponsible censorship administered by petty bureaucrats can do to freedom of thought and expression. The censors played no favourites. Any written material (to say nothing of moving pictures) that held up to ridicule or attacked the idea of monarchy, reflected on the dignity of law enforcement officers, presented politically dangerous thoughts, or threatened Japanese morals (for example, the kiss in movies) was ruthlessly destroyed or hacked to pieces in order to remove the offending bits.

Suppression drove all rival political ideologies, particularly communism, far underground in Japan. As has been pointed out already, the attack against communism was much more vicious than that against democracy and liberalism. The latter were driven underground by informal means, rather than by the deliberate methods that the police used against the communists. But the technique of suppression was not enough to insure that all Japanese had the proper thoughts. The number of dissidents who actively supported dangerous thoughts was relatively few. What was necessary in addition to suppression was to indoctrinate the great mass of the Japanese people with the positive ideas which would make loyal subjects out of them. The government arm that was delegated to carry out this important function was the Education Ministry.

The establishment and development of a nationwide system of education, where one had never existed before, were certainly among the outstanding accomplishments of the new government in Japan. The educational system was one of the proudest boasts of pre-war Japan, and the object of much amazement on the part of non-Japanese educators. But what one group failed to mention and what the other failed to notice was that it was a state-controlled system for the fostering of literacy, not of education in the true meaning of the word.

The Japanese educational system was designed for the indoctrination of the young of Japan. The fundamental aim was to create a uniformity of attitude toward the divinity of the emperor, the greatness of the Japanese nation and people, and the glorification of the military ideal, the importance of obedience to parents and other types of authority, and the necessity for the subordination of the individual to the state. The process is started in the grade schools as a part of what is known as ethical training. Of course, the usual subjects for youngsters are also taught, but it is one of the major functions of the school system to make sure that all the young become good subjects of the state.

Although grammar school education was (and is) compulsory, entrance into secondary and higher institutions of learning is difficult. The government has not lavished the same amount of care on the development of middle schools, where attendance is optional, as it has on the grammar schools. The result has been that competition to enter middle schools has been vicious, particularly since candidates have to pass difficult entrance examinations. Bright young grammar school students in pre-war Japan had to pass through an ordeal of preparation for entrance examinations to good middle schools, that rivals the discipline through which American graduate students have to go in order to win advanced degrees.

In middle schools, too, the process of indoctrination continues with particular emphasis on military training. In these schools, as well as in higher institutions of learning, Japanese mythology is taught as unchallengeable historical fact.

Students desirous of a first-rate university education had to enter government-controlled higher schools (roughly comparable to the junior college in the United States) in order to prepare for entrance into Imperial Universities, also government-controlled. Competition to enter both higher schools and Imperial Universities was also great. As middle-school registration was only a small percentage of that of grammar schools, so only a small percentage of middle school and higher school students advanced to higher levels.

It was in the higher schools and universities that the pre-war Japanese student had his best opportunity to become acquainted with the ideas that have inspired the rest of the world. As a matter of fact, some courses in some of these schools probably were as intellectually stimulating as courses in any university in the world.

But even in these schools pressure was exerted to keep dangerous ideas at a minimum. Since the government controls all schools, either directly or indirectly, it could and did exert pressure on professors who were known to be more progressive and more liberal than was consistent with their duties as subjects. Professors were also subjected to intimidation by chauvinists. An attempt was even made on the life of the famous and courageous Dr. Minobe Tatsukichi, Japan's greatest authority on constitutional law, who had advocated the theory that the emperor was only an organ of the state. In addition, he felt impelled to resign his seat in the House of Peers, which he had been given in recognition of his distinguished intellectual contributions to the state. His books were prohibited in universities, and three representative copies of his works were destroyed in a feeble imitation of the Nazi "Burning of the Books," by a group of "patriots" whose stupidity was even more monumental than that of their Nazi counterparts.

Another check on the development of true intellectual activities in Japanese universities was the fact that in pre-war Japan a university education was much more a course of training for a career than is the case in the United States. In Japan the university student trained himself for a career with the government, or with one of the large business firms. Even a career as a teacher or research scientist led inevitably either to a university which was under government control or to a position with a large firm. Neither the government nor a business firm would have been anxious to take on any bright young man if he were contaminated with the wrong ideas. The result, of course, was an informal, invisible, but nevertheless effective check on the free development of the "wrong" type of intellectual curiosity.

Thus, the Japanese educational system, from top to bottom, was ideally designed for the nurture of the kind of ideas that were suited for the development of docile, easily-led subjects who would support the aims and the ideals of the government.

Within the framework of these legal limitations, police restrictions, and ideological controls it is obvious that the subject in the modern Japanese state has as little participation in his government as he had under the old feudal order. The appearance of greater participation, as demonstrated in an elective lower house in the parliament and the suffrage, was illusory. Neither the experience with government nor the ideological foundation for participation in government were present to convert illusion into reality as far as the new "rights" granted the Japanese people were concerned.

The new governmental machinery was also tailored to fit the demands of the new rulers of Japan, and conformed to the pattern of Japanese political tradition. It formed a fitting counterpart to the new position of the governed in Japan.

Japan's new oligarchy was different from the old that had controlled the country. It was composed neither of nobles of the blood, nor of a caste of hereditary warriors. It was made up of men, drawn from all classes of Japanese society, but bound together by a set of common ideas: authoritarian government at home, and imperialistic expansion abroad.

The new oligarchy was much stronger and more powerful than its predecessors, for it had as its aim the rigid control of the entire nation. It was, as has been pointed out previously, the logical culmination of the development of Japanese history. The ideas and the forms of the new authoritarian state were both implicit and explicit in the traditional Japanese concepts of state organization and of political philosophy.

The powers of government in the new Japan were concentrated in a few organizations, both executive and advisory, to which both the legislative and judicial branches of the government were subordinated. In modern Japan the powers of government were concentrated in the Cabinet, the Privy Council, the *Genro* (or Elder Statesmen), the officials connected with the emperor and the imperial family and the bureaucrats, the thousands of government career men and petty officials who were charged with the actual task of operating the government. The legislative branch of the government was not only severely circumscribed in its powers, but also was split sharply into a conservative, oligarchic House of Peers and a pseudo-representative Lower House. The judiciary, in sharp contrast with the American system, was specifically enjoined from reviewing the work of other branches of the government.

The Constitution is singularly vague on the functions of the executive arm of the government, the branch that has become by far the most powerful. This is perhaps natural, when one considers the fact that it was the deliberate design of the founders of modern Japan to make the emperor the formal source of all political power. If this view were to be consistently adhered to, then it would be a contradiction to enumerate the powers of and limitations on the executive branch of the government. It is likewise entirely possible that Prince Ito and his fellow politicians clearly perceived the fact that the power of the executive branch could flourish best if it were unembarrassed with specific grants or specific limitations of powers.

The Cabinet, which has been the principal executive arm of the government, is not specifically mentioned in the Constitution. Article LV defines the duties of the Ministers of State: *"The respective Ministers of State shall give their advice to the Emperor, and be responsible for it. All Laws, Imperial Ordinances and Imperial Rescripts of whatever kind, that relate to the affairs of the State, require the countersignature of a Minister of State."* When one considers the important rôle of the Cabinet in Japanese affairs, this is indeed a casual statement of the duties of its members. However, although this article says little, Prince Ito dignified it with his longest comment. Because of the light it sheds on both the theory on which the framers of the Constitution based their work, and on the rôle of the executive in Japanese politics, his comment is worth extensive quotation.

In summarizing the considerations that entered into the formulation of the position of the Ministers of State, Ito says: "Thus, in our Constitution the following conclusions have been arrived at: *First,* that the Ministers of State are charged with the duty of giving advice to the Emperor, which is their proper function, and that they are not held responsible on His behalf; *secondly,* that Ministers are directly responsible to the Emperor and indirectly so to the people; *thirdly,* that it is the Sovereign and not the people that can decide as to the responsibility of Ministers, because the Sovereign possesses the rights of sovereignty of the State; *fourthly,* that the responsibility of Ministers is a political one and has no relation to criminal or civil responsibility, nor can it conflict therewith, neither can the one affect the other."

It is not difficult to see that Ito was primarily concerned with establishing the emperor as the source of the executive powers of government. Note that the people have absolutely no voice in controlling the acts of the executive. On the one hand, the ministers are not responsible to the people for the advice that they give the emperor; and on the other, the people cannot hold the ministers responsible for their executive acts. Notice that the phrase "indirectly responsible" means absolutely nothing as far as popular political powers are concerned, for the people are indirectly concerned only in so far as they are the "children" of the emperor. The third point listed above eliminates any possibility of doubt as to the nature of the "indirect responsibility" to which the people can hold the ministers accountable.

The Ministers of State are not only solely responsible to the emperor, but also, according to Ito's views, they are responsible individually to the emperor and not to the Minister President of State (the term which Ito uses for the prime minister). Ito declares: "As to the other Ministers of State, they are severally held responsible for the matters within their respective competency: there is no joint responsibility among them in regard to such matters. For the Minister President and the other Ministers of State, being alike personally appointed by the Emperor, the proceedings of each one of them are, in every respect controlled by the will of the Emperor, and the Minister President himself has no power of control over the posts occupied by other Ministers, while the latter ought not to be dependent on the former. In some countries the Cabinet is regarded as constituting a corporate body; the Ministers are not held to take part in the conduct of the government each one in an individual capacity, but joint responsibility is the rule. *The evil of such a system is, that the power of party combination will ultimately over-rule the supreme power of the Sovereign. Such a state of things can never be approved of according to our Constitution.*" (Italics are the present writer's.) In view of what has been said previously, in regard to the oligarchic nature of the Japanese government, the implications of the last two sentences of the above statement are crystal clear.

In regard to the second important duty of the ministers of state, namely, the countersignature of state papers, Ito says: "*First,* laws, Imperial Ordinances and Imperial Rescripts that relate to affairs of the state can be put into force only by virtue of the countersignature of a Minister or of Ministers of State. Without it, they can take no effect; and when issued through any other than a Ministerial channel, none can be carried out by the functionaries charged with its execution. *Secondly,* the countersignature of a Minister or of Ministers of State, attests the right of the said Minister, or Ministers to carry out the law, Imperial Ordinance or Imperial Rescript in question, and also his or their responsibility for the same."

The first of these considerations is undoubtedly designed to act as a check on the possibility of successful *coup d'état.* If, for example, a group succeeded in gaining control of the person of the emperor, it would be powerless, constitutionally, that is, to negate the structure of government as set up by the oligarchy. In other words, if a politically ambitious clique managed to gain temporary control of the emperor, it could not constitutionally alter the government without the consent of the Ministers of State, who, presumably, would be on the side of the controlling oligarchy. Ito knew how the position of the emperor had been utilized in past Japanese history and evidently envisaged the provision as a safeguard against seizure of the government through mere control of the emperor. Of course, this constitutional provision would not stand in the way of ambitious plotters, but it would make their work more difficult, and it would provide a handy means of undoing their work on the grounds of unconstitutionality in the event that they were later driven out of power.

In his comments on the countersignature provisions, Ito makes the significant point that mere countersignature does not limit the responsibility of the signing minister, but declares that, "when a mistake has been committed by the Government, responsibility should not be confined to the countersigning Minister or Ministers, but those Ministers also who, though not the countersigners, have been consulted about the matter, ought to be held responsible for the mistake." Though this comment might be taken to be contradictory to the previous statement that there is "no joint responsibility" among the ministers, such is not the case. This provision is interpreted to mean that the ministers are responsible to the emperor for their mistakes, but are responsible to the people for neither their mistakes nor for their positive acts.

Because of the special position of the War and Navy Ministers the cabinet has been virtually a two-headed organization, one concerned with the administration of civilian affairs and the other with military and naval affairs. The result has been that the military has been in a position to dominate the decisions of the cabinet as a whole.

Although there is nothing in the Constitution which forbids the appointment of a civilian as head of either the War or Navy Ministries, it has been made mandatory that these two posts be filled by only admirals, vice-admirals, generals, or lieutenant-generals. In 1895 Prince Yamagata, one of the leading statesmen of Meiji Japan, obtained the approval of an imperial ordinance to that effect. It is now the rule that only officers of those ranks on active duty can be appointed to these posts. This provision is innocent enough on the surface, as it ostensibly only insures that Japan's armed forces be directed by professionals, but actually it has proved to be the instrument by means of which the Army and the Navy (but the Army to a greater extent) have controlled Japan's government. By refusing to continue to serve in the cabinet or by refusing to permit their associates to serve in the cabinet, generals and admirals have successfully blocked legislation or policies which they did not favour and the appointment of men to cabinet positions who might be unsympathetic to their cause.

This "invisible" government has been one of the most effective weapons used by the military in gaining their undisputed control of the government. It is clearly extra-constitutional, but at the same time it must be remembered that "constitutionality" is not a part of the Japanese scheme of government and that there could be no enlightened public opinion which might have attacked this technique on the grounds that it contravened the constitutional operation of government. However, it must be noted that Ito in his commentaries must have had something of this general nature in mind when he placed the emperor in supreme command of the armed forces. In 1891 he is reported to have written that military and naval men should fill the offices in order to prevent parliamentary or political interference, and to avoid the decline of the imperial prerogatives.

Emperor Meiji's rescript to soldiers and sailors, granted in 1882, charges the Japanese military to refrain from participating in politics. The passage in question reads as follows: "Unattracted by the opinions expressed by the public, and regardless of politics, you should devote yourselves to your allegiance as your principal duty, esteeming fidelity weightier than mountains and death lighter than a feather." During the 1920's this passage was often quoted by those who were attempting to curtail the political activities of the military. However, the Army insisted that its sole business was national defense, but at the same time interpreted the phrase "national defense" widely enough to include everything in Japanese government.

The second executive arm of the government treated in the Constitution is the Privy Council. However, the Privy Council is not an executive body, but rather an advisory group. Article LVI of the Constitution says: *"The Privy Councillors shall, in accordance with the provisions for the organization of the Privy Council, deliberate upon important matters of State, when they have been consulted by the Emperor."* It is to be noted that the organization of the Privy Council is not determined by the Constitution itself, but by "the provisions for organization of the Privy Council." It was the aim of the drafters of the Constitution to place the seal of constitutional approval on an instrument which they had already devised as a part of the new oligarchy a year before the Constitution was promulgated.

Although the Privy Council was cloaked with constitutionality, it was quite obviously designed to act as an extra-governmental check on the operation of the government. From the standpoint of its constitutional position, it might well never function at all, for if it pleased the other advisers of the emperor not to call it into session, it would never have anything to do. In practice, it has served to function as another check on widening of the basis of the government.

The membership of the council is limited to twenty-six, a president, a vice-president, and twenty-four councillors. In addition, the Ministers of State are *ex officio* members. The twenty-six permanent members are men who have distinguished themselves in the national service as administrators, diplomats, judges, educators, generals, or admirals. It is to be noted that the great majority of members would naturally tend to be extremely conservative if not reactionary. Only those whose careers have proved them to be "safe" have been admitted into membership. All members are nominated by the emperor with the advice of the prime minister, which means that in actual practice they are nominated by the prime minister himself. This method of nomination is an additional safeguard against the inclusion of any "undesirable" individuals. As long as its personnel remains conservative, if not reactionary, it can effectively stifle any liberalizing influences in the field of Japanese politics. It both strengthens the hold of the oligarchy on the Japanese government and keeps whatever popular elements might develop at arm's length from the sources of ultimate political power.

The *Genro,* or Elder Statesmen, have disappeared from the sphere of Japanese politics, but for almost half a century they played a major rôle in the shaping of Japanese policy. This group came to an end in 1940, when Prince Saionji Kimmochi, who for almost twenty years carried the unofficial title of "the Last *Genro,*" died. The *Genro* had no legal, constitutional, or official status as a governing body in Japan, and yet its influence was great. How this group arose no one knows exactly. Indeed, there is not always agreement even as to the number who are to be honoured by inclusion in this select group.

It is usually agreed that seven men have been members of this group. They are Prince Ito, Prince Yamagata Aritomo, Inouye Kaoru, and Katsura Taro, all of the Choshu clan; Oyama Iwao and Matsukata Masayoshi of the Satsuma clan; and Prince Saionji. Ito, Yamagata, Inouye, Oyama and Matsukata are regarded as having belonged to the original group. All seven are men who played major rôles in the politics of the Meiji period. It is thought that the five original elder statesmen met as an informal advisory group to Meiji. Their prestige, plus the work that they had accomplished, apparently enabled them to mingle with the Emperor on virtually equal terms. Their prestige would naturally give their advice tremendous weight.

The *Genro* undoubtedly determined much of Japan's policy from the early 1890's, when it is believed that they first began to sit, until Saionji's death in 1940. The latter was unable to take an active part in Japan's politics for more than a decade before his death. Nevertheless, he was consulted whenever a new prime minister was to be nominated and at other times of political crisis. On several occasions he traveled to Tokyo in order to confer with the Emperor himself. At other times a high official, the personal representative of the Emperor, journeyed to the Prince's summer home some miles southwest of Tokyo to obtain his opinions. His importance is attested by the fact that his name was found several times on assassins' lists. It was only by chance that the aged Prince escaped assassins' bullets during the February 26 incident. It is said that he escaped into the hills on the back of one of his faithful servants.

The Prince, one of the small number of court aristocrats who took an active part in the restoration struggles of 1868–9, was regarded as one of the last remaining bulwarks of liberalism in Japan. He is known to have blocked the nomination of men to the premiership who were regarded as extremists. His liberal outlook, in spite of his aristocratic background, is attributed to the fact that he spent some years in France at the end of the nineteenth century when he became firmly converted to democratic principles. One of the primary reasons for Prince Konoye's being regarded as a liberal was the fact that he was Saionji's principal protégé.

The *Genro* as a political institution disappeared with Saionji's death. It is ironical that this body, which was conceived by the leaders of Meiji Japan to maintain absolutist control of Japan's government, ended by becoming the last outpost against the worst absolutism that Japan has ever known. The *Genro* are gone beyond the possibility of recall, for it is impossible to conceive of a rôle for them in the Japan of the future, no matter what might be its political complexion. Whether they have been a force for evil or for good cannot yet be determined. As an individual, Saionji did much to stave off the present evil days.

The Minister of the Imperial Household, the Lord Keeper of the Privy Seal, and the Grand Chamberlain, all officials closely connected with the emperor, played important rôles in Japan's politics in the 1930's. It was they who controlled access to the emperor, for it was through them that audiences were arranged and other affairs concerning the emperor carried out. Until the 1930's these men were regarded as constituting one of the few remaining barriers to an out-and-out totalitarian régime in Japan. They were older men, who had been at least sympathetic to the liberal tradition that had been imported into Japan in the nineteenth century. Their political significance is also attested by the fact that they were the objects of assassination. It might be argued that attacks on men so closely associated with the emperor would be skirting perilously close to *lèse majesté,* but the assassins cloaked their acts in high patriotism by declaring that they were motivated simply by the desire to remove the emperor from the counsel of men who were guilty of misleading him, of giving him advice not in accordance with the ancient traditions of Japan.

Below the level of these special groups, the Cabinet, the *Genro,* the Privy Council, the special ministers and groups closely associated with the emperor, is the bureaucracy, the mass of individuals who fill the government offices which are actually charged with the details of administration. Japan's government in the modern period has been characterized by an excessive amount of bureaucratic control. From the very nature of the Meiji Restoration, one would expect that the government of modern Japan would be top-heavy with bureaucracy. In Tokugawa Japan the life of the individual, no matter what social class he might belong to, was minutely regulated. The spirit, if not the letter, of these controls was carried over into the new Japan, and of course required a considerable staff of administrators. The complexity of the new government demanded a greatly increased personnel. Tokyo Imperial University, Japan's leading university, was charged with the special duty of training men for the government service.

The bureaucracy *qua* bureaucracy has not played a decisive rôle in Japanese politics. From its ranks have risen a few men who have, in their time, played important rôles in Japanese politics. As a part of the Japanese structure of government, it has never affected Japan's policies decisively. Its political importance arises from the fact that it is composed of a solid backlog of individuals who can be relied upon to carry out any policies that the government itself might deem wise. The Japanese people are in a very real sense conscious of the impingement of the bureaucracy on their daily lives, for policemen, teachers, and a multiplicity of other minor officials are an integral part of the bureaucracy.

As might be expected, bureaucratic control of Japanese life has increased greatly in the past ten years, during the drive toward the complete totalitarian state. Government control bureaus and regulation of Japan's economic life have increased tremendously since the outbreak of the war with China. There is not a Japanese, from millionaire to beggar, whose life has not been in some way affected by this bureaucracy. Although it is made up largely of civilians, it includes in its ranks many military men in the rôle of "technical experts."

The twenty-two articles of the third chapter of the Constitution deal with the Imperial Diet, the Japanese national legislative body. The two houses of the Diet, the House of Peers and the House of Representatives, do not have equal powers. It was obviously the aim of the drafters of the Constitution to have the House of Peers act as a constant and inescapable check on the Lower House. For example, the latter can be dissolved by imperial order, but the former cannot be. The House of Peers was definitely an aristocratic body which could be depended upon to keep the more democratic Lower House under control.

The supreme position of the executive arm of government in Japan has reduced the legislative branch to an extremely subordinate rôle. To-day the legislative arm of the Japanese government is scarcely more than an appreciative audience, viewing the accomplishments of the executive and expressing its approval not by the polite clapping of hands, but by the less direct method of automatically voting approval of every executive act that is placed before it. In a nation with no tradition of self-government, with no tradition of representative government, it is little wonder that the Japanese legislature has fallen short of what should be its rightful position under the terms of constitutional government as it is understood in the Western sense.

Nevertheless, in spite of its present impotent rôle, the Japanese Diet has proved to be the most vocal instrument of Japanese government, and the only vehicle through which discontent with the trend toward authoritarianism has been expressed in recent years. Its primary function in the history of modern Japanese politics has been to act as a symbol of what might have been in Japan had the psychological lag between the forms of representative government and the political experience of the Japanese people not been so great.

The Diet has been the target of a consistent "smear" campaign on the part of the reactionary nationalists of Japan ever since the Manchurian "Incident" of 1931 determined the direction of development of Japanese political activity. However, it must be admitted that its conduct provided its detractors with more than enough ammunition for an effective campaign of defamation. Bribery, frequent fights (including the tossing of live snakes), numerous factional disputes, and other aspects of representative government at its worst, scarcely served to give it a respectable standing. Had the Diet been given the power and the dignity that it should have had under a system of true constitutional government, it is possible that it would have risen above the level of mediocrity and worse that was to bring about its eventual complete emasculation as an organ of government.

It was obviously no part of the plan of the architects of the modern Japanese state to grant the legislature more than an absolute minimum of political power. The limitation of the sovereignty of the legislature was accomplished in three ways: 1, by creating a conservative reactionary House of Peers to act as a counterbalance for the House of Representatives; 2, by writing into the Constitution effective checks on the powers of the House of Representatives, which were granted in other sections of the same document; and 3, by effectively limiting the suffrage, a move which has already been described.

The Japanese Diet is bicameral, being composed of the House of Peers and the House of Representatives. The drafters of the Constitution did not wish to set the two houses on a footing of political equality. Article XXXIV of the Constitution reads: *"The House of Peers shall, in accordance with the Ordinance concerning the House of Peers, be composed of the members of the Imperial Family, of the orders of nobility, and of those persons who have been nominated thereto by the Emperor."*

In the extremely idealistic words of Ito's commentary, the House of Peers was supposed to be a "body of Nestors." He says: "The members of the House of Peers, whether they be hereditary, elected or appointed ones, are to represent the higher grades of society. If the House of Peers fulfills its functions, it will serve in a remarkable degree to preserve an equilibrium between political powers, to restrain the undue influence of political parties, to check the evil tendencies of irresponsible discussions, to secure the stability of the Constitution, to be an instrument for maintaining harmony between the governing and the governed, and to permanently sustain the prosperity of the country and the happiness of the people. The object of having a House of Peers is not merely admittance of the higher classes to some share in the deliberations upon legislative matters, but also representation of the prudence, experience and perseverance of the people, by assembling together men who have rendered signal service to the State, men of erudition and men of great wealth." Naturally, the House of Peers has fallen far short of this grandiose description of its rôle in Japan's political life, but it has served as a check on the "evils" that Ito enumerated.

The membership is made up of the following categories: imperial princes; peers of the order of prince and marquis, who are seated by virtue of their birth; representatives of the peers of the order of count, viscount and baron, who are elected from their respective orders; men of erudition or distinguished service who are nominated by the emperor; four members of the Imperial Academy, elected by the membership and nominated by the emperor; and representatives of the highest taxpayers in each prefecture, who are elected from their own number. In regard to the number from each group, there can be no set limit for either of the first two categories; eighteen counts, sixty-six barons and sixty-six viscounts are to be elected from their own number; and not more than sixty-six of the land's highest taxpayers. The group of imperial nominees cannot exceed one hundred twenty-five. All elected members serve for seven years; all others for life. There is no established proportion between the number of titled, and the number of non-titled members.

It is easy to see that a governing body made up of such men could not but be conservative. The aristocrats and the high taxpayers would be certain to be reactionary. The imperial nominees include, of course, statesmen and army and navy men, because these are the groups most likely to perform "meritorious services to the state." The statesmen, given Japan's political history, would be without exception for the established order. Those appointed for their erudition, and the four men who are elected by the Imperial Academy, constitute the only sources through which a possible leavening element of liberalism could infiltrate. But even if a few were admitted, it is easy to see that it would be very difficult for them to alter the preponderantly reactionary spirit of the upper house.

Government finances are removed from legislative control by Chapter VI of the Constitution. Although it is provided that "the expenditure and revenue of the State require the consent of the Imperial Diet" and that "the budget shall be first laid before the House of Representatives," the Diet does not have any effective control over government finances. Article LXVII reads: *"Those already fixed expenditures based by the Constitution upon the powers appertaining to the Emperor, and such expenditures as may have arisen by the effect of law, or that appertain to the legal obligations of the Government, shall be neither rejected nor reduced by the Imperial Diet, without the concurrence of the Government."* Lest there be any doubt as to the nature of this article, Ito says in his commentary: " 'Already fixed expenditures based by the Constitution upon the power appertaining to the Emperor, include all the expenditures which are based upon the sovereign powers of the Emperor, as set forth in Chapter I of the Constitution, to wit: ordinary expenditures required by the organization of the different branches of the administration, and by that of the Army and Navy, the salaries of all civil and military officers, and expenditures that may be required in consequence of treaties concluded with foreign countries." The government can also "take all necessary financial measures by means of an Imperial Ordinance" in the event that the Imperial Diet cannot be convoked owing to the "external or internal condition of the country, in case of urgent need for the maintenance of public safety." However, in this event, the Imperial Ordinance must be submitted to the Diet for approval at its next session.

Article LXXI has proved to be the most potent financial weapon in the hands of the government. It reads: *"When the Imperial Diet has not voted on the Budget, or when the Budget has not been brought into actual existence, the Government shall carry out the Budget of the preceding year."* This constitutional provision makes it impossible for the legislative branch to bring the executive branch to heel by refusing to provide for its financial needs.

Ito and his aides subordinated the judicial branch of the government to law, just as they subordinated the rights of the Japanese citizen to law. Article LVII declares: *"The Judicature shall be exercised by the Courts of Law according to law, in the name of the Emperor. The organization of the Courts of Law shall be determined by law."* The powers and functions of the judicial branch can be limited in any way that the rulers of Japan see fit. The phrase, "in the name of the Emperor," obviously places the decision of the courts above criticism.

The right of the citizen to protect himself against arbitrary acts by the administrative authorities is severely limited, if not completely eliminated, by Article LXI, which reads: *"No suit at law which relates to rights alleged to have been infringed by the illegal measures of the administrative authorities, and which shall come within the competency of the Court of Administrative Litigation specially established by law, shall be taken cognizance of by a Court of Law."* This definitely bars the judiciary at large from reviewing the acts of the administrative authorities.

Ito made it clear in his commentary on this article that the executive branch of the government was to be absolutely free of any interference on the part of the judicial. He says: "Were administrative measures placed under the control of the judicature, and were courts of justice charged with the duty of deciding whether a particular administrative measure was or was not proper, administrative authorities would be in a state of subordination to judicial functionaries. . . . Administrative authorities carry out measures by virtue of their official functions, and for these measures they lie under constitutional responsibility, and it follows that they ought to possess power to remove obstacles in the path of these measures and to decide upon suits springing from the carrying out of them. For, should the administrative be denied this power, its executive efficacy would be entirely paralyzed, and it would no longer be able to discharge the responsibility put upon it by the Constitution." He also points out that only men trained in administrative procedure are qualified to pass on administrative policy; hence, review of their acts must be kept from the hands of men with only judicial training. The aim of this restriction on the power of the judiciary, like that of so many provisions of the Constitution, is to keep the government entirely under the control of the executive oligarchy.

The Authoritarian State

The machinery of state in the new Japan was much more complex than that of the Tokugawa *bakufu,* but all power continued to be concentrated at the apex of the political structure. The government continued to be of the few, by the few, and for the few. The oligarchy made its rule palatable by pressing home the point that it was working for the glory of the emperor, the state, and hence, the whole people.

The authoritarian state created the ideal conditions for the mass acceptance of the ideals of militarism and aggression that were held up before the Japanese people by the leaders of modern Japan. The people accepted the decisions for war and aggression that were made by the narrow ruling oligarchy and they accepted without complaint the sacrifices that grew out of these decisions. They did so not only because they had been forced to do so and indoctrinated to do so, but also because they were acting as their political traditions and their political attitudes had disposed them.

Chapter VII

BACKGROUND OF WAR

When the feudal period came to an end, the warriors lost their special privileges as a class, indeed they disappeared as a separate and distinct part of the population. But the ideology of the class became that of the nation. Men whose ideas were essentially those of the vanished warrior class carried the largest share of the burden of building the new government in Japan. They constructed an authoritarian state that was ideally suited for purposes of war. What is perhaps even more important is the fact that they made Japan into a nation of warriors, not in the classical sense of the term as old Japan had understood it, but in the more dangerous sense, that all Japan accepted the ideals of war and its use as an instrument of national policy.

The whole concept of war and of the bearing of arms was changed with the fall of the Tokugawa shogunate and the collapse of the feudal order. No longer was the bearing of arms a jealously guarded privilege of a few select members of the population. Under the new system all men became soldiers. Mass conscription changed a mark of social distinction and political power into a duty and an obligation to the state.

The feudal order resulted naturally in the glorification of the warriors and all they stood for, but there were certain fundamental weaknesses in the system when viewed from the standpoint of men interested in the furtherance of war and militarism as instruments of national policy. The greatest fault of the warrior class, from this point of view, was the fact that it was not an army. In addition, the Tokugawa régime, although of, by, and for warriors, did not favour armies. Its control of the country was so complete that it did not require a large army in the formal sense of the term. It did not allow others to maintain armies, for they were dangerous to Tokugawa rule.

Even had it been possible to raise large bodies of men under the old régime, they still would have fallen far short of the demands of even nineteenth century warfare. They had no real weapons. The sword was still the weapon in which the warrior placed his greatest trust, although firearms had been imported in the sixteenth century. It was his "soul," and was regarded as his most prized possession. The Japanese had a few pieces of artillery, which had been built either on the model of the artillery pieces brought into the country in the late sixteenth century or had been cast under the direction of the Dutch who were allowed to remain in the country. These weapons were no match for what the West had developed. The bombardments of the Choshu forts and of Kagoshima in the 1860's were proof enough of that. Whatever faith in their traditional weapons might have lingered in the hearts of the warriors was certainly swept away in 1877, when an army of despised conscripts, armed with the best weapons in Japan, smashed the proud forces of the Satsuma clan which were still fighting more or less according to the old rules.

The system of universal male conscription, instituted in 1872, guaranteed that the army would be of the nation; for this meant that virtually no family would be without at least one member who was a trained soldier. Every able-bodied male knew that the state was going to demand that he devote time to learning the profession of the soldier. Women had to send their sons, fathers, brothers, and husbands off to fight and die for the country. Only by accident or ill fortune could one escape discharging this debt to the state.

Men were only one of the requirements of the new national army. It also needed modern arms, the factories that could make them, and a transportation system that could deliver them. The nation's economy was vitally affected by the development of the modern army. A large proportion of the civilian population contributed indirectly, as well as directly, to the maintenance of the army. Workers, contractors, businessmen, manufacturers, financiers, all had an interest one way or another in the Army and Navy. The nation had to pay for the new army, too. Much of the national budget was devoted to the building, arming, supplying, and maintenance of the Army and Navy.

Modern Japan had a national army, but this vast new organization because of its very extent had to be kept busy. An army not employed in the business of war would be a truly expensive luxury, so expensive that Japan, a relatively poor country, could not continue to support it. Popular discontent might even develop, if the people had to continue to pay heavy taxes in order to maintain an army that did not fight. Its very closeness to the mass of the people made it necessary for the rulers of Japan to find work for it to do.

In the early years of modern Japan the Army had perhaps its best justification. The stress and strain of the destruction of the feudal order and the shift to a quasi-modern state inevitably brought in its train dislocations which might have proved serious had not the government had under its control an army that was able to maintain relative peace and order within the country during those critical times. Japan also needed an army for protection from the threat outside her borders. For some time after the opening of the country there was danger that foreign arms might reduce Japan to the same semi-colonial status that was rapidly being forced on China. These threats were enough to justify the building up of an extensive armed force.

By the 1880's foreign intervention in Japanese affairs had virtually disappeared, and the new structure was secure against any active internal opposition. But by that time the new armed strength of Japan was firmly established. All Japanese had a stake in it and all were involved one way or another in its operations. The passage of time and the grim succession of wars firmly fastened this new national army on the Japanese people and the Japanese state.

With the immediate need for a modern army eliminated, the Japanese government had to seek occupation for the Army. The leaders of the new Japan were not averse to such plans, for they were men who had been born and bred in an atmosphere of militarism. The Army was dominated by men from the Choshu clan, and the Navy by the Satsuma clan. With the armed forces of the country controlled by men from these warlike clans, it was to be expected that work would be found for them outside the country when their immediate utility at home had disappeared.

The philosophy of conquest found its earliest expression, after the Meiji period had started, in an abortive attempt to invade Korea in 1873. A bitter debate developed within Japan over the question of whether Korea should be invaded or not. The Koreans had refused to send tribute, and leaders of the government were hot to avenge the fancied insult to Japan. An expedition was about to be sent out, but the return of the famous Iwakura mission from Europe and America brought the project to an end. The Iwakura group, impressed by what it had seen in the Occident, counseled a policy of waiting. They recognized Japan's weaknesses as well as they did the strength of the West. They knew that Japan had to proceed cautiously. The nation was not yet strong enough to follow the policy of conquest and exploitation that the West was implementing in China.

In 1874, more or less as a sop to those who had been disappointed in their hope to invade Korea, an expedition was sent against Taiwan because of attacks that had been made against Japanese there. The expedition won its few skirmishes with the native population, but did not win Japan any territory or prestige. From this small beginning grew Japan's plans of conquest. The steady succession of wars, all profitable, converted most Japanese to the idea that war and militarism were not only necessary and inevitable, but also profitable.

Universal conscription brought almost every family into actual contact with war. Veterans' associations, under Army control, maintained the martial spirit in men after they had been demobilized. Propaganda built up in the minds of many Japanese the complete acceptance of the ideas of the military. School children were told of the heroic deeds of warriors in ancient times. They were schooled in martial exercises that had become firmly entrenched in the Japanese tradition. They were taught to honour the men who wore the uniform of the emperor's army. They were given military drill in the schools. As the pace of the program of militaristic aggression against China accelerated, they were exposed more and more to stories, fictional, quasi-fictional, and otherwise of the deeds of the men at the battlefront.

Patriotic groups of one sort or another kept the war spirit alive among the older groups. The controlled press likewise kept up a steady barrage of propaganda. In addition, all groups and individuals suspected of harbouring anti-war sentiments, or even ideas that might contain the seeds of discontent with war, were ruthlessly suppressed.

Business and businessmen had no reason to quarrel with war as an instrument of national policy. Their business was so closely bound to the policies of the government, as has already been pointed out, that they had little, if any, reason to stand against the tide of militarism that was sweeping over the country.

When Japan struck at China in 1937 and at the United States and Great Britain in 1941, there was no group in the country that stood against a policy of war. It is not an exaggeration to state that the nation stood as one behind the policy of aggression that was bringing Japan to her doom. Isolated individuals there may have been who saw the danger that was inherent in the program of the militarists or who might have disagreed with those who were exalting militarism and war, but there was no effective group at any level in Japanese society that could have altered the program that was losing Japan all the friends and all the influence that she had once possessed.

What were some of the factors that lay behind the development of war and militarism in Japan? Many of them have already been described. The warrior tradition, the dominant rôle of the military in the creation of the new Japan, the threat of foreign invasion, the planned, carefully controlled nature of the Meiji Restoration, all led Japan along the way toward militarism and war. But there were also other factors which developed both outside and inside Japan. Some had no relation to Japan at all; some were turned into effective pro-military propaganda; some were purely accidental; some were in essence unfavourable to the government, but were turned to the advantage of the policy of aggression.

Japan was brought back into contact with the outside world as an indirect result of the fever of expansion that swept through Europe and the United States in the eighteenth and nineteenth centuries. Although the country was not opened by force of arms, and although the strictures on its sovereignty were indeed minor when compared with those that were imposed on China, Japan's leaders were keenly aware of the fact that it was armed might that had awed them into admitting the hated "barbarians" and had forced them to negotiate treaties on a basis of equality. Equally powerful was the sight of China being partitioned by the Western powers.

Japanese leaders, predisposed to militarism, were thus given convincing proof that force as an instrument of foreign policy spoke loudly and yielded large returns. The example of the West was, in the eyes of Japan, one to be followed in foreign relations as in other things. The most striking proof of the efficacy of force as the language of diplomacy was given Japan in 1895 in the "Three-Power Intervention."

As a result of her successful war against China in 1894–5, Japan demanded the cession of the Liaotung peninsula. China was forced to agree, but three powers, France, Germany, and Russia, stepped in and forced Japan to give up what she considered to be her rightful spoils of war. Russia then moved to take over control of the peninsula. Here was an excellent example of the manner in which might made right in the Far East in the latter part of the nineteenth century. Japan had been forced to give up by force what she had won by force, and on top of that saw her spoils gobbled up by a nation more powerful, at least at the moment, than she was. This occurrence rankled in Japanese breasts, and led to a Japanese resolve to persevere in building up her strength.

Another situation that created favourable circumstances for the development of Japanese militarism and aggression was the fact that China, Korea, and Russia were all weak at the moment when Japan was just beginning to feel her own strength. China was in the throes of a dynastic change that marked the end of the rule of the Manchus. The pressure of Western imperialism on China added a complicating factor to the turmoil of dynastic change. The death struggles of the Manchu dynasty took more than half a century. The birth of the new Chinese Republic was complicated not only by extreme internal social, economic, and political disorganization, but also by the presence of Western and Japanese imperialism.

Korea had been weak for some centuries, and her weakness was compounded by the feebleness of China, for previously China had been a protector of the Korean kingdom. Korea was no match for the Japanese. Japanese "peaceful penetration" and Japanese-promoted intrigue within Korea sapped the strength of the already weak kingdom, and it was no task at all for Japan to assimilate Korea in 1910 after she had forced both China and Russia to recognize her "paramount interest" in the peninsula.

Russia, though stronger than both China and Korea, was also no match for a determined, well-organized Japan. The Russian Far Eastern empire in Siberia was scarcely more than undeveloped frontier. Russian penetration into Manchuria was deep, but not well-planned, and not integrated into the Russian economy as a whole. More crucial than the relatively superficial nature of its interest in the Far East was the fact that the Russian imperial régime was rapidly coming to an end. Shaken by disorder at home, its strength sapped by corruption and intrigue, Imperial Russia did not have at its command sufficient strength or sufficient interest either to establish firmly its interests in the Far East or to fight a major war such as the one with Japan.

Weak neighbours contributed greatly to Japan's success in her early wars and the resulting increase in her militaristic spirit. Purposeful, efficient Japan was able to defeat the armies of both Russia and China and to bring Korea into her empire. These victories also gave Japan confidence in her program of aggression. They provided a background of heroic achievement which fed the propaganda of the militarists. There were no defeats to raise doubts in the minds of the people as to the desirability of war as an instrument of national policy.

Not only did Japan profit from the fact that her immediate neighbours were weak, but also the drive to militarism was aided tremendously by other outside developments. From the end of the first World War almost until the day of Pearl Harbor Occidental attention was centred on its own affairs, and what Japan was doing in the Far East was of secondary interest to the governments of America and Europe, and of almost no interest at all to the peoples of the West. The depression, the post-war revulsion of feeling toward war, and all it stood for, and the Nazi drive to power and aggression aided Japan immeasurably by shifting Western attention away from her own aggression in Asia.

The depression was an immediate event of such importance to both governments and peoples that there was little time for foreign events which were taking place in distant places of the world. Unemployment, hunger, and want were problems which formed a screen behind which Japan operated almost unnoticed. Japan, too, was hit by the depression in the 1920's, but the major program of aggression was set in motion in the early 1930's, when the economic problem was bearing most heavily on the West.

Of equal if not greater importance was the fact that none of the democracies was willing to use war to stop war. The cost of the World War in blood and treasure and human degradation was so great that no one wanted to see a repetition of war on such a scale. No one liked what Japan was doing in Asia, but no one was willing to become embroiled in war with Japan in order to stop her aggression. The attitude was not simply one of revulsion from war. It was composed also of genuine pacifism, a muddle-headed softness that often masquerades as pacifism, appeasement, it's-too-far-away-from-here-to-matter, a desire to continue to do business with Japan's merchants, and a misguided belief that the "fundamentally decent" elements in Japan would stop the militarists. No democratic government was willing to oppose Japan with force, and no people would have supported its government if it had adopted such a policy.

While these negative attitudes aided Japan's militarists greatly, other positive acts played into their hands by presenting them with propaganda arguments that made it seem as if Japan were being persecuted economically, and thwarted in its ambitions. The American Exclusion Act of 1924 and the Canadian and Australian attitudes toward immigration from Asia supplied Japan's chauvinists with some of their most powerful arguments. These attitudes were described as being insulting to the Japanese people, for they implied, so the Japanese propaganda line ran, that the Japanese were an inferior race. The impact of this line can be gauged when it is placed beside Japan's own racial theories, that is, that Japan was a land of the gods and the Japanese were descended from the gods. The argument was all the more effective for being emotional and illogical.

The exclusion laws were also given an economic aspect. The Japanese argument in this regard ran as follows: "Japan is suffering from over-population. She has more people than her land can support. These people should be allowed to emigrate to areas where land is available. The United States, Canada, and Australia have vast areas which are virtually unpopulated. Yet they bar Japanese from entering, thereby forcing a lower standard of living on Japan and selfishly allowing great areas of their own land to remain undeveloped." The argument was a standard one for years, used both at home and abroad, to justify Japan's expansion on the Asiatic continent. Overlooked were the reluctance of the Japanese to emigrate and the government's deliberate policy of encouraging the growth of the population in order to keep the size of the population at a level deemed necessary by the military.

Another powerful economic development that reinforced the government's propaganda was the Western practice of erecting tariff walls not only to keep Japanese products out of their home lands, but also out of their colonial possessions. During the early 1930's Japan's light industries made tremendous strides, particularly in the field of textiles and light consumers' goods. Japanese labour was cheap and the system of household industries reduced production costs to levels where Japanese goods were flooding into areas where the populations had little purchasing power. But competition with goods of other nations forced the latter to raise tariff barriers against the cheaper Japanese products. Again the effectiveness of this in Japan's internal propaganda is obvious. The people were told that the other nations were attempting to starve them by closing markets to their products, markets that they needed if they were to continue to live.

Another economic factor that played into the hands of the militarists was Japan's relative poverty of raw materials. Japan is not a country with all the raw materials at its command that are necessary for a well-balanced structure of heavy industry, especially one which is designed to service a modern army and navy. The country lacks certain types of coal and iron ore and oil reserves, to mention only the more outstanding requirements of a modern army. The Army deliberately set out to gain control of such resources in China. The first major move was the penetration of Manchuria; then came the creation of the state of "Manchoukuo"; and finally the drive into China.

The Army then made further use of the lack by telling the people that the nations standing in its way were attempting to strangle Japan by cutting her off from access to vital raw materials. The result of this was that the people felt that they were being deprived of something that was rightfully theirs, by the machinations of China, the United States, and Britain.

Developments inside China were also turned to the advantage of the program of the militarists. The steadily growing nationalism of China during the 1920's and early 1930's was jeopardizing Japan's special position in China. Japan enjoyed the special treaty rights that other foreign powers had in China, but in addition, because of her geographical proximity to the continent, had also developed much more extensive interests, both legal and illegal. The Chinese grew ever more resentful of the position of the Japanese.

The natural development of a national consciousness among the Chinese took the form, among other things, of a violent anti-Japanese movement, sponsored both officially and unofficially. Thus, the Japanese militarists were able to tell the Japanese people, first, that Japanese legitimate interests in China were being threatened by Chinese who failed to understand Japanese aims; and second, that the anti-Japanese elements in China would have to be wiped out before the two countries could live together as "peaceful" neighbours. Thus, the Japanese people were told not that the militarists were implementing a program of imperialistic expansion in China, but that the Japanese Army was simply trying to protect Japanese rights in China, and to eliminate certain Chinese groups which were "standing in the way of peace in the Far East."

The upsurge of Russian interest in the Far East was also used by the militarists to create a war psychology among the Japanese people. The victory over Russia in 1904–5 had not driven her out of the Far East. It created new causes for fear and distrust between the two countries. The growing strength of the Russians in the Far East, as expressed in the drive to industrialize Eastern Siberia, was another cause for fear in Japan.

The militarists used Russia, its Far Eastern strength and its ideology, to impress the people with the necessity of maintaining large armies for the "defense" of Japan against possible Russian attacks. The Japanese people were never allowed to forget that Russia was a dangerous potential enemy. One of the arguments for the invasion of Manchuria and the creation of the puppet state of "Manchoukuo" was that Japan had to have on the continent a buffer state between herself and Russia.

Thus a complex of developments outside Japan contributed both directly and indirectly to the propaganda arguments that were used by the Japanese government to justify in the eyes of the Japanese people both a policy of militaristic expansion abroad and the maintenance of a large Army and an expensive Navy for the purpose of carrying out that policy.

Finally, the insularity and chauvinism of the people were great contributing factors in the development of the spirit of militarism in Japan. Cut off from the flow of more liberal ideas that swept through the West after the first World War, and ignorant of the potential power of the United States and Great Britain, the people of Japan were not conscious of their limitations and of the limitations of the Japanese armed forces. Fed by victories over relatively inferior opponents, the Japanese people felt that the Japanese Army and Navy were as great as their propaganda said they were. They had never experienced the desolation and ruin that war brings in its wake. The weakness of China, Korea, and Russia had saved Japan itself from being visited by the destruction of war.

Indeed, the very fact that no battles were fought on Japanese soil undoubtedly contributed greatly to the acceptance of war and militarism. The Japanese people had never known the terrible destruction of war and saw it only through the propaganda of the military. To them war was only a succession of glorious deeds, and of sacrifices for the sake of the nation, which were made to appear to be something far grander than they actually were. The complete military defeat of the Japanese armies on the soil of Japan will make the Japanese people realize, for the first time, the devastation that their armies have wrought on the continent. They will be able to see that the militarists who have been living by the sword will have to die by the sword, and that it was they who brought Japan to ruin.

Japan's chauvinism was fed by the propagation of the idea of emperor worship and of the divinity of the Japanese islands and of the Japanese people. The successes of the Japanese Army and Navy reinforced these attitudes, for it was the standard line of the militarists that the "Imperial Virtue" was responsible for military successes. The armies were built up as the instruments through which the imperial virtue was to be spread throughout the world. It became the duty and responsibility of every Japanese to spread the glory of the emperor by serving the armed forces either directly or indirectly.

These factors, operating both inside and outside Japan, contributed to the growth of militarism and the use of war as a national policy. Some of the factors, of course, had little or nothing to do with Japan, but they all played into the hands of the men who ruled Japan. They were used by them to further the spirit of militarism that had flowed through Japanese life as a strong and enduring current for many centuries. They made war acceptable to the Japanese people. But one of the greatest contributing factors to the rôle of war in modern Japan was the success that accrued to Japan as a result of the waging of war.

In the last half century Japan has averaged better than one major war a decade. The first Sino-Japanese War of 1894–5, the "Manchurian Incident" of 1931–2, and the current war which began in 1937, all involved China. The war of 1904–5 was against Russia. Japan's participation in the first World War was directed against Germany. Finally, late in 1941 Japan invaded Southeast Asia, the Philippines, the Netherlands East Indies, and the islands of the Southwest Pacific, a move which aligned all great powers save Russia and Germany against her.

These wars were not wars of defense, although they were treated as such in Japanese propaganda. They were wars of aggression, each of which added something to the wealth of Japan, temporarily at least. They were the logical expression in foreign affairs of the ideas of the authoritarian state. They were the extension beyond Japan's borders of the militarism that had so long been characteristic of Japan. Although there is no definite proof that the makers of modern Japan deliberately adopted war as an instrument of national policy, the manner in which each war led logically to the next hints strongly that there was a master-plan behind the whole program of conquest.

When one regards the great gains that Japan won by means of war, it is not surprising that the Japanese people developed a positive attitude toward it. It was through war that Japan gained international prestige, territory, raw materials, wealth, and glory.

Until the war with China began in 1937 the Japanese people had every reason to believe that war was right, and that it was to their advantage to follow their military leaders into whatever venture they might attempt. A brief review of the wars in which Japan was involved prior to 1937 will indicate the great gains that accrued to the nation from them.

Japan did not begin her program of expansion prematurely. It has already been described how plans for an attack on Korea in the early 1870's were cancelled when the Iwakura Mission returned to the country with news of the strength of the West and Japan's relative weakness. The more impetuous members of the warrior class who were in favour of the blow at Korea were governed by their blind faith in their strength, but Iwakura and his fellows knew that Japan could afford to wait until success was assured. They knew that if Japan struck too soon, and failed, it would mean a great set-back. Their counsel prevailed and Japan waited for two decades before striking at the continent.

It was in 1894 that Japan challenged her great though weak neighbour, China. The issue was joined over the status of Korea, which was independent, though acknowledging Chinese suzerainty. Japan had recognized Korea's independence when a formal treaty was negotiated between the two countries in 1876. But Japan was definitely eyeing the peninsula, and China was anxious that it remain within the Chinese sphere of influence. China had protected Korea from outside aggression, as on the occasion of Hideyoshi's attempt to conquer the peninsula, and had aided the Korean rulers to maintain order within the country. In return for this, the Korean court paid tribute to the Chinese court, and when a new ruler came to the throne Korea asked China to recognize and to invest the new sovereign with the power to rule.

Although the immediate cause of the war was the situation in Korea, conditions in both China and Japan contributed to the outbreak of hostilities. China was desperately trying to retain at least nominal control over Korea, perhaps in the hope that if she succeeded she would regain some of the prestige that she had been losing in the face of the steady inroads that the Western powers were making on both her rights and her territory. Perhaps China was also desirous of warring against Japan because she underestimated the strength of the latter.

Japan, on the other hand, was anxious to gain prestige not because of growing weakness, but because of growing strength. Japan's leaders had been building up the country's military and naval strength steadily over a period of more than a quarter of a century. They were eager to test the efficacy of their new weapons, in battle. They felt that their new military machine was ready for the test of war, if not against the Occident, at least against a weakened China. But pressing internal problems also were driving Japan into war.

The Constitution had been promulgated in 1889, and the Diet had sat for the first time in the following year. It was proving to be a political instrument not amenable to the control of the oligarchy. In 1891 it was dissolved because of its opposition to the government. The third session, a special session in the spring of 1892, witnessed a bitter battle between the House of Peers and the Lower House over the budget. The fourth session was marked by another struggle over the budget, which was finally resolved only because the Emperor intervened. The next session was also dissolved. The sixth session saw the Lower House presenting an address to the Throne which impeached the Cabinet. The Emperor refused to accept it, and the Diet was again dissolved.

These bitter battles between the Diet and the Cabinet, which had the power to suspend it, and between the two Houses of the Diet were producing a crisis in the government. The House of Representatives, which was designed to be more ornamental than useful in the structure of the government, at least according to the Constitution and the plans of the oligarchy, was proving to be unexpectedly obstreperous and was threatening the power of the oligarchy.

But the war with China came at the very time when the crisis reached its height, just after the address impeaching the Cabinet had been submitted to the Emperor. The declaration of war (on August 1, 1894, two days after a Japanese sinking of a Chinese transport) immediately stilled the bitter battle that had been raging in Japan. There is room for suspicion that Prince Ito and his fellows were more than willing to see Japan go to war in order that their internal position be strengthened. Certainly the war tided them over a situation that was rapidly developing into a crisis for the oligarchy.

The war was short. China was beaten in little more than half a year. An armistice was agreed on late in March, 1895. The treaty of peace was concluded in Shimonoseki on April 17, 1895.

The Treaty of Shimonoseki marked a milestone in the development of Japan. The war had given Japan a tremendous amount of prestige. Few in the Occident had expected Japan to win. China's territory was huge compared with Japan's, and China's manpower seemed to be sufficient to overwhelm Japan by sheer weight of numbers. But few recognized the inherent weakness of China. Against the determination, the organization, the arms, and the discipline of its smaller neighbour, China was helpless. The rapid succession of victories and the quick triumph of Japan amazed the world. Tiny Japan was respected as having much more strength than anyone suspected.

The terms of the treaty placed the seal on the completeness of Japan's victory. China was forced to recognize Korea's independence, another step toward eventual Japanese assimilation of the latter. China had to give up the Liaotung peninsula, Taiwan, and the Pescadores islands off Taiwan, thus giving Japan invaluable bases for later expansion. Japan was forced to give up its claim to the Liaotung (now known as the Kwantung peninsula) peninsula by the three powers, Russia, France, and Germany, but the feeling aroused in Japan by this move was perhaps more important to Japan than the temporary loss of the territory. China was forced to pay an indemnity of ¥300,000,000, thus not only making Japan's war virtually costless, but also providing additional capital for the expansion of industry at a critical period in her history. A new treaty of commerce and navigation was to be negotiated in order to give Japan also the rights and interests enjoyed by the Western powers in China. In addition, Japan was also granted a virtually unrestricted right to build up her own industry in China. These were the major gains that accrued to Japan as a result of her war with China.

An aggressor nation could scarcely hope for a better war. It was short, which meant that it was exhausting of neither men, materials, nor machines. It resulted in substantial territorial, political, and economic gains. It added greatly to Japan's international prestige. And no enemy soldier set foot on Japanese soil.

Victory over China assured Japan of a dominant position over at least one of its Far Eastern rivals, but Russia still remained to be reckoned with. For years Russia had been regarded as the great threat to Japan's security from the north. To this traditional fear was added the rivalry between the two nations on the continent. Each was eager to build up influence and strength there. The inevitable clash of interests was to come in Korea, and China's Northeastern Provinces, more commonly known as Manchuria.

It was in these peripheral areas that China's influence was weakest. They were closest to Japan on the continent and thus more inviting. Finally, they lay in the path of Russia's expansion to the south. For Imperial Russia the bleak areas of Siberia were not promising fields for empire. In Korea there were not only ice-free ports, but also a better climate, more available natural resources, and in general a more promising field for exploitation. It was natural then that the interests of Russia and Japan should clash in Manchuria and Korea, where China's control and interest were weak, and where theirs had a greater chance to develop.

Russia's participation in the Three-Power Intervention in itself was sufficient justification, in Japanese eyes, for war. Japanese resentment against France and Germany was not as intense, for their interests in the Far East were neither as great as Russia's nor did they come into as violent conflict with Japan. Russia heaped injury on insult by leasing Port Arthur and Dairen on the Liaotung peninsula from China in 1898.

Russian and Japanese interests in Korea continued to conflict. The two governments in 1896 and 1898 warily reached agreements which ostensibly were designed to bolster Korean independence, but which were really aimed at maintaining a rough balance of influence. Japan perhaps was the gainer in these transactions, for in the 1898 agreement Russia promised not to "impede the development of the commercial and industrial relations between Japan and Korea."

In 1896, China and Russia signed an agreement by which the latter was enabled to construct the Chinese Eastern Railway, which was to supplement the eastern end of the Trans-Siberian Railway. This was a major gain for Russia in Manchuria, both economically and politically. During the Boxer Rebellion of 1900 Russia occupied most of Manchuria, and after assuring the other powers that she would withdraw her forces, failed to do so.

The tension finally broke, and the two nations were at war in 1904, Japan again striking the first blow without the formality of declaring war. The war lasted about a year and a half. This time the struggle was much more bitter than the war with China, but again Japan was victorious. Again Japan gained great prestige, for no one expected her to topple Imperial Russia, which was then regarded as one of the greatest of the world powers.

Japan's Navy crushed the Russian fleet, though not without heavy losses of its own. The Japanese armies, fighting in Korea and Manchuria, defeated the Russians in every major land engagement, but did not succeed in crushing the imperial armies. The Japanese expelled the Russians from Korea and were pushing them steadily back in Manchuria when fighting ceased. But Japan was perhaps even more eager than Russia to bring hostilities to an end. Men and materials were being devoured at a rate far greater than that of the Sino-Japanese War a decade earlier, and Japan's economy was beginning to stagger under the burden of replacing Japanese losses. Had the Russians held out for a few more months the result of the war might have been different. Overextended supply lines, ineptness in the field, poor staff work at home, and the general corruption and decay of the imperial régime made Russia weaker than Japan in the long run.

The treaty of peace was negotiated in Portsmouth, New Hampshire, in September of 1905, to the displeasure of both the Russian and the Japanese people, each feeling that its envoys had allowed the other to gain far too much. However, on the balance Japan was the principal winner, although she was not successful in gaining all that she had asked in her original demands at Portsmouth.

The result of the war was another major step forward in Japan's advance to a position of dominance in the Far East. Russia was forced to recognize Japan's "paramount political, military and economical interests" in Korea, a step which brought still closer Korea's doom. Japan took over the Russian lease of the Liaotung peninsula, thus gaining a base for major operations in Manchuria, which were eventually to split it completely away from China. Even more important, Japan gained control of the South Manchuria Railway, which was to be the instrument by means of which she was destined to develop her empire in Manchuria. Russia turned over to Japan the southern half of the island of

Sakhalin. In 1875 Russia had gained control of the entire island, by recognizing Japan's right to the Kuriles. Russia also agreed to grant Japan certain fishing rights along Russian possessions in the Japan, Okhotsk, and Bering seas.

The gains to Japan from the treaty far offset the loss of the indemnity which Japan had originally demanded from Russia, and which Russia refused to pay. The failure to gain the indemnity infuriated the Japanese people, who demonstrated violently against the government when it became known that Russia was not to indemnify Japan for the costs of the war. Since the war had almost caused a financial collapse in Japan, it is not surprising that the people (or more properly certain leaders) wanted an indemnity. But the foundations for a continental empire were laid by the war, and this was of much greater value to Japan than a cash indemnity would have been.

Japan's hand against Russia had been strengthened immeasurably in 1902 through the conclusion of the Anglo-Japanese agreement, signed on January 30, 1902, and in force for almost twenty years, after being renewed and altered in 1905 and 1911. The original document was in effect an agreement stating that England would recognize Japan's special interests in Korea, and Japan would recognize England's in China. Of course, both nations pledged that they recognized the independence of both China and Korea and in addition declared "themselves to be entirely uninfluenced by any aggressive tendencies in either country." In addition, the two parties agreed that "it will be admissible for either of them to take such measures as may be indispensable in order to safeguard those interests if threatened by the aggressive action of any other Power, or by disturbances arising in China or Korea, and necessitating the intervention of either of the High Contracting Parties for the protection of the lives and property of its subjects." They also agreed that if either party became involved in war "in the defense of their respective interests" the other would remain neutral and would use its good offices to prevent others from joining against its ally. In the event that another nation joined the war against either ally the other would immediately come to the assistance of its partner. Russia was the obvious object of the last two points.

The Anglo-Japanese agreement really marked the coming of

age of Japan as a great power. In this instrument the nation negotiated on a footing of equality and entered into a partnership with the greatest power in Europe at that time. This occurred less than half a century after Japan's doors had been opened by Commodore Perry. The first renewal of the agreement came in 1905 while the war with Russia was still going on, although it was not published until a few weeks later, after the Treaty of Portsmouth had been signed. In the new agreement it was provided that if either nation became involved in war "in defense of its territorial rights or special interests" in Eastern Asia or India the other would immediately come to its aid.

The new agreement placed mild limitations on Japan's earlier "right" to paramount position in Korea. It was agreed that Japan could take any measures she wished in Korea, "provided always that such measures are not contrary to principle of equal opportunities for the commerce and industry of all nations." Britain also agreed to enter Japan's war against Russia in the event that another nation joined forces with Russia against Japan. In the renewal of 1911, the clauses regarding Korea and India were eliminated, primarily because Korea had by that time been incorporated into the Japanese empire, as were those regarding the Russo-Japanese War. The alliance finally came to an end in 1921, as a part of the agreements reached at the Washington Conference.

Japan participated in the 1914–18 war on the side of the Allies and gained benefits far out of proportion to the efforts that she expended in helping to defeat Germany. The Anglo-Japanese Alliance paved the way for the participation of Japan in the war on the Allied side, although there are indications that in 1914 Great Britain was unwilling to see Japan join her as an ally because of the gains which might accrue to Japan as a result.

Upon her declaration of war Japan immediately started to expel Germany from Chinese soil. Chinese permission was not asked before Japan launched her attack on the principal German base of Tsingtao on the Shantung peninsula. The Chinese announced the establishment of a war zone on the peninsula to which all fighting was to be confined. But the Japanese soon fanned out from the war zone. The Japanese forces occupied Tsinan, one terminus of the Tsinan-Tsingtao railway, built by the Germans; seized all German properties; and took over complete control of the railway and of the customs, although their control over the latter was soon surrendered. Japan revealed no intention of returning control of the Kiaochow concession to China although she had announced in her ultimatum to Germany that it would be turned back to China. The Japanese offered the argument that the territory was really a rightful conquest and that since Japanese lives and Japanese money had been expended in expelling the Germans, Japan had won legitimate control of it. Japan did not finally retire from Shantung until 1922, as a result of the Washington Conference settlement.

The Japanese occupation of the German holdings was completed in November of 1914, and two months later Japan presented the infamous "Twenty-one Demands" to China. The effect of these demands, if the Chinese had agreed to all of them, would have been to make China a virtual Japanese protectorate. Japan failed to force her demands on China at the time, but in later years resorted to other means to dominate China.

Japan took advantage of European preoccupation with Europe's own troubles at this time in order to submit the demands. This technique of taking advantage of Occidental preoccupation has been frequently resorted to. The nature of the Japanese intentions was best indicated by the circumstances under which the demands were presented to the Chinese government. The Japanese Minister, Hioki Eki, presented the "Demands" to President Yuan Shih-k'ai, not through regular diplomatic channels, but directly to the President, and apparently virtually ordered him to keep them secret. But the Japanese plans failed. The news leaked out and foreign pressure helped to modify Japanese demands.

The Twenty-one Demands were divided into five groups. The first group, consisting of four articles, covered Japan's position in the Shantung peninsula, and in effect would have converted that Chinese area into a Japanese holding. The seven articles of the second group would have made Manchuria and Eastern Inner Mongolia into Japanese preserves. Japanese subjects would have been given special rights in these areas, and China would have been forced to consult Japan in the event that other governments requested railway or financial privileges in these areas. The two articles of group three covered certain Japanese mining holdings in China. Group four, a single article, was designed "with the object of effectively preserving the territorial integrity of China." China agreed "not to cede or lease to any other Power any harbour or bay on or any island along the coast of China," a move designed to prevent any other nation from challenging Japan's paramount position in China.

The fifth and final group of seven articles would have placed "influential Japanese" in the Chinese government as political, financial, and military advisers; given Japanese hospitals, temples, and schools the right to own land in the interior of China; placed Japanese in virtual control of the Chinese police system; given Japan control over Chinese armaments; granted Japan the right to construct certain railways in China; placed Japan in a position to veto the participation of foreign capital in the development of Fukien province; and given Japanese the right to preach in China. The last articles were so bare-faced in their infringement on Chinese sovereignty that the Japanese attempted to deny that they represented anything more than Japanese "wishes."

Japan was forced to back down in regard to many of the demands, but others were agreed to in two treaties, that of May, 1915, respecting Shantung, and another signed concurrently respecting Japanese rights in South Manchuria. Under the first treaty China agreed to abide by any agreement made by Japan and Germany regarding Shantung. The second treaty gave Japanese subjects certain rights in South Manchuria and more limited ones in Inner Mongolia. In notes accompanying the above treaties the Chinese government agreed to give preference to Japanese subjects in the employment of advisers, to consult with the Japanese government if it proposed to negotiate certain loans involving South Manchuria and Inner Mongolia, and to keep foreigners and foreign capital out of Fukien. In return Japan agreed to turn back to China the Kiaochow Leased Territory provided that the Chinese government made certain concessions regarding it.

Japan made economic gains out of her participation in the first World War that were at least as great as her political ones. Because of her limited participation in the war, she became one of the chief manufacturing centres for the Allies. Not only did her industrial structure expand greatly in order to satisfy these new demands, but also her gold profits were tremendous. She lost some of this economic ground during the severe depression that later struck the country, but she gained much in the form of an increased development of her industrial structure.

Japan also occupied the German-held islands in the Pacific soon after the beginning of the war. She was given a mandate over these islands at Versailles, after secret negotiations in 1917 between Great Britain and Japan had resulted in the former's recognition of the latter's rights not only to the islands but also to Shantung.

But in spite of the gains that Japan made during the first World War, one of the results was a temporary setback to the Army. The Army suffered a blow because of the failure of the so-called Siberian Intervention. In 1918, after the collapse of Russia, the Allies planned an expedition into Siberia, ostensibly to rescue some Czechoslovakian prisoners attempting to escape from Russia, but actually to keep an eye on Russian affairs in Siberia following the Revolution. Apparently both Great Britain and France wanted Japan to go into Siberia alone, but the United States objected. As a result it was agreed to send an Allied force, including American, British, French, and Japanese troops. Each was to send 7,500 men, but the Japanese sent far in excess of that number, estimates ranging from 25,000 to 100,000.

The Japanese troops ranged far and wide through all of Eastern Siberia and the northern part of Sakhalin. The Japanese aim seems to have been to create rather than to control disorder in the region, in order to provide an excuse for continued occupation. This military expedition cost the Japanese government an estimated half billion dollars and the net result was zero, although the Japanese forces remained in Siberia from 1918 until 1922, and in northern Sakhalin until 1925. The Army was severely criticized inside Japan for its part in this affair, and this was the sole occasion, until the present, that it emerged from a military venture without a considerable amount of added prestige.

Japan's next major blow was the "Manchurian Incident" of 1931–2. The struggle was inevitable. As a result of its victory over Russia in 1904–5 and the partial success of the Twenty-one Demands, Japanese penetration in Manchuria continued steadily. The spear-head of this penetration was the South Manchuria Railway, a semi-official Japanese company, which had charge not only of the railway itself but of virtually all Japanese activity in Manchuria. By 1931 Japanese investments in the South Manchuria Railway Zone were estimated at something more than a billion and a half yen, a stake more than worth defending. Japanese railway guards were permitted to protect Japanese lives and property within the Railway Zone, a narrow strip on either side of the railway, but the Japanese authorities interpreted the protective rôle of these guards very liberally. They were frequently sent out of the Zone into Chinese territory for the purpose of apprehending men who were suspected of having committed acts against Japanese persons and property.

This Japanese conduct could not but be galling to China, particularly since Chinese nationalism had been growing steadily under the Republic, and the Chinese were coming to be more and more resentful of the presence of foreigners on Chinese soil and the existence of the unequal treaties. The Chinese government was more and more eager to assert full sovereignty over Manchuria. The Chinese also began to develop Manchuria in areas outside the Railway Zone. Japanese interests, including the Government, declared that these developments, particularly the construction of new railway lines, threatened the Japanese investment in Manchuria.

The combination of growing Japanese aggression in Manchuria and of steadily developing Chinese nationalism could not but end in open conflict. On September 18, 1931, the Japanese Army authorities charged that a Chinese attempt had been made to derail one of the crack Japanese express trains on the S.M.R. Using this incident as a pretext, and there is abundant reason to believe that the incident was Japanese-inspired and Japanese-committed, the Japanese Kwantung Army, which was charged with the duty of policing Japanese interests in Manchuria, moved swiftly. The key Manchurian cities were speedily occupied and Chinese forces in Manchuria were mopped up. Within a few months the Japanese were supreme in Manchuria. But the Kwantung Army did not resort to the crude device of absorbing this vast area of some 300,000 square miles into the Japanese empire. Instead, they created the "free and independent" state of "Manchoukuo." The Japanese argument was that Manchuria had never been a part of the Chinese Empire, and that the Japanese Army simply assisted the Manchurians to gain their independence from the corrupt and inefficient rule of the Chinese government. The first step was the establishment of local and provincial administrations under the "guidance" of the Japanese Army. But as a result of a "spontaneous demand for an independent government" which had never existed before the invasion, the Kwantung Army proclaimed "Manchoukuo" a new nation on February 25, 1932, with Henry Pu-yi, the last Manchurian Emperor of China, as the Chief Executive. The form of this new government was a republic, but the Japanese masters of the puppet state apparently thought that a republic was too un-Japanese, and so in 1934 the "Empire of Manchoukuo" was established and Henry Pu-yi was set on the throne as the first emperor, with the reign name of Kang-te.

In "Manchoukuo," as in Japan, sovereignty resides in the emperor. Although Japan has maintained the fiction that "Manchoukuo" is independent, the actual rulers of the country are the numerous Japanese advisers who stand behind each "Manchurian" who has been given office in the government. The commander-in-chief of the Japanese Kwantung Army, who is *ex officio* Japanese ambassador to "Manchoukuo," is the all-powerful controller of the country.

Naturally Japan did not allow "Manchoukuo" to develop her own economic destiny. The breaking away of the area from Chinese control was the signal for the flooding of the area with Japanese businessmen and Japanese capital. The S.M.R. immediately began to expand its holdings greatly. One of its first steps was a program of railway construction, especially in those areas which abutted on Siberia. In addition, "Manchoukuo's" heavy industries were greatly expanded, not only to take care of the increased demands of the Railway, but also to build up the "national defense" of the new country. The S.M.R. was, of course, kept under strict control of the "government," which meant control by the Kwantung Army. During the late 1930's, however, the holdings of the S.M.R. were gradually reduced. It was made more and more into a strictly transportation company, while its industrial functions were taken over by the Manchuria Industrial Development Corporation and other Japanese companies which were working in close co-operation with the Japanese Army authorities. The great emphasis on the development of heavy industries was decided upon so that Japan could have a supplemental industrial structure on the continent for the supply and maintenance of its armies.

Although Japan's great industrialists were given the major share of the work of developing this new Japanese holding, the government also held out to the people glowing economic prospects which were supposed to grow out of this new seizure of territory. Japanese propaganda at the time of the "Incident" declared that "Manchoukuo" was a vast treasure-house, control of which would guarantee Japan's economic future. It was pointed out that the stores of raw materials would guarantee Japan's military strength and that the vast undeveloped areas of "Manchoukuo" would help relieve the population pressure within Japan.

Glowing pictures were painted of the country as a site for Japanese colonization. Hard-pressed Japanese farmers were told that in Manchuria there were vast farms which would be theirs virtually for the asking. The area was painted in all the romantic colours of a frontier region which was a challenge to the spirit of adventure and enterprise of all Japanese. Plays, novels, moving pictures, and success stories were used by the government in an attempt to encourage emigration. The Japanese government was eager to develop the areas in the border region opposite Siberia, where the settlers would be potential fighters in the event of a war with Russia, and it was also desirous of relieving the pressure on the land in Japan proper. Grandiose plans were announced throughout the 1930's for the settlement of millions of Japanese in Manchuria over a period of several decades. Information on this program is scarce, but apparently the government's program did not meet with an enthusiastic welcome from the people.

The Japanese people have never been eager to migrate to distant lands. The climate of Manchuria is inhospitable. Agricultural methods in Manchuria for the most part differ greatly from anything that the average Japanese peasant has known. In fact, the entire way of life in Manchuria was completely different from that of Japan. In order to combat these latter difficulties, the government attempted the experiment of transplanting whole villages from depressed areas in rural Japan to the continent. Another difficulty attached to the immigration program was its expense. The farmers themselves were in no position to finance the expensive job of moving themselves and their families to the new country and of starting out on an entirely different type of farming. Government subsidies aided, but the very farmers who might be most desirous of bettering their lot were unable to help themselves because of their poverty.

On the whole, however, the Army profited from the "Manchurian Incident." It won a major victory in a short time, with few casualties and at little expense. It gained control of an immense area of land. It successfully sold the Japanese people on the idea that the venture was undertaken in order to help "liberate" the "Manchurians" from Chinese domination. It gained access to badly needed raw materials. Last, but not least, it discovered that it could pursue its policy of aggression with no interference, other than verbal chastisement, from the Western powers.

But the move was not without its dangers. Japan had created a 1500-mile land frontier with Russia, where none had existed before save for a few miles in Sakhalin and in the extreme northeast corner of Korea. By moving into Manchuria Japan automatically created the necessity for the strategic expansion of railways on the Russian frontier, and for the development of heavy industry in the area. Of more immediate consequence was the fact that Japan, by this move, practically guaranteed that there would be a major war with China. The recovery of the Northeastern Provinces became one of the rallying cries of the Chinese.

For five years after the "Manchurian Incident" an uneasy peace, or rather absence of armed hostilities, existed between China and Japan. But Japan's designs on Chinese territory became ever more apparent, and China became increasingly conscious of the effect of Japan's aggression on her integrity as a nation. The new struggle began on July 7, 1937 as a result of a local clash between Chinese and Japanese troops not far from Peking. The initial incident was small, but the fighting spread rapidly and grew in intensity. War was not declared between the two nations until almost four and a half years later, when China formally declared war on Japan after the attack on Pearl Harbor.

Again the Japanese Army had great and spectacular victories to present to the Japanese people. Japanese forces quickly overran North China, were momentarily checked at Shanghai by the gallant Chinese armies, but soon swept up the Yangtze River to disgrace themselves forever at the rape of Nanking, and then overwhelmed the great Wuhan cities. By the end of 1938 Canton, the key city of South China, was also in Japanese hands. In less than a year and a half Japan controlled all of China's major pre-war industrial centres and showed herself clearly superior to the Chinese armies in frontal combat. But Japan soon found that although she controlled key points and key routes of communications she had not conquered China. The Chinese armies withdrew, it is true, but behind them the guerrillas took up the fight and kept the occupation forces in a constant state of uneasiness. And the Chinese spirit of resistance to the invader remained unbroken.

Again the immediate economic gains from Japan's early victories were great. The great Japanese monopoly capitalists moved in behind the army and played a major rôle in the exploitation of China. They, with Army assistance, controlled the looting of China's resources, and flooded the Chinese markets with Japanese goods. Thousands of small businessmen followed them into China, even though the Army instituted a policy of controlled migration. The Japanese communities in Shanghai, Peking, Tientsin, and other North China areas grew by leaps and bounds. Again there was tangible evidence that the policy of aggression paid great dividends.

But still the war in China dragged on its weary way. By every indication it should have been over. Japan had won the battles. Japan had gained control of China's pre-war industrial centres. China's armies were ill-equipped, ill-fed. Yet they fought on. China did not sue for peace nor for a cessation of hostilities. Japanese armies had to be maintained in the field, and Japanese soldiers had to fight and die, while Japanese civilians at home had to continue to sacrifice to support the cost of Japanese aggression. Japan was the victor and yet not the victor. She had won the battles but not the war.

Japan's Army and Navy had one more trump card. They attacked Pearl Harbor, and swept into Southeast Asia and the Southwest Pacific. They involved Japan in war with the United States, Great Britain, and almost all the rest of the world, save for a handful of neutrals and her two unnatural allies, Germany and Italy.

In six months Japan's Army and Navy had won Japan an empire greater than the wildest dreams of the most extreme chauvinists. One after another Thailand, Malaya, the Netherlands East Indies, the Philippines, Burma, and dozens of scattered islands came under Japanese control. French Indo-China had become a virtual Japanese protectorate even before Pearl Harbor. The wealth of natural resources that fell into Japan's lap as a result of these conquests was greater than any average Japanese could conceive. The victories won over the United States and Great Britain, particularly, were as dazzling as they were intoxicating. In the spring of 1942 most Japanese must have believed firmly that Japan was the greatest and strongest nation in all the world. Here was the fulfillment of all the dreams of empire that had ever been dreamed by any Japanese. The China "Incident" must have been swept into the background. But the empire, though won, was not yet secured.

The almost constant state of crisis since the opening of the country had served to keep the Army and Navy in the forefront of government activities. The very fact of war had served to entrench the militarists and those who thought as they did in positions of power. Nevertheless, civilian elements in the government began to come to the fore during the 1920's and there was a period when it seemed as if civilians might succeed to the positions of policy determination within the government.

The economic depression of the 1920's which necessitated retrenchment in arms expenditures, the unsuccessful venture into Siberia with its resulting loss of prestige for the Army, the current of revulsion against war that swept through the world following the war of 1914–18, and the advent to positions of influence of civilian Japanese not connected with the clans that had dominated the development of modern Japan, all contributed to the growth of civilian influence in the government. It was at this time that the highest point of party government was attained in Japan. It seemed for a time that Japan was on the threshold of a system of responsible government, dominated by political parties who were responsive if not to the mass of the people, at least to certain groups, namely the industrialists whose interests at the time were not governed by militarism and aggression. As has been repeated so often in these pages, the vital element of mass acceptance of the idea of responsible government, of government responsive to the will of the people was lacking in Japan.

The high point of civilian influence in the government occurred during the London Naval Conference of 1930, when the civilian elements of the government under the leadership of Premier Hamaguchi Yuko succeeded in imposing their will on the determination of Japan's naval policy. In October, 1929, the London Naval Conference was called for the purpose of limiting the size of the navies of the world. Japan, of course, was invited.

The Japanese delegation to the Conference was given instructions to the effect that Japan's fundamental naval policy was aimed at defense and security, and did not include aggressive intentions toward other powers. In addition, the delegation was specifically enjoined to obtain a seventy per cent ratio with the United States in eight-inch gun cruisers and in all auxiliary craft; to oppose either a radical reduction or the abolition of submarines, and to insist on the maintenance of Japan's submarine strength, which was not less than that of either the United States or Great Britain.

But Japan was not able to gain all these points. Senator James Reed of the United States and Ambassador Matsudaira Tsuneo, representing Japan in London and one of Japan's official delegates to the conference, agreed on the so-called "Reed-Matsudaira Compromise." Japan, while not abandoning her claim to a permanent seventy per cent ratio in heavy cruisers, was to receive only a sixty per cent ratio. But the United States agreed not to build up to full strength in this category until 1936, and until that date Japan was actually to enjoy a seventy-two per cent ratio in tonnage and an eighty per cent ratio in numbers. The compromise also included submarine parity between the two navies, but at a level lower than their present tonnage. This agreement immediately precipitated a struggle between the Foreign Office and the Navy Ministry in Tokyo.

The Foreign Office was eager to make the Conference a success even at the expense of the instructions given the Japanese delegation. The Japanese naval technical advisers at London wanted to reject the compromise immediately, even though it might mean the wrecking of the Conference. The Navy Ministry in Tokyo upheld this stand. Matsudaira had apparently actually arranged the compromise without reference to his technical advisers. The Foreign Office in Tokyo immediately overrode the Navy Ministry's views and instructed the Japanese delegation to accept the compromise, but not to commit Japan against any alteration or compromise in the future.

Premier Hamaguchi, commenting on the decision, declared that in arriving at the decision he had considered the "guiding spirit" of fostering international peace, the nation's economic and financial condition, and Japan's need for national defense. The treaty was finally ratified as it was agreed to by the Japanese delegates.

The victory of the Foreign Office was a major one for the civilian arm of the Japanese Cabinet, and it posed a problem of tremendous import for Japan's future. That problem was, briefly: does the Cabinet as a whole control government policy in so far as it affects problems of national defense or are the War and Navy Ministries supreme in considering such problems? On this occasion the Cabinet imposed its will on the Navy Ministry, but the potentialities were ominous for the Army. If the civilian branches of the government could make this interpretation stick, it would mean that they could control any and all aspects of the Japanese armed forces. The next move might be one to slash the size of the Japanese Army itself.

The London Naval Conference was not only the final victory of the civilians in the government over the armed forces, but it made inevitable a further struggle over the question. Six weeks after the ratification of the Treaty, Hamaguchi was shot by a super-patriot for his part in the negotiation of the London Naval Treaty. Hamaguchi lingered on for almost a year before dying. His fate was symbolic of that of the civilian moderates in Japanese government. Less than a year after the London Naval Conference the "Manchurian Incident" was to deal a death blow to the moderates.

If a definite date can be placed on the beginning of the major drive of the militarists toward empire and complete domination of Japan, it is probably September 18, 1931, when the "Manchurian Incident" started. The "Manchurian Incident" was not only an expression of the militarists' policy of aggression on the continent, but it also marked the beginning of their campaign to bring Japan itself completely under their control. The invasion of Manchuria really broke the power of the civilian elements as a force in Japanese government.

The seizure of Manchuria from China has been denounced as Japan's first major act of aggression against China, an act which paved the way for the present war. However, the internal consequences of the "Incident" were as great as the external ones. If it was an act of aggression against China, then it was also a major step in the direction of the establishment of an authoritarian régime at home. In a very real sense the "Manchurian Incident" was the militarists' answer to the London Naval Conference.

The steadily increasing tension between China and Japan in regard to the latter's holdings in Manchuria has already been described. But the political situation inside Japan was also building toward a climax.

The conflict over the question of disarmament was clearly highlighted in an address delivered by War Minister General Minami Jiro on August 4, 1931, to the heads of Army divisions. The significance of this address is clearer when it is recalled that it was delivered just six weeks before the outbreak of the "Manchurian Incident." Minami declared that the Army reform that had just been carried out represented the minimum strength of the Japanese Army in terms of its needs. No further reduction was possible, and the money that had been saved by the reduction should be used for other purposes, especially the mechanization of the Army, he said. In regard to expenditures, he declared that those who criticized the Army for being extravagant frequently overlooked the Army's sacrifices.

He also bitterly attacked the whole idea of disarmament, then the subject of world-wide discussion. He asserted that those who advocated disarmament in Japan were indulging in propaganda inimical not only to the interests of the Army, but of the nation as well. He expressed the hope that the divisional commanders he was addressing would "co-operate with the authorities in correcting such mistaken views and in disseminating correct information regarding the situation of the officers and men" under their command. A final section of his speech dealt with Manchuria and Mongolia. He declared that those two regions had important relations with Japan in the fields of politics, economics, and national defense. He said that as far as Japan was concerned the situation in those regions was serious and was being steadily aggravated. This unfavourable state, he added, was due to the change of the international situation and the decline in Japanese prestige due to the "decrease of the Japanese people's courage and spirit."

Six weeks later, immediately after the "Mukden Incident" which opened the attack on Manchuria, the clash between the Army and the civilian branches of the Cabinet broke out. The Cabinet's view of the situation was that the Incident was purely local and could be handled by the Cabinet through normal diplomatic channels. The Cabinet in Tokyo actually killed an Army order issued by War Minister Minami calling for reinforcements to be sent into Manchuria from Kwantung Leased Territory and Korea. Premier Wakatsuki, a civilian, was backed principally by Foreign Minister Shidehara and Finance Minister Inouye, both regarded as anti-militarist and liberal in outlook, as was Wakatsuki.

The Army, however, completely ignored the Cabinet's moderate attitude. It took the stand that the Chinese were entirely to blame for the situation and consequently the world powers could not object to any action taken by the Japanese. China, the Army argument ran, would demand that the Japanese Army withdraw before any negotiation, but that the latter would not agree to this. Meanwhile, although the Cabinet had killed the Army order for the sending of reinforcements, General Hayashi Senjuro, later to become what was perhaps Japan's most inept premier, took the responsibility of sending reinforcements on his own. The reinforcements were sent, of course, and the Army program for the occupation of Manchuria was carried out without let or hindrance.

The Foreign Office, while the Army moves were going on, was vainly attempting to force Japan to remain faithful to her commitments in the Nine-Power Pact, signed at the Washington Conference, under the terms of which Japan had pledged herself "to respect the sovereignty, the independence and the territorial and administrative integrity of China." Japan had also signed the Kellogg-Briand Pact in 1928, pledging not to resort to war as an instrument of national policy. However, she wriggled out of the latter commitment by declaring that this war was one of "defense," a type of war which was recognized by the Pact.

From this struggle the Army emerged supreme. Not only had it done exactly what it desired to do, but it also treated the Cabinet with contempt by overriding both its desires in the matter and its attempt to keep Japan within the limits of its treaty commitments. The civilian branch was not only powerless before the Army, but also discredited. The Army had again been successful in using force in Japan's foreign relations. Henceforth the major decisions of the Japanese government, almost without exception, were made by the Army, the Navy, or men in sympathy with their programs.

The Army's successful defiance of the civilians in the government was a large stride forward in its drive to power in Japan. Within a few months there began an informal, but highly effective, campaign which was to drive the moderate civilians in Japan still farther from positions of power and influence. This was a deliberate campaign of terror, carried out by Army and Navy personnel acting unofficially, and by chauvinistic civilians whose ideals were identical with those of the armed forces. Assassination, attempted assassination, bombings, inflammatory speeches, and pamphlets all served notice on moderate civilians that their counsel was no longer desirable in Japan. The public opinion represented by liberal politicians and industrial leaders was soon suppressed.

Early in 1932 Finance Minister Inouye and Baron Dan, head of the great Mitsui interests, were both assassinated. These murders were merely the prelude to the "May 15 Incident." On that date in 1932 twenty-five Army and Navy officers broke into the Premier's official residence and assassinated Premier Inukai Ki, a civilian moderate. Almost simultaneously bombs were thrown at the residences of the Lord Keeper of the Privy Seal, the Grand Chamberlain (both officials close to the Emperor), and at the Tokyo Metropolitan Police Headquarters, the headquarters of the Seiyukai Party, and at the Bank of Japan and the Mitsubishi Bank. Virtually no damage was inflicted by any bomb. Later it was discovered that plans had also been made to attack five power stations supplying electricity to the Tokyo area, but these attacks did not come off.

The men who were involved in the murder of the Premier were brought to trial, but not to justice. The trial became in effect a gigantic parade of chauvinism. The accused were allowed to deliver long lectures on the "purity" of their patriotic motives. The press reported every word of the testimony and the murderers were made into virtual national heroes because of their "patriotism." A few of the men were given prison sentences, ranging downward from life, but by 1940 all but one were free.

The naval cadets involved in the murder gave as their primary motivation the results of the London Naval Conference. They declared that they were aroused by the "encroachment on the Supreme Command by the civil authorities." They asserted that Admiral Kato Kanji, then Chief of the Naval General Staff, had intended to submit a memorandum to the throne on the Conference, but that the Lord Keeper of the Privy Seal and the Grand Chamberlain had prevented it from reaching the Emperor.

But the motives of the plotters were far more complex than mere dissatisfaction with the results of the London Naval Conference. Their chauvinism had operated powerfully to drive them to their plot. They were dissatisfied with the 5–5–3 naval ratio of the Washington Conference and the position of inferiority in which it placed the Japanese Navy. They were "insulted" by the inability of the Western powers to regard with a sympathetic eye the Japanese grab of Manchuria. They felt a deep resentment toward the American Exclusion Act, they said.

Economic conditions influenced the plotters. There was distress in the rural districts of Japan, and out of this grew their vague feeling of dissatisfaction with the existing social and economic systems of Japan. The plotters, and their predecessors in the earlier assassinations, attempted to overthrow what they called the "capitalistic oligarchy." They demanded state control of finance and industry, both as a measure to eliminate the capitalists and as a device to insure the more efficient arming of Japan. They were dissatisfied with the capitalistic system in Japan and wanted to overthrow it; but they wanted to supplant it not with a "dictatorship of the proletariat," but with a "dictatorship of the state." Their cure for the economic ills that were besetting Japan was not socialism or communism, but the complete diversion of the energies of the state to conquest and aggression.

The "May 15 Incident" marked a long stride toward the domination of Japan by the military. The assassinations indicated that no prominent civilian was safe from attack by extremists either in or out of the services. The conduct of the trials of the men involved in the assassinations showed that actual and potential victims of assassins not only lacked the protection of law, but that public opinion was definitely against them. The attack on the capitalists meant that it was not healthy to be either a businessman or a spokesman for the protection of the interests of big business. The attacks on political party headquarters and the attempt to involve the parties in the corruption of the businessmen also indicated that parties were in a position where they could no longer play a dominant rôle in the politics of Japan. The attack on the groups within Japan that might possibly stay the sweep toward power of the militarists was bearing fruit.

The culminating point of the career of the assassins of the 1930's was the "February 26 Incident" of 1936, which was in actual fact more of a small-scale mutiny than an outbreak of controlled lawlessness like the "May 15 Incident." Early on the cold, stormy morning of February 26, 1936, the new group of assassins loosed a floor of terror on Tokyo. Viscount Saito Makoto, Lord Keeper of the Privy Seal; General Watanabe Jotaro, Inspector-general of Military Education; and Takahashi Korekiyo, Finance Minister, were murdered. A Colonel Matsuo was also assassinated because he was mistaken for his brother-in-law, Premier Okada. Admiral Suzuki Kantaro, Grand Chamberlain, was severely wounded. Prince Saionji and Count Makino Nobuaki were also on the assassins' list, but both escaped. Army units occupied the Metropolitan Police Headquarters, the War Ministry, and the Diet Building. Rumour said that they also surrounded the Imperial Palace and made the Emperor a virtual prisoner. The Tokyo *Asahi,* regarded at that time as Japan's foremost liberal journal, was attacked and some of the presses put out of commission. Tokyo was placed under martial law and heavy units of the Japanese Navy moved into Tokyo Bay to meet any emergency. The mutiny lasted four days before being suppressed without additional bloodshed.

The instigators and actors in the "2–26 Incident," as it became known, moved almost too far and too fast for the militarists. They were not allowed to become the pampered darlings of the chauvinists as had the actors of the "May 15 Incident." Some of the mutineers and some civilians who had been involved with them were speedily brought to trial. There was no foolishness this time. The Army was too vitally concerned with the problem of the mutiny. Thirteen officers and two civilians were executed. Something like forty additional officers were given prison sentences.

That the mutiny was no free-lance plot of a few super-patriotic young officers was proved by the involvement in the case of Major General Mazaki Jinsaburo, vice-chief of the General Staff. Mazaki worked closely with the young officers involved in the mutiny, and seems to have acted as a kind of go-between for them and the Army authorities. He was brought to trial, but was acquitted in September, 1937, because of "insufficient evidence." A Tokyo English-language paper described his opinions as follows: "When he looked at the domestic and international situations, he was concerned over the friction between the military and civil services and between those in high places and those in low places. He also was aware of serious defects in national defense and war preparations, which he feared would entail disadvantages in supporting diplomacy. The only manner in which the situation could be remedied, it seemed to him, was to bring about the formation of a truly strong Cabinet that would possess the moral force and power necessary for enforcement of national policies. He was accustomed to voicing concern over the possibility that if weak and wavering men occupied high places in the government and showed themselves weak in diplomacy, there could be no guaranteeing that there would not be bloodshed, the future of the nation being so beset with sources of worry."

The Army itself did not allow itself to lose face because of the mutiny in its ranks. As a matter of fact, it actually made capital of the incident. The Army admitted that Army men were involved in the affair, but declared that the fundamental causes for their action lay outside the Army. Army circles were quoted in the press as saying, "In order to eradicate the possibility of such occurrences, the people must co-operate with the Army." Thus, by implication at least the Army was taking the line that the people at large were as responsible for the mutiny as the Army itself.

The Army was reported to have put forth a two-point policy which was necessary in order to prevent the recurrence of another "incident." The two points were "clarification of national policy" and "stabilization of national life." An examination of the contents of these two points reveals the road which the Army was laying out for the nation.

"Clarification of national policy" involved an attack on Westernism in Japan. The things of the West had to be examined "to make sure all is in accord with the proper conception of the State and proper moral principles." As an inevitable corollary to this anti-foreign pronouncement, there was the statement that the national education policy would have to be changed and textbooks revised. Again we have the combination of attack on ideas from the outside and the nurturing of the "pure" Japanese way of life.

"Stabilization of national life" was really a thinly disguised program for putting the nation on a war footing. The Cabinet system, according to these Army demands, had to be strengthened and the authority of both Houses of the Diet and of the Privy Council had to be curtailed. The control of the Army over the Cabinet makes the reason for this move clear.

Measures had to be taken to equalize the tax burden and to increase the amount of government revenue. The Army plans for Japanese industry were even more ambitious. State control over industry had to be strengthened. Foreign trade had to be promoted, especially in order to insure adequate supplies of raw materials from abroad. Japanese industry had to be spread over larger areas by encouraging traders and manufacturers of moderate means and by developing a plan of farm aid through a program of rural industries.

National life was to be additionally stabilized by the expansion of "national defense." The air force had to be expanded. Mechanized armaments had to be increased. The forces in "Manchoukuo" had to be enlarged. More divisions had to be added to the Army. Weapons had to be modernized. Materials for military operations had to be collected and stored. Finally, the foreign policy had to be renovated. The chief aim of the new policy was to be "stability in East Asia."

It is hard to see how the Army could be so ungrateful as to execute a handful of young officers who had been involved in the "Incident." The stain on the Army's honour made by the "Incident " was small indeed when compared with the immense propaganda use that the Army was able to make of the affair. Not only did it escape with reputation virtually untarnished, but it also involved the people in its own failure to maintain discipline by placing on them the responsibility for allowing a "provocative" situation to develop.

The Army and the super-patriots had not, however, joined in actual legal combat with the forces that might be expected to oppose it. It had succeeded in driving out of power the men who had been successful in forcing the London Naval Treaty on the nation. It had almost eliminated the demands for disarmament, for a more moderate foreign policy, and for the control of the Army by the civilian arm of the government. But all this had been accomplished by extra-legal means. A real test of strength in the formal arena of politics had not yet been joined. That was to come early in 1937.

In January, 1937, the Army brought about the downfall of the Hirota Cabinet, prevented a highly popular statesman, Lieutenant-General Ugaki Kazushige, from assuming the portfolio of premier, and forced the formation of a Cabinet which it believed would follow the policies that it favoured. All this grew out of a criticism of Army policy delivered by a courageous Diet member.

After War Minister Count General Terauchi had resigned in a huff because the Army had been charged with meddling in politics in violation of the Emperor Meiji's injunction to Army and Navy men to stay out of politics, the Hirota Cabinet fell because, of course, no other Army man would willingly serve as Army Minister as long as the "insult" to Army honour went unchastised.

Following the resignation of the Cabinet, Ugaki received the imperial order to form a new Cabinet. Although an Army man, he belonged to the more conservative wing. He was responsible for a reduction of the size of the standing army in the mid-1920's, but it appears that this move was more in the direction of increased efficiency than a blow to the military. After his retirement from the Army, he was appointed Governor-General of Korea, and is recognized as being one of the more humane and progressive individuals to fill that office.

Ugaki had been given the imperial command and was hailed as the man of the hour by the press, and public opinion seemed to be entirely in his favour. Yet in spite of all these factors he was forced to abandon his attempts to form a Cabinet. The sanction of the Emperor, the backing of the people, and the willingness of others to serve as ministers under him meant nothing at all, for the Army had decided that he was not a fit man to serve as premier. His ideas were not "correct." Ugaki invited three different generals, all men of influence and representative of the dominant opinion in the Army, to serve as his War Minister, but all refused. Consequently, Ugaki was forced to admit defeat. Angered by the thwarting of his plans, Ugaki asked that he be relieved of his rank as a general on the retired list, because he felt that if he were called to active service he would not be able to carry out his duties. It was said that he wrote to a member of the Privy Council voicing his regret at the situation in the Army, and declaring that Japan stood at the crossroads of fascism and parliamentary administration. The man who finally received the nomination and succeeded in forming a cabinet was General Hayashi Senjuro, who had defied the Cabinet and sent "reinforcements" to Manchuria in 1931. Hayashi was generally regarded by Japanese observers as being the most inept person ever to hold the premiership.

The implications of this incident are worth careful analysis. Terauchi's actions indicated two things quite clearly. First, the Army was not going to tolerate any criticism of its actions; and second, it had ready at hand an extremely effective instrument for avoiding searching questions. Terauchi's resignation did not impair the position of the Army in any way. Of course, he had to retire as War Minister, but the solidarity existing among the top military leaders meant that his policies were not repudiated and that all that was involved was the nomination of another individual of like opinions to see that the Army policy was continued.

In regard to the question of the Army's refusal to co-operate with Ugaki it might be thought that that action constituted an act of disloyalty to the Emperor. Had not Ugaki received his orders from the Emperor himself? Was he not then, to all intents and purposes, the agent of the Emperor? The Army did not take this view. They, in terms of their arguments, were not opposing the imperial will by opposing Ugaki. They were defending the best interests of the country, and therefore the imperial person, by opposing Ugaki. He did not think in the proper terms, hence, he was dangerous to the nation. Thus, it was entirely within the limits of their loyalty that they opposed Ugaki. The argument, from a strictly logical point of view, was perhaps tenuous; but the

Army was not interested in logic; it was concerned with its own position.

It should be quite apparent that because of their independent position, the Army and Navy were in a position to dictate to the rest of the Cabinet exactly what they wished. Men were not lacking who saw the danger of this situation as far as liberal government in Japan was concerned, but like their fellows in other parts of the world they did not have the same unity of purpose, the same positive drive to power that their political adversaries possessed. There was to be no necessity for a repetition of this dramatic interference on the part of the Army in the affairs of the Cabinet.

The Army showed clearly by its conduct in this case that it was supreme in Japan. The structure was still not perfect, but there was no other group in Japan, governmental or otherwise, which could now challenge the position of the militarists. It was they who would from that time on make the decisions for Japan, both at home and abroad.

On July 7, 1937 the Army struck at China. This was the first step toward Japan's eventual involvement in war against most of the rest of the world. Four and a half years later came Pearl Harbor. The war in China was connected clearly with the strike at the United States, the Philippines, Southeast Asia, and the islands of the Southwest Pacific. The long years of war on the continent had brought only territory to Japan.

There had not been the quick victory with great winnings that had characterized Japan's early wars. The Japanese industrial machine was able to support a much longer war than had been the case during the war against Russia, but it could not go on indefinitely. The Japanese people saw that although Japan had won all the battles (according to Japanese propaganda at least), the Army was still far from winning the war. Generalissimo Chiang Kai-shek and the Chinese people showed no inclination to sue for peace. The Army's propaganda had trumpeted long and loud that Japan was not fighting the Chinese people, but Chiang and his Anglo-American supporters. The Japanese people apparently believed this propaganda completely, but the Chinese people did not. The realities of the invasion and occupation were too stark, too ever-present to be offset by sweet words which fell far short of matching realities.

Four years of war had deprived the Japanese people of more and more of the few liberties they had had. It had forced their standard of living down to levels much lower than what the country had known even during times of depression during the 1920's. An increasing number of men were failing to return from China or were coming home disabled. The pressure of war was becoming greater on the life of the people at home. The war in China was, in short, a stalemate. The early optimism which had existed during the brilliant drives through China in 1937 and 1938, was beginning to give way to a feeling of resignation, if not depression.

Japan was becoming further isolated internationally as a result of her aggression in China. The more the Army became involved in China the less it was disposed to recognize the rights that other nations had built up there for decades. Japanese attacks on American and British nationals and property became more frequent. Japanese propaganda at home began to blame the United States and Great Britain for the Japanese failure to "liquidate" the China "Incident." The assistance that the two countries were giving China was a convenient excuse for the militarists to explain their failure to defeat the ill-armed and ill-equipped Chinese Army which, by all rules, should have capitulated months before. The militarists did not mention the valuable war supplies they themselves were getting from the United States and Great Britain.

Japanese aggression and terror in China were also creating, particularly in the United States, a growing anti-Japanese reaction. Press criticism became sharp. Although the United States had been supplying Japan with many of the materials that she needed in her war against China, the government, with public support, began gradually to cut off such supplies. This, in turn, was seized upon by Japan's propagandists as evidence that the United States not only failed to "understand" Japan's motives in China, but was actually standing in the way of the realization of Japan's "legitimate ambitions" in China.

As Japan began to look toward the south, the United States, Great Britain, and The Netherlands began to stand more firmly together in formulating plans for the possibility of a common defense against Japanese aggression. Their increasingly sympathetic attitude toward China brought into existence the so-called ABCD (American, British, Chinese, Dutch) grouping in the Far East.

Japan seized upon this situation as "proof" that Japan was being encircled by these potential enemies. The closer military co-operation of the three powers was backed up by economic steps that either cut off or reduced the amount of vital raw materials that Japan was getting from the still free areas in Asia. Thus, on two counts Japanese propaganda was able to persuade the people that they were being throttled by a combination of unsympathetic powers.

Though Japanese propaganda was enlarging on the potential military danger to Japan of the four powers, Japanese espionage must have known well how little prepared the Philippines, Malaya, and the Netherlands East Indies really were to resist a determined, well-planned, and well-co-ordinated attack by Japanese forces.

Japanese agents must have also submitted encouraging reports on the situation in the rest of the world. Russia, with whom Japan had concluded a neutrality pact in the spring of 1941, was quailing before the mighty blows of the Wehrmacht. With astonishing speed Germany had overrun vast stretches of Russian territory, including some of Russia's key industrial areas. The occupation of Moscow itself seemed a not-too-distant prospect. Russia was definitely in no position to become interested in developments in the Far East.

Germany was supreme in Europe. She dominated the continent and was beating back Russia steadily. Italy, if not as powerful as Germany, was not a liability to Japan's cause.

Great Britain was in a precarious position. She seemed on the verge of losing complete control of the Mediterranean. Germany's submarine campaign was taking a heavy toll of British shipping. British air power was able only to peck at Germany's Festung Europa. There seemed to be little chance that Britain would be able to launch an invasion of the continent that would beat back the Nazi conquerors.

Internal conditions in the United States must have been encouraging to the Japanese militarists. The anti-war sentiment in the United States after the first World War was stronger than it had been anywhere else in the world. It had reduced the American Army almost to the vanishing point. It had shackled the American Navy. It had prevented the full development of American potential air power. It had created in the American people a very real desire never again to become involved in the quarrels of the rest of the world. It had resulted in a renunciation of military force and all that it stood for.

Isolationism was strong in this country. Great sections of the people wanted to become involved in no one's affairs. Europe and Asia could stew in their own juices as long as they did not bother the United States. No one wanted war. No one wanted to fight for other peoples. Japan saw clearly enough what that meant in Asia. American words denounced Japanese actions in China, but American actions were conspicuously missing.

To Japanese militarists, steeped as they were in war, it must have seemed unlikely that the American people could shed almost overnight the convictions that it had developed over two decades. Only a few months before Pearl Harbor, the Selective Service Act came within a single vote of being repealed. If the move had gone through, even the handful of men who had already been mobilized would have been sent back home.

Japanese military attachés in the United States must have been very gleeful indeed when they clipped from American newspapers and sent back to Tokyo pictures of American equipment that was used in summer manœuvres in 1941. Stovepipes labelled "anti-tank gun," two-by-fours marked "artillery," spoke eloquently of the state of American armaments at that time.

The industrial situation within the United States was also favourable to Japan. Industry was carrying on business as usual in spite of the fact that the government was attempting to build up national defenses. Labour strife was frequent. Neither capital nor labour was interested in the problems of war production. There was no indication that American industry could turn quickly and efficiently to the problem of arming the country. Selfishness at both ends of the structure would effectively stand in the way of effective production.

The American standards of living, notoriously the highest in the world, also must have given the Japanese militarists a sense of security when they were planning their new war. Soft living, luxury, and extravagance when balanced against Japanese austerity could not but lead the militarists to believe that, even if aroused, the American people could not produce fighting men with the courage or the stamina to withstand the attacks of the Japanese soldier. There is little reason to doubt that the Japanese Army was certain that the American soldier could not develop into an efficient fighting unit. The whole American attitude toward discipline, toward military training, toward war itself, was the very antithesis of that of the Japanese. There is little wonder then that the Japanese tended to underestimate the fighting potential of the American.

Thus, the militarists were faced with a situation in which the war in China had reached a stalemate that might eventually lead to their discrediting, if it was not broken. They were also undoubtedly victims of their own propaganda, believing that they were being encircled and strangled by the ABCD powers. Their reading of the international situation must have revealed to them that the Axis powers in Europe were militarily of great strength and that the Allies could not hope to break that strength. It showed also that the United States, Japan's most dangerous enemy, was in no position to wage a major war. Russia, her traditional enemy, was pledged to neutrality toward Japan and was also in dire military straits in Europe. In this situation the military must have decided that only a stroke of great boldness and brilliance could save Japan from the bankruptcy of her hopes in China. If the drive to the south was successful, the dreams of empire would be realized and not only would the China Incident be finally liquidated, but also Japan's enemies crushed forever.

Although it was to the advantage of the militarists to gamble Japan's future in the greatest military venture the country had ever undertaken, it would be a grave mistake to assume that they had forced an unwilling people into a war, against their wishes. Tradition, history, the success in war, chauvinism, insularity, Japanese belief in Japanese propaganda, and "thought control," plus all the other factors that have been described in these pages, created attitudes in the Japanese out of which arose the ambitions of the militarists and which led to an acceptance of those ambitions by the masses of the people.

Military defeat will lead to the elimination, at least temporarily, of the militarists, that is, the Army and the Navy. But much more must be brought about in Japan if the conditions which have permitted the growth of militarism and war are to be eliminated.

Chapter VIII

THE FUTURE OF JAPAN

The defeat of the Japanese Army and Navy will not alone mean the end of Japanese militarism. The crushing of her military strength is one of the necessary conditions for the uprooting of Japan's militarism, but it is also only one of the conditions; it is not in itself the final act.

A purely military defeat of Japan will mean the end of the current war in the Pacific, but such a defeat will be only partial. Japan can still emerge from this war as Germany did from the war of 1914–18, defeated but with all the potentialities for bringing about a later and greater holocaust. The complete defeat of Japan will be attained only when the political, economic, and social conditions that have created Japanese militarism and aggression have been eliminated.

Japanese militarism is not the Japanese Army and Navy. It is not a few generals and admirals. It is not the willingness to die for the emperor. It is not the plots of a few evil men. These are only its surface manifestations. It is really a way of life and a set of attitudes held by the Japanese, not because they are born with them but because they have inherited them from centuries of Japanese historical development. Modern Japanese militarism is the product of a combination of age-old social, political, and economic factors. In past Japanese history nothing short of a revolution could have eliminated militarism and the conditions which gave rise to it. That revolution did not occur. To-day the approaching military defeat of Japan is creating the foundation for the attack on both the oligarchy and militarism which have for centuries dominated Japanese political life.

We do not yet know the shape that defeat for Japan will assume, though we are sure that it will be inevitable and smashing. The manner in which defeat is inflicted on Japan and she is forced to accept unconditional surrender will play an important rôle in determining the future of the country, not only in terms of Japanese internal development, but also in regard to her relations with her neighbours and the rest of the world.

What the United Nations are planning in the way of peace terms for Japan has not yet been revealed. They are, however, pledged to the unconditional surrender of Japan. The phrase, "unconditional surrender," is ambiguous even though it is uncompromising in its simplicity. It is ambiguous because it goes no farther than the enemy's act of laying down his arms. It means that we shall force the enemy's surrender, but the doctrine of unconditional surrender does not in itself imply that we shall take the necessary and fundamental steps to prevent the enemy from waging war again in the future.

The United Nations cannot enunciate genuine peace terms for Japan until the time that they know what kind of a Japan will be left for them to deal with. The amount of devastation wrought on Japan, and the type and extent of social, economic, and political change that the stress of war may bring to Japan are all unknown factors. The degree of political wisdom that the United Nations can bring to bear on the problem of Japan is also of crucial importance.

The worst type of war that could be fought against Japan in terms of the post-war world order that the United Nations seem honestly striving to build, and in terms of Japanese national interest, would be a war of annihilation, a war in which Japan would not agree to unconditional surrender. Assuming that the United States continues to bear the major burden of the offensive against Japan, this would result in the loss of thousands of American lives and the expenditure of a tremendous amount of American national wealth. The same would hold true for other members of the United Nations to the degree in which they participate in the war against Japan. It would also result in the effective destruction of Japan as a nation. A war of annihilation would mean that most of Japan's cities and towns would be bombed into complete ruin; that the Japanese economic structure would be pulverized; and that so many Japanese, both civilians and military personnel, would be killed in battle that Japan would cease to exist as a nation.

This is the kind of total, uncompromising, fight-to-death war that Japan's militarists would like us and their people to think that we are going to have to fight. But although we shall have to keep the possibility in mind until the war is finally won, it is unlikely that the war will assume this form when it is finally carried to the shores of Japan.

A clue to the possible course of events in Japan has been furnished in the battle of Saipan. In the intense, bloody struggle on that island, many Japanese took the fantastic course of committing suicide rather than fall into American hands. The horrible and macabre quality of these acts has served to obscure the more significant fact that more than fifteen thousand civilians did come over to our lines during and after the fighting. This is not the mass, national *harakiri* that some experts predict will occur when the Battle of Japan is opened.

The very intensity of the chauvinism of both the military and civilian extremists is an argument against a course of action on their part which would lead to the total destruction of the Japanese nation. National extinction would mean not only that they could not avenge the defeat that will be inflicted upon them, but also that Japan could never attain the world domination that they have envisaged for her. Those who believe so blindly in Japan's destiny will not be willing to die before its attainment. Neither will they want to render it impossible for succeeding generations to make it manifest in the event that the current attempt fails. They can plan and wait, wait for the day that they hope will come when the vigilance of the rest of the world relaxes, as it has on so many occasions during Japan's recent career of aggression.

We must remember that although Japan has some twelve centuries of fairly reliable recorded history, she is a young country as far as her relations with the rest of the world, excluding China, are concerned. As a force in world politics she is barely half a century old. Her leaders would naturally feel that Japan can afford to wait. The promise of world domination, dim as it might seem in the face of defeat, will act as a powerful deterrent on many Japanese when it comes to a question of choosing between a doubtful future and the blackness of present annihilation.

At the other end of the scale from national annihilation lies the prospect of a negotiated peace, which would be to the long-term interest of the rulers of Japan to conclude, if they could. To us this would be catastrophic. In order to avoid this disaster, we must remember that what may appear to us to be harsh peace terms may not appear so in the long-range plans of the men who control Japan. Faced with the prospect of absolute and complete destruction of the economic structure of the country and the loss of much of its manpower, it is conceivable that the Japanese government might express its willingness to accede to unconditional surrender. They could agree to the mass surrender of the armies of Japan, the surrender (or scuttling) of the Japanese fleet, the demilitarization of Japan, and the temporary policing of Japan by occupation forces. In the eyes of the United Nations this might seem to be complete victory and unconditional surrender, but it would not be to the Japanese. It would be humiliating, but it would not be final.

Such a peace would leave untouched the internal structure that has made Japanese militarism and aggression possible. Not only would the conditions that have given rise to militarism remain, but also there would be added the powerful motivation of revenge and the desire to make the next war completely successful. What is more, the leaders of Japan would know that if we agreed to such a half-way peace we would still be ignorant of the basic foundations of Japanese life, and that at some time in the future our interest in the problems of the Far East would again lag and the doors would once more be opened for a resumption of their career of aggression. One of our most powerful weapons against the recrudescence of militarism will be complete understanding of Japan, not only for our own defense, but to serve notice on Japan that we know her and that our knowledge not only reinforces our determination, but also gives us the strength to see to it that she shall not again let loose aggression against her neighbours, be they near or far.

Between the two extremes of war-to-the-death and what would from the Japanese point of view be an eventually profitable negotiated peace lie many other possibilities, all of which will be conditioned first by the manner in which the United Nations carry the war to Japan, and second by the manner in which the Japanese population reacts when war is actually brought home to the islands.

We are definitely pledged to carry the war to Japan's shores, and to occupy the country for an indefinite period of time. If the invasion and the occupation are characterized by bitter and vicious fighting and by fanatical resistance to our forces, the prospects for the future will not be bright. We should have resisted to the end, and we should have refused to knuckle under to the administrators that would have been brought in to govern us, had the Japanese mounted an invasion of the United States in the early months of the war. We can scarcely expect less from the Japanese, especially since so many of them have been so thoroughly indoctrinated in the belief that their land is divine. We can look forward to bitter resistance not only from the armed forces, but also from a substantial percentage of the civilian population.

Once fighting has ceased in Japan we shall be faced with the new problem of administering the areas which we have decided must be occupied. The prospect is not a pleasant one for those who have been selected for this duty. The coming of the Westerners to Japanese shores in the nineteenth century resulted in a campaign of assassination and intimidation on the part of the Japanese die-hards. Those Occidentals had come to Japan peacefully and were there because of agreements negotiated between the governments concerned, but the Japanese reaction was bitter. It will be infinitely more so after the invasion of the country by armed force.

The men who will bear the major responsibility for the administration of Japan presumably will be individuals selected not only for their courage and professional training, but also for their knowledge and understanding of the ways of men. We know too that the number of Americans who have the necessary professional training and a knowledge of the Japanese (who most assuredly are not Europeans in outlook) is infinitesimal. The training of the administrators-to-be will be as thorough as it possibly can be under the circumstances, but there is bound to be friction arising out of failure of the administrators and of the population to understand each other's actions. We can expect that for months no administrator can feel safe in his job and few United Nations military personnel will be in a position to feel a sense of security.

There are too many extreme chauvinists in Japan. Such post-combat friction is certain to compound the bitterness arising out of the actual invasion.

We shall be regarded as enemies when we land on Japanese shores and we shall be regarded as enemies after the fighting has ceased. This will not create an atmosphere in which peace terms can be discussed calmly and rationally.

We can impose a cessation of hostilities on Japan because we have at our command the necessary force to beat down Japanese military resistance. But we cannot impose the conditions of peace on the Japanese people. First, there is nothing in the American tradition (assuming that Americans will carry the major share of the burden of administering Japan) that has fitted Americans for the task of ruthlessly uprooting the ideas of a people and of supplanting them with new ones. We have helped to change the ideas of the Filipinos, but the Philippines were an American possession, not an enemy country, and their struggle for independence, which began long before we gained control of the islands, had given them a political consciousness that was not too unlike our own. We have never had a tradition of ruthlessness designed to further the attainment of political goals, either at home or abroad. If we went into Japan with the idea of encouraging the political co-operation of the Japanese, we would handle the intransigeants with kid gloves. We might impose the death sentence on a few, but for the rest our punishment would be merely prison sentences. We would not resort to mass executions or to political terrorism in our attempts to make the Japanese abandon the type of political philosophy that has made them dangerous. In other words, we would not use force and terror, their own weapons and the only ones they understand, against the extremists in Japan.

More important than our lack of inclination to force new ways on the Japanese is the fact that the Japanese people, though politically immature, are not politically unsophisticated. They have been sedulously indoctrinated with the ideas of Japanese chauvinism. Their political attitudes are mediæval, narrow and bigoted, but they have been given something to fight for in the terms of Japanese political philosophy. Their desire to protect their land from the "defilement" of foreign feet is as strong as our desire would be in the face of a foreign invasion that threatened to kill the liberties that we have come to cherish as an integral part of our lives.

In our eyes emperor worship and the belief that Japanese soil is sacred are not worth fighting for, but they give a political content to the Japanese resistance to our invasion. We cannot confront them suddenly with an alternative political system and expect them to welcome it, any more than Japan's militarists could have expected us to become overnight a nation of emperor worshippers, after the military conquest of the United States.

If Japan is to become a peaceful nation and if she is to assume a new, though minor, position in the society of nations, the task of preparing her for her new rôle must be a co-operative one. To-day we are preparing the way for the new Japan; to-morrow the Japanese must assume the task.

At present, paradoxical as it may seem, we are working harder for the liberation and the reconstruction of the Japanese and their country than they are themselves. The destruction of the military power of Japan is the first step in the re-orientation of the Japanese toward a politically more mature philosophy of government. We shall continue to bear the major share of the work until the Japanese military machine is crushed and the Japanese people indicate their willingness, if they have it, to accept unconditional surrender. From that time on our task will become less important and that of the Japanese people more so. It is only the Japanese people themselves who can bring about the final regeneration of their nation and themselves, so that they can live in peace with the rest of the world. It is they who must destroy the attitudes and the institutions which have made the authoritarian state and its aggression possible. If the people begin this work of destruction soon enough, it will not only ease the task of crushing Japanese militarism but will also pave the way for co-operation between representatives of the people and our administrators.

The forces that led Japan into war against most of the world and that have made her name synonymous with aggression and treachery have grown directly out of Japanese history. Consequently, Japan must make a complete break with her past if she wishes to regain the confidence of the world. Whether Japan can do this by methods short of revolution is debatable. But the break with the past must be of such a nature that it can scarcely be described by a term short of "revolution." The political and economic oligarchies, emperor worship, and the strictures on the inflow of foreign ideas must be abolished. If this comes to pass, the consequences cannot be described by a word less than "revolutionary."

What Japan must go through is the political, economic, social, intellectual, and moral equivalents of the French Revolution, the Russian Revolution, the Reformation, the Industrial Revolution, and the Renaissance. It is only thus that much of the primitive and mediæval deadwood that encumbers Japan's political and economic orders can be cleared away. This she can do only with the encouragement of others outside her borders, but the major part of the responsibility must be shouldered by the Japanese. To pile such a program on top of military defeat makes the future of Japan seem indeed dark. Yet it is the test through which Japan must pass if she is to attain political maturity.

There seems to be little chance that such a break with her past will take place in Japan. Japan, as has been pointed out so many times in these pages, has never known a true revolution. But to say that since one has never occurred a revolution will never occur is false reasoning. A revolution, if such it may be called, may not follow the classic pattern of the French and Russian Revolutions, yet certain factors are building toward an unprecedented situation in Japan which may lead to a dramatic break with her past.

First, what are the factors which will work against the appearance of revolution in Japan? The Japanese seem to have an almost unrivaled political solidarity which, of course, centres around the emperor. Such solidarity argues that there is little chance for political cleavage to develop out of which violent political dislocation would eventually evolve. We must remember, however, that the very fury of the efforts of the state police to eliminate all non-Japanese political theories indicates that those who knew Japan best, namely her leaders, were unsure of the stability of the people if they were offered a choice of political systems.

The large and efficient Japanese police systems, the state police under the control of the Home Ministry and the gendarmerie under control of the Army, have been and will be effective checks on the development of political discontent. They are in possession of the weapons and they are backed by the authority of the state.

But the Japanese people have chafed under the rule of the police. The petty officiousness of the police has been felt in one way or another by most Japanese. There is nothing in this relationship to date that would indicate that the Japanese public will rise without provocation against the police, but there is a tiny seed of discontent that may possibly arrive at sudden and violent flowering if other conditions within Japan foster attacks on authority. But even so the weight of power as expressed in control of weapons will be definitely on the side of the police.

The rigid system of censorship and suppression of printed material that has operated in Japan has also undoubtedly kept at a minimum the flow of ideas that might seriously challenge the foundation of the present order.

In addition, the tremendous inertia of tradition, custom, and patterns of political and economic thought and behaviour will serve to hold in check violent and widespread outbreaks against the present system. The riots of the peasants during the Tokugawa period do not form a political tradition in Japan. They were simply events symptomatic of the unhappy state of the people of that time. They had no real ideological foundation and as a consequence there is nothing in Japanese tradition that would support the use of popular violence against the established order.

These are powerful arguments to offer against the possibility of a revolution in Japan. Under normal circumstances they would be sufficient to safeguard Japan against the violence of revolution, as they have in the past; but the most important thing about Japan's present position is that it is absolutely unprecedented in Japanese history. Many factors, such as the threat of foreign invasion and severe economic dislocation, have been present previously. But the combination in which they are now appearing and the fact that there are new ones never before known in Japan, argue that the unprecedented situation to-day may have unprecedented results.

First of all, Japan is standing on the brink of invasion and of complete military defeat. In the thirteenth century the Mongol hordes succeeded in establishing bridgeheads in northern Kyushu, but they were driven off and never really invaded the country. In the late sixteenth century Japanese armies were forced to evacuate the Korean peninsula after a tactical success, but a strategic failure. At that time they fell back to a Japan that was strong and politically unified. Japan has won all her wars in the modern period up to the present; now she is not only going to lose a war but also will see before her a Japanese army and a Japanese navy that have been decisively defeated and actually crushed in battle. If the Japanese militarists have thrived on victory, defeat will seriously undermine their position for the first time in Japanese history.

After a triumphant career of aggression the Japanese militarists have been engaged in an unprofitable war with China for almost eight years. The Japanese people have seen their standard of living deteriorate steadily since 1937, and at a rapidly accelerating rate since the first flush of the great victories of early 1942. They are seeing, first hand, for the first time, what the devastation of modern war is. Now they know what has been visited on the people of China for years by the Japanese Army and Navy. They know that the policies of the Japanese militarists have resulted in the deaths of more and more Japanese men with nothing to show for it. Military defeat, disregarding the possibility of a desperate war-to-the-death development as outlined above, will inevitably bring with it a revulsion of feeling, no matter how temporary, in regard to war and the bearing of arms.

The unrelenting pressure of military defeat will undoubtedly intensify the normal social, economic, and political dislocations of war which are already evident in Japan. The economic situation within Japan is as unprecedented as the military situation. Japan has been swept with civil war with all the consequent devastation and suffering that follow in its wake. Japan has been plunged into the depths of economic depression with starvation and privation bearing heavily on the population. Such periods of economic dislocation have arisen out of Japanese domestic crises for which Japanese and internal Japanese developments alone were responsible. But the economic dislocations that have been visited on Japan during the past eight years have grown directly out of the policies of foreign aggression that have been favoured by the most powerful groups within Japan. Thus, there is a situation in which Japanese within Japan can be held accountable for the suffering of the Japanese people, because of the miscarriage of plans which demanded the expansion of Japanese power outside of Japan itself. The argument is a tenuous one, but in a situation such as that which Japan is approaching it might possibly be used with telling effect against the present rulers of the country.

Steady deterioration in Japan's economy, especially in so far as the livelihood of the people is concerned, will provide arguments for a political attack on the present régime. Empty bellies and cold backs constitute far more powerful political arguments than soap-box oratory. The Japanese have always had less than Western countries and they have been able to get along with less, but economic privation will create a situation in which politically unorthodox arguments will have a far greater appeal than under normal circumstances.

Two factors above all others support the view that sweeping change within Japan is possible. For the first time in Japanese history during a period of crisis the Japanese people, by and large, are literate, and in addition Japan has known ideas which are totally foreign to the accepted political philosophy of the country. The Japanese government, as has been described, deliberately fostered the educational system in order to make the masses of the people more susceptible to the doctrines that were being imposed on them. Mass indoctrination in the tenets of Japanese chauvinism could not be effectively carried out unless the Japanese population had attained a level of literacy which would make it possible. How well the rulers of modern Japan have succeeded in this task is only too evident.

As a consequence of the policy of the promotion of literacy, the Japanese people for the first time are in a position where they can be counter-indoctrinated. They can now be exposed to ideas which they have not known before. The problems of counter-indoctrination are tremendous, yet the possibility is there.

The existence of non-Japanese political ideas may play an important rôle in the future changes within Japan. Although all ideas that seemed to have the potentiality of undermining the accepted order have been driven underground, the fact remains that living Japanese on all levels of society have studied and discussed such diverse political philosophies as democracy, socialism, and communism. The ideas have been abroad in the land, even though on a limited scale, and have found Japanese converts. Consequently, for the first time there is the possibility of the development of a genuine ideological cleavage within Japan. It is to be noted that the political ideologies mentioned above all challenge the basic ideas of political and economic oligarchy that have been the foundation stones of Japanese authoritarian society. This is not to argue that we can expect a Japanese revolution overnight, but it is designed to indicate that the potentialities of ideological cleavage do exist in Japan.

If genuine revolution is to come in Japan, the problem of leadership is the principal difficulty. In pre-war days it was fashionable to say that Japan would be saved by the "liberals." This group was never clearly defined. The consensus of Western opinion seemed to be that the liberals in Japan consisted of a few courageous Diet members who would occasionally challenge the soundness of the plans of the military, a few Japanese big businessmen who, because they were educated in the West, and seemed to derive their dividends solely from peaceful trade would not let a program of aggression alienate all of Japan's friends, and a few Japanese intellectuals who likewise thought as Occidentals did. When the crucial time came, these liberals did not stand in the way of aggression that had been laid out by the militarists and chauvinists who were the real rulers of Japan. They lacked the vital driving force of conviction that animated their opponents within Japanese society. They held their views as individuals, not as members of a cohesive group that would fight for their ideals. Their political philosophies were intellectual exercises, not articles of faith. The communist and socialist leaders from whom leadership might be expected have been ruthlessly silenced.

On the other hand, there have been many students, professors, and others who, given the proper conditions, might possibly emerge as leaders of an opposition to the miltarists. They have known, and perhaps still cherish, ideas which would form the foundation for an active attack on the militarists and all they stand for. They are anonymous and they have been driven underground. The chances are not great that they will become the leaders of the new Japan, and yet their very existence inside Japan is a new factor in the development of Japanese society.

The prospects for a genuine revolution within Japan are not bright, yet the flow of events is creating a situation in which a powerful protest against the established order may be possible, and there are individuals in Japan who might have the proper ideology and the right qualifications for leadership to fit them to lead the attack against the established order. It is impossible to predict with certainty the possibility of revolution in Japan, yet we must not overlook it.

If Japan is to break with its past, what must be accomplished in order to make Japan a nation which can live within the framework of a stable world order and which can contribute to the maintenance of world peace? The historical factors which have made Japan an aggressor have been described in detail. It is with her historical past that Japan will have to break if her people are to have genuine happiness and if she is again to be accepted as an honourable member of the family of nations.

The defeat of the Japanese Army and Navy will not be only military in character. It will have political repercussions as well. For the first time in seven centuries the military will be removed from a position of political power, for the military elements that have dominated the Japanese political oligarchy since the end of the twelfth century will have been crushed. But this alone will not be sufficient. The whole structure of oligarchic government must also be eliminated. As long as the political control of Japan is in the hands of a few individuals, be they militarists or democrats, there will always remain the possibility that the major decisions in Japanese government will again be made by individuals from the same mold as those who have brought so much suffering not only to Japan, but to her neighbours as well. The basis of government in Japan must be widened for the protection not only of the Japanese people, but of the rest of Asia and of the rest of the world.

The task of destroying the formal aspects of political oligarchy will be comparatively simple. The defeat of the Japanese Army and Navy will automatically eliminate many of the officers who have been responsible for the policies of Japan in recent years, either as planners or as the ruthless field officers who have led the Japanese forces. Death in battle or suicide will break the back of the present officer clique, although it will not end the possibility of the recrudescence of like-minded officers later on. Military defeat will also bring to an end the power over the government of Japan that is now in the hands of the War and Navy Ministers who, as has been pointed out, are in key positions to control both the personnel and the policies of the Japanese Cabinet.

The Privy Council, the repository of reaction, has no true organic connection with the government. It has simply acted as a brake on the growth of less autocratic, more responsive features of government and governmental policy. It initiates no policy, but acts simply in an advisory and review capacity. Its personnel and the manner of its choosing guarantee that few progressive measures will receive Privy Council approval.

The House of Peers of the Diet will also have to be either eliminated or else reduced to a completely powerless position in the Japanese governmental structure. It, too, is a reactionary stronghold. It has been to the interest of the Peers to defend the established order and to prevent widespread popular participation in government.

Besides the reduction in the power and influence of the War and Navy Ministries two other major changes will have to be made in the administrative system. First, the police must be removed from the control of the central government. Both normal police functions and censorship and "thought control" must be taken from the hands of the central government. The system of state police has given the oligarchy an all too effective means for the control of Japanese society. The censorship and thought control functions of the state must be reduced drastically in scope and removed from their association with the police. The removal of the bonds of thought control will permit the free importation of the ideas that Japan must have, if she is to orient her national thinking in new and fruitful directions. The police system must be converted so that it will more nearly resemble the local system that is established, say, in the United States. Although the maintenance of law and order is a highly important function of the police, the system as it has operated in Japan has been not so much in the direction of law and order as such, as in the direction of the suppression of all thought and action which have been deemed, at the arbitrary discretion of the state, to be dangerous to the established order.

Likewise state control over education as it has existed in Japan under the Ministry of Education must be abolished. While it is true that state control is at least partly responsible for the rapid construction of a modern system of education, it is likewise true that that control has enabled the government to institute a long and systematic program of indoctrination in the importance of conformity to the oligarchic order. The fragmentization of control over education, although it may reduce the efficiency of the reconstruction of the Japanese educational system, will check the danger of the development of a new type of ideological indoctrination simply by making impossible the maintenance of a monolithic structure of thought. It will no longer be possible to use exactly the same text-books with exactly the same ideas in all parts of the country.

Certainly the re-education of the Japanese will be one of the most difficult of tasks. The pressure of war on Japanese society has already done much to undermine the educational structure of Japan. Defeat will do more. Violent social and political dislocation will bring Japanese education to a state near chaos. It will then be possible to begin from the ground up in the re-orientation of the Japanese mind and the reconstruction of the Japanese educational system. The task will be long and difficult, but the result may finally be an educated people rather than a merely literate one.

The House of Representatives of the Diet will have to be revitalized, so that it will truly represent the interests of the Japanese people. Certain constitutional reforms, such as the return to the hands of the House of the control of the budget, will be necessary. The elimination of some of the outmoded political institutions of Japan will in itself automatically result in the increase of power of the House. The great essential, however, will be the political education of Japanese people so that they will be able to understand and to make workable a system of democratic government.

The crux of the problem of political reform in Japan is the political education of the Japanese people. To-day they are mediæval in their political thinking. They have proved that they cannot live in peace with their neighbours and with the rest of the world as long as their political thinking is in terms of that of the Middle Ages. Their mastery of the techniques of modern war has made their political backwardness thrice dangerous.

The Japanese people have never been allowed to rule them-

out of geographical propinquity, efficient shipping services, and cheap labour, that enabled her to supply goods for the Asiatic markets where purchasing power was low. It will be a knotty problem in economics, politics, and ethics for the United Nations to decide whether or not Japanese light industry should be permitted to revive to the extent that it can service the Asiatic market, at least until the rest of Asia can build up its own consumers' industries to the point of at least semi-self-sufficiency.

The post-war economic future of Japan is not bright. Indeed, the internal economic problems will probably be of a nature much more difficult to solve than the political problems. Yet they must be solved if Japan is to build a political structure that will guarantee internal stability and peaceful relations with the rest of the world. The destruction of the present economic oligarchy will be the first major step in that direction. Some of the destruction will be carried out by the military action of the United Nations; the rest must be done by the people of Japan.

If the destruction of the political and economic oligarchies is a major condition for the reconstruction of Japan, then a great modification of the position of the emperor is basic. He is the foundation of the political oligarchy, besides being the centre of the greatest concentration of wealth in Japan. He has been made the foundation on which internal authoritarianism and external aggression have been built. If he disappears, or if his present position is modified so as to be almost unrecognizable, much will have been done to clear the way for a better political order in Japan.

It is impossible to foresee what will happen to the present Emperor and to the Imperial Family. The best solution to the problem would be a revolutionary wave which would destroy the whole imperial institution as that of Russia was destroyed during the Revolution there. Such a revolutionary act would be the ideal means of disposing of the emperor, for the Japanese themselves would have destroyed him. There would then be no tradition of a hated foreigner destroying the sacred institution of the emperor. The worshippers of the emperor would not be driven underground to plot a restoration of the institution and to drive out a hated invader. If the Japanese did rise against the emperor, it would mean that there would be inside Japan a vigorous anti-imperial-institution movement which could be relied upon to subdue any possible restoration movements. It would also result in civil war within Japan over a fundamental question of political ideology. Such a civil war would be a most healthy development for Japan's future stability. A civil war fought on these lines would be bloody and painful for Japan. It might take years for the nation to recover a degree of political stability. But it would be a healthy purge that would rid the country of the most dangerous element of its political mediævalism. It would also tend to break down the carefully nurtured idea that all Japanese are bound together in common worship of a common ancestor, the Sun Goddess, and of a common ruler, the Emperor. If Japanese fights against Japanese over the question, it will reveal a fundamental ideological cleavage which will destroy the monolithic structure of political thought which has been the strength of the oligarchy in modern Japan. It would also assure the development of a reasonably complete revolution in Japanese political attitudes by channeling political thought in basically new directions.

Thoroughness of indoctrination of the great mass of the people, rigid police suppression of any possible anti-imperial movements, and the absence of a firmly rooted rival political philosophy make it unlikely that in the immediate future the emperor will become the target of a revolution. However, we must not forget that the conditions of war and the effect of a crushing military defeat may result in a combination of circumstances that will foster a violent reaction against the imperial institution.

At the opposite end of the scale from a revolutionary attack is the possibility that the United Nations will take care to maintain the emperor in his present key position in the event that a violent Japanese reaction against him does not develop. It can be argued that the emperor can be manipulated politically for the purposes of the United Nations, as he has been on numerous occasions in the past by the Japanese oligarchy. It is conceivable that the victorious United Nations would assume the position that as long as Japanese attitudes toward the emperor remain unchanged, his name would be sufficient to command obedience to the laws and the regulations that the conquerors of Japan would promulgate for the people. For example, the emperor could be used to order the Japanese Army and Navy to lay down their arms. If they failed to do so, they could be charged as being rebels against the imperial authority and will, and could be hunted down as such.

If this program is followed by the United Nations, it can succeed only if their representatives in Japan are as ruthless as they are intelligent in their manipulation of the emperor. They must be prepared to persecute those who act against the expressed will of the emperor as ruthlessly as the present rulers of Japan have acted toward those Japanese who have challenged the position of the emperor. They must be sure that their ultimate goal is the destruction of the imperial institution, or at least its reduction to a relatively harmless position. If the United Nations plan to use the emperor, they must understand and see clearly the implications of their failure to act wisely. The manipulation of the institution is not its destruction. If the purpose or the vigilance of the conqueror of Japan wavers, then it will be possible for unregenerate chauvinists to emerge and to use him as they have in the past, as the symbol of the power of Japan and of her "right" to rule the world.

Assuming that the imperial institution will continue to exist and that it will not be destroyed by revolution, it is still possible that the emperor can be "denaturalized," so that he is no longer as dangerous as at present. One of the most effective means of doing this would be to make him "human" once more. He could mix with his people. He could speak on the radio. He could abolish many of the primitive rites which are still a part of his duties. He could end the court rituals that have been retained in order to surround his position with mystery and awe. He could command his subjects to treat him as if he were one of them. He could abolish the stilted and honorific language which must now be used in referring to his activities. He could command that he be known by his personal name and not by the impersonal title of "Tenno Heika" (freely, "His Majesty, the Emperor"). By thus reducing himself to the level of all human beings, he would get rid of much of the mystery that gives him his rôle of god-on-earth. Another result would be that he would become a purely political institution and not a god, a part of whose divinity is expressed in quasi-political acts. He could become the legitimate target of assassins' bullets. His powers could be circumscribed by the popular institutions of government.

Yet such a procedure would still be a compromise. It would not eliminate the evil or the potentiality for evil that lies in the imperial institution as it now stands. There would always be the possibility that at some future date the institution could again be perverted to the uses of the chauvinists.

The direct and simple method of execution of the Emperor and all the members of the Imperial Family by the victorious United Nations would be the surest way of creating a dangerous underground restoration movement in Japan. The Japanese could find someone somewhere who could be presented as having a drop of imperial blood in his veins. Such a move on the part of the United Nations would not only make the work of administering Japan infinitely more difficult, but would also create the conditions for a relatively speedy revival of Japan's dangerous nationalism.

The Japanese people themselves must be encouraged in every way to rid themselves of the imperial institution. In the name of the emperor they have been cajoled into fighting wars of aggression and into accepting all the sacrifice and sorrow that war entails. They must be made to realize that the continuity of the nation and the happiness of the people are of far greater importance than the emptiness of the imperial institution.

The substitution of new values and of new ideas for the forces in Japanese politics and economics that have driven the country into war is another necessary condition for the reconstruction of the country. The abolition of the political and economic oligarchy and the destruction or complete renovation of the imperial institution will create an ideological vacuum in Japan that must be filled from without. We have seen how war and aggression have grown directly out of the forces that have molded Japanese history. We have seen how the ideological content of historical change in Japan has not been affected by the apparently revolutionary material changes that have come over Japan at periods of crisis.

When complete military defeat has been inflicted on Japan, every effort must be made to inject into Japanese life foreign political and economic ideas, many of which have already been known in Japan, even though they have been driven underground. The concepts of communism, of liberalism, of democracy, of socialism must be permitted to flow into Japan. A restricted number of Japanese have already known such ideas, but the masses of the people must be allowed to come into contact with them. Japan's political philosophy has been built on oligarchy and authoritarianism. It will be discredited by military defeat and internal chaos. European brands of fascism and authoritarianism will also have been thoroughly discredited, if not erased. The Japanese people will have to turn to other ideas for the necessary inspiration for the political and economic reconstruction of their country. Such ideas may not be adopted by the Japanese exactly as imported. The difference between the foreign concepts that will form the basis of the new Japan and what will eventually develop may be as great as the differences between American, French, and Swiss democracy.

The enthusiasm with which some Japanese adopted Occidental ideas before the campaign of repression went into high gear indicates that a truly substantial number of Japanese might welcome foreign concepts once the barriers have been battered down. We can expect that these foreign political, social, and economic ideas will not be fully understood by many, for the reason that they have grown out of environments far different from Japan's. Nevertheless, the Japanese will probably cast about desperately for new ideas once the old forms have been shattered.

The injection of new ideas may mean as great social chaos within Japan as military defeat will mean political and economic chaos. The institution of the family may suffer as greatly as it did in Russia in the early days of the Revolution there. If so, then a great stride will have been taken in the direction of the breaking down of the attitudes of authoritarian government. The destruction of the hierarchy of relationships within the family will be the first step in the destruction on all levels of social relationship, of the idea of absolute subservience to authority. If younger brother no longer bows to elder brother, if sister no longer bows to her brothers, if the narrow concepts of filial piety no longer are binding within the family, then the individual will have taken a long step in the direction of the control of his own life within the sphere of social relationships on the family level. This will mean in turn a loosening of the class relationships within the framework of society outside the family. On the highest level of authority, it will mean also an unwillingness to obey unquestioningly the dictates of the state.

The degree of social chaos in Japan will be great, if our victory is to have more than purely military significance. Chaos is not an agreeable state of society to be contemplated in any nation, friendly or enemy. But it must come to Japan if the Japanese people are to reject finally and completely the institutions that have brought them to their present unfortunate state. Internal chaos must be a form of expiation for the Japanese people. It will be the political adolescence through which Japan must pass if she is to attain the maturity that will fit her to be one of the family of world nations. The less chaos arising out of violent political, economic, and social change there is in Japan in the post-war period, the more certain it will be that Japan will again become a threat to world peace.

It will be a test of statesmanship of the victorious United Nations to allow Japan to pass through a period of disorder and dislocation that is necessary if she is really to be defeated and if she is to rebuild herself along sane and orderly lines in the future.

The problem of the future of Japan is not a problem of Japan alone. It is bound inextricably with the problem of the future of Asia and with that of the future of the world, unless as was indicated above the war is to end in the complete annihilation of the Japanese people.

Military defeat of Japan will not change the geographical fact of her location as a part of Asia. Post-war Asia will be almost as different from pre-war Asia as post-war Japan will be from pre-war Japan. Unless we adopt the unrealistic policy of a complete permanent quarantine and isolation of Japan from both her Asiatic neighbours and from the world, we must consider Japan as a part of the new Asia that has been rapidly developing since the outbreak of the war in Asia in 1937.

The pressure of the war in Europe and the fruition of carefully laid plans for its internal development, have made of Siberia an important part of Asia for the first time in history. Though Russia has been in Siberia for three centuries, in both Russian eyes and in the eyes of the rest of the world Siberia has been considered as nothing more than a vague concept. It had geographical meaning, but no organic geographical connection with the rest of the world. The settling of the area, the development of its natural resources, the erection of a structure of heavy industry, and the linking of the area to North America through the extensive development of air routes, have made Siberia into an integral part of a world economic and political complex.

The strained neutrality between Russia and Japan, the war in the Pacific, and the concentration of a tremendous amount of Russian effort on the war in Europe have retarded the development of relations between Siberia and the rest of Asia. Those relations are bound to grow rapidly in the post-war world, unless Russia is pursuing the most unlikely and unrealistic course of making Siberia a self-contained, self-sustaining economic area.

Another factor that must be kept in mind is the possibility of Russia's entry into the war in the Pacific. Since Pearl Harbor Russia has maintained a scrupulously impartial neutrality in regard to the war in the Pacific, partly out of respect to her neutrality pact with Japan, but primarily because of her grave commitments in her war against Germany. It would be most unnatural for Russia to remain long out of the war in the Pacific once the Nazis are crushed in Europe. The defeat in the Russo-Japanese War has long rankled in Russian breasts and has not been written off as a mere blunder on the part of old Imperial Russia. Russian dislike for the Japanese brand of fascism has not been less intense, but only more carefully hidden, than her hatred of the European brand. Relations between Russia and Japan have been strained since the Japanese seizure of Manchuria. Armed clashes and diplomatic disputes have been frequent between the two countries since the creation of the long frontier along the Amur river. Russian participation in the final defeat of Japan would give Russia military, political, and diplomatic stature in Asia roughly comparable to the position she has won in Europe as a result of her long, bitter struggle against the Nazis. The Russians are not likely to adopt the rather unrealistic view that Russia's European prestige will automatically give her the necessary power to play a major rôle in post-war Asia.

The military results of Russian participation in the war in the Pacific are fairly obvious. Great weight would be added to the military power already being brought to bear against Japan. New air bases would be made available for United Nations attacks on

Japan. It would be possible to bring great pressure to bear on Japanese armies in Manchuria. Submarine action against Japanese shipping could be intensified still more.

The political results are not as clear. If the war against Japan should be won primarily by means of a sea-borne invasion, it would mean that the United States alone would bear the major burden of dictating the terms of peace to Japan and of administering Japan during the transitional period from war to peace. If considerable numbers of Chinese troops are employed in the final drive, the Chinese voice will be louder in the peace, but active Russian participation will create still different conditions for the formulation of the peace. A different political philosophy and different types of political and economic interests in Asia, will inevitably lead the Russians to propose peace terms for Japan which would not coincide with ours, or China's.

Russia's rôle in Asia has become much more important in recent years, and her stake in its future has become much greater. We shall not know how this will influence the future of Asia until the war has been won and Russia has given some clear indication of the manner in which she proposes to participate in Asiatic affairs.

China's position has changed greatly since 1937. She is at once weaker and stronger than she was when Japan began her major attack on her. These long, bitter years of war have undermined seriously her entire internal structure. Japan speedily seized China's major cities in which what little industry she had was located and through which flowed the great part of her foreign trade. During most of the war against Japan China has been fighting only with blood and sweat. She has not had the weapons to wage war on anything resembling even terms. In virtual isolation from the rest of the world and cut off from her own principal sources of wealth, her internal economy has been virtually strangled. Inflation has gripped the country for some time, and the standard of living of the masses of the people has been forced steadily downward.

Japanese invasion has deprived China of virtually all of the pitifully small industrial structure she had built up prior to 1931. Japanese retreat in China will probably result in the destruction of what industrial facilities now remain even in occupied China.

Politically, China was unified in the first years of the war because of the Japanese invasion, but that spiritual unity which once seemed so close to attainment for the first time in almost a century in China largely evaporated in the struggle for power between the Kuomintang party in Chungking and the communist group in North China. The Kuomintang under Chiang Kai-shek became the symbol of resistance against the Japanese, and it was the Generalissimo who became the great leader of the Chinese people in the eyes of the world. But the very stake that he and his party had in the future of China forced them to adopt methods for the retention of power, that came dangerously close to being totalitarian in nature. The communists, on the other hand, claimed that they were fighting a true people's war against the Japanese invader, and pointed to their record of guerrilla resistance as proof. The split has become progressively wider with the development of the war, and it is impossible to determine whether or not the question of their relations can be solved without recourse to civil war.

A third disruptive factor within China is the puppet governments which have been established by the Japanese in North and Central China. The latter, its capital in Nanking, is treated by the Japanese as the legitimate government of all China. These puppet régimes have been in existence for several years, long enough for them to have developed vested interests, political and economic. The task of dispossessing them will not be simple.

The steady internal disintegration of China under the relentless Japanese invasion has been balanced by the dramatic renovation of her international position. For more than a century China was in the position of a semi-colonial nation because of the strictures on her sovereignty imposed by extraterritorial rights, special territorial concessions, the loss of tariff autonomy, the right of foreign powers to station foreign troops on Chinese soil, and loss of control over her coastal and inland waters. Decades of internal strife and her loss of international prestige had reduced China to the rôle of a third-class power. Her resistance to Japanese aggression and her importance to the United Nations war effort against Japan resulted in the restoration of almost full control over her internal affairs. Both the United States and Great Britain, since Pearl Harbor, have given up their special treaty rights in

China. Other nations have followed suit. With the defeat of Japan China will have regained full control of her internal affairs and will be free of external interference.

China has also been admitted to a footing of equality with the United States, Russia, and Great Britain in the councils of the United Nations. She has been given (and has earned) a position as one of the so-called "Big Four." But her newly won international prestige is out of proportion to her internal strength. Her position vis-à-vis her allies is one of prestige rather than of true power. She cannot expect to enjoy the full benefits of her newly won international position until she has solved the pressing internal problems that have been brought about not only by Japanese aggression, but also by her own failure to solve her internal political disputes.

In post-war Asia China will be a free and independent power, a position that she has not enjoyed since the institution of the system of unequal treaties in the mid-nineteenth century. But the development of post-war Asia will be influenced by the manner in which China will be able to solve her great internal problems. The extent to which China is weak and disunited will determine the relative strength of Japan's post-war position. The weaker Japan can leave China when she is finally forced to withdraw, the better will be Japan's chances of retaining the semblance of a position of leadership in Asia. From present indications the problems of post-war reconstruction in China will be even greater than those of Japan. Yet the rôle of China in the future of Asia and of the world will be potentially much greater and much more important than that of a defeated Japan.

The war in the Pacific has also brought great changes to the rest of Asia. After Pearl Harbor Japan quickly gained control of the Philippines, the Netherlands East Indies, French Indo-China, Malaya, Thailand, and Burma. There is a strong temptation to view these areas in the same way that we have viewed the occupied countries of Europe: namely, as areas which have been enslaved by a brutal invader and which will welcome his expulsion and the consequent return to the *status quo ante bellum* with unrestrained joy. We can be sure that the Japanese in most areas that they have occupied have not made themselves popular. We know that their record in China has been as black as anything that the Nazis have compiled in Europe. We shall probably find, as other areas are liberated, that they followed the same pattern there.

The big question mark in the rest of Asia is whether or not the people will be as happy to welcome the *status quo ante bellum* as they will be to hail the departure of the Japanese. Two of Japan's most potent and most used propaganda slogans in Asia since Pearl Harbor have been "Asia for the Asiatics!" and "Down with Anglo-American imperialism!" We cannot deny that the record of Occidental imperialism in Asia was not one of which to be proud. It denied self-rule to the local populations. It retarded the economic development of colonial areas. It exploited the local populations by forcing them to produce crops for a world market which enriched only the owners. It was practised in most of Asia by individuals whose arrogance toward the peoples with whom they lived made them extremely unpopular. The Japanese, although introducing an Asiatic imperialism, have apparently created conditions within occupied areas which might result in something less than an enthusiastic welcome for the return of the former rulers of those countries.

Japanese propaganda has reached more Asiatics during the past few years than ever before. It is probable that many have developed a sense of grievance against their former masters whether it was justified or not in terms of the actual record. The Philippines will gain true independence as soon as the Japanese invaders are driven out. Thailand will probably again become independent. But French Indo-China, Malaya, Burma, and the Netherlands East Indies are apparently to revert to their former colonial status. They can scarcely be expected to accept that status with more willingness than they revealed before Pearl Harbor. In these areas there were independence movements of varying degrees of strength even before the Japanese invasion. The absence of their former masters may have been regarded as a state more favourable than before, even though the hated Japanese have replaced them.

We must recognize the fact that post-war Asia cannot exist half-free and half-colonial. We have returned sovereign rights to China, a fact that will not be missed by the politically conscious in colonial Asia. We have proclaimed the Atlantic Charter as a great document governing the relations between man and man. We have repeated again and again that we are fighting the war for the liberation of all men from tyranny. Japan has been sedulously planting the seeds of an all-Asiatic Asia and has been utilizing to the utmost the anti-Anglo-American imperialism argument. The full implications of the above will not be lost on the politically conscious Asiatics in those areas which will revert to a colonial status after the war.

Assuming that the free nations of Asia, China, the Philippines, Thailand, and Japan, will attain a reasonable degree of internal stability, then the greatest potential source of trouble in Asia will be in the colonial areas where the politically conscious will remember the ideals for which the United Nations have declared that they have been fighting this war and will demand a greater share in the self-government which they will believe to be their rightful heritage.

The problem of the colonial areas is not a Japanese problem nor an Asiatic problem. It is a world problem because it involves the relationships between European powers and millions of the peoples of Asia. Europe may in time attain a reasonable degree of stability, and Asia can look forward to the same goal, but purely regional stability will not solve the problems of inter-regional relationships that are bound to arise out of the colonial problem if it remains unsolved.

The colonial problem is a knotty one. Great Britain, France, and the Netherlands will not willingly let slip the great investments that they have made in Asia. They will not consider Japanese occupation as having had the legal effect of dispossessing them of their colonial holdings. They will earnestly work for the restoration of the *status quo ante bellum*. Not only the wealth of a substantial number of their citizens depends on the re-establishment of the colonial system, but also their national economic existence is largely bound up with their colonial possessions. The considerations of self-interest will inevitably tend to overshadow the larger issue of independence and freedom of substantial numbers of the human race.

On the other hand, the colonial areas themselves are much more likely to have a heightened degree of political consciousness as a result of the Japanese invasion. Resistance against the Japanese invader whose arrival was much more violent than that of the previous masters, and the very absence of the old colonial rulers who had kept a firm rein on all aspirations to freedom, have created conditions which have no doubt encouraged the development of an even greater desire for independence from any rule whatsoever, Japanese or otherwise. From another view, immediate independence, as desirable as it might be from all points of view, is not completely practical. It is unfortunate, but true, that the colonial system resulted in the linking of the welfare of the peoples in colonial Asia to the general economic structure of the world. A pre-war collapse in the price of rubber, for example, affected the rubber factories of Akron, Ohio, but not nearly as much as it did the livelihood of the populations of Malaya and the Netherlands East Indies. Immediate independence, without due consideration for the economic problems that it would involve, might in the long run prove to be even less happy than the present state of political semi-servitude.

If the problems of intra-Asiatic and European-American-Asiatic economic relations can be solved, then there will be every reason to expect the amicable settlement of the political problems that are involved in the continuation of the colonial system. It would be indeed tragic if the next war in Asia is to be fought over the question of whether the colonial system should or should not continue. The solution of the colonial problem will be one of the major problems in the creation of a global peace which we hope will be the successor to the present global war. Such a solution will be a major step toward Asiatic stability, which in turn will encourage the development of a peaceful Japan. If it is the major responsibility of the Japanese people to rid themselves of a system which has forced them to adopt militarism and aggression, then it is the major responsibility of the victorious nations in this war to work to create conditions both in Asia and in the rest of the world under which it will be possible for the Japanese to follow the new course of national destiny which they must perforce adopt if they are to enjoy the full fruits of the internal changes that they must bring about.

The expiation of the Japanese people for the destruction and tragedy that they have visited directly on Asia and indirectly on so many in distant parts of the world must be long. Only a part of it will be endured in the period which will lead to the final crushing of Japanese military power. Japan must be visited with the same kind of destruction that she has carried to China and other occupied areas. The Japanese people must be made to taste to the full the bitter dose of defeat, with all the destruction in life and property that it entails. Only thus will they know the terrible consequences to which the authoritarianism and aggression that their leaders plotted for them will lead. They must in addition endure the internal chaos that will ensue if the outmoded political, social, and economic institutions of the country are to be swept away. Crushing military defeat from without and the turbulence of civil war will be a terrible price for the Japanese people to pay, but pay it they must if they are to prove that they can again be accepted with full trust by the rest of the world.

The task of encouraging the Japanese people to rehabilitate themselves politically is only one of the problems connected with the building of a structure of world peace. The job is one that calls for all the intelligence, statesmanship, and good-will that the world can muster. The problems that we have conquered in winning the war against Japan have been tremendous. Had we been less persevering in our planning, less intelligent in our application of our plans, less industrious in the construction of our weapons, less daring in their use, and less imaginative in the conception of the strategy that is defeating Japan, the war might well have been one of exhaustion in which Japan could have hoped for a negotiated peace which would have allowed her the time and the opportunity to exploit Asia and her peoples as she wished, and to have strengthened herself for the task of dominating the world.

We shall have to bring to bear on the problems of Asia and of Japan at least as much intelligence, boldness, daring, and, in addition, sympathy, wisdom, and good-will, if we are to construct the new and peaceful world the hopeful among us see in the future. We must solve the problem. The alternative will be another war.

INDEX

Index

Index

The text of this book is set on the Linotype in Baskerville. The punches for this face were cut under the supervision of George W. Jones, the eminent English printer and the designer of Granjon and Estienne. Linotype Baskerville is a facsimile cutting from type cast from the original matrices of a face designed by John Baskerville, a writing-master of Birmingham, for his own private press. The original face was the forerunner of the "modern" group of type faces, known today as Scotch, Bodoni, etc. After his death in 1775, Baskerville's punches and matrices were sold in France and were used to produce the sumptuous Kehl edition of Voltaire's works.

This book was composed, printed, and bound by The Plimpton Press, Norwood, Mass. The binding scheme is based on original designs by W. A. Dwiggins.

THIS BOOK HAS BEEN PRODUCED IN FULL COMPLIANCE WITH ALL GOVERNMENT REGULATIONS FOR THE CONSERVATION OF PAPER, METAL, AND OTHER ESSENTIAL MATERIALS.